Design for Six Sigma

To the memory of my father, a designer BC (Before Computers).

Design for Six Sigma

Launching New Products and Services Without Failure

GEOFF TENNANT

Gower

Published by
Gower Publishing Limited
Gower House
Croft Road
Aldershot
Hampshire GU11 3HR
England

Gower Publishing Company
131 Main Street
Burlington VT 05401-5600 USA

Reprinted 2002

Geoffrey Tennant has asserted his right under the Copyright, Designs and Patents Act 1988 to be identified as the author of this work.

British Library Cataloguing in Publication Data

Tennant, Geoff
   Design for Six Sigma : launching new products and services without failure
   1. Quality control 2. Product management
   I. Title
   658.5'62

ISBN 0 566 08434 1

Library of Congress Cataloging-in-Publication Data

Tennant, Geoff.
   Design for Six Sigma : launching new products and services without failure / Geoff Tennant.
     p. cm.
   Includes bibliographical references.
   ISBN 0-566-08434-1 (hardback)
     1. Quality control–Statistical methods. 2. Experimental design.
     I. Title.

TS156.T448 2002
658.5'62–dc21
                                          2001040539

Typeset in 9/13pt Utopia by Bournemouth Colour Press, Parkstone and printed in Great Britain by T J International Ltd., Padstow.

Contents

Appendix 181

List of figures and tables

FIGURES

TABLES

List of abbreviations

CMM	capability maturity model
CTP	critical to process
CTQ	critical to quality
DCCDI	define – customer – concept – design – implement
DFSS	Design For Six Sigma
DMADV	define – measure – analyse – design – verify
DMAIC	define – measure – analyse – improve – control
DMAIIC	define – measure – analyse – improve – implement – control
DOE	design of experiment
DPMO	defects per million opportunities
EMEA	error mode effect analysis
FMEA	failure mode effect analysis
HOQ	house of quality
JIT	just in time
MGP	multi-generation planning
MOT	moments of truth
NPI	new product introduction
PDA	personal digital assistant
PDCA	plan – do – check – act
QFD	quality function deployment
QMS	quality management system
RAD	rapid application development
RPN	risk priority number
SPC	statistical process control
TIPS	theory of inventive problem solving (TRIZ)
TQM	total quality management
VOB	voice of business
VOC	voice of customer
VOE	voice of employee
WAP	Wireless Application Protocol

Preface

From the moment I first heard about Six Sigma I knew that it was the salvation of both business and customer. Here, at last, was a proven and powerful methodology that both allowed and encouraged organizations to remove once and for all the reasons for defects from processes, products and services. Having worked for the majority of my paid employment in the field of systems design and development, I understood all too well the value of preventing the defect from happening in the first place and Six Sigma improvement was like a breath of fresh air. Naturally I looked beyond the idea of patching up or improving bad processes, towards the high ideal of getting everything right in the first place. I have long been a firm champion of the end customer, and have never been able quite to accept the business need to overly manage customer expectation, rather than to proactively deliver what was wanted and needed.

It is almost exactly a year since beginning work on my first book – *Six Sigma: SPC and TQM in Manufacturing and Services*. As the cycle of creation and commercialization of one work closes with final printing, the creation of the next generation work is well under way. Writing a book is indeed very much about designing and launching something new, both a product and service, to a commercial marketplace. The sharp reader would certainly ask, 'did you use the Design For Six Sigma approach for this book?' The answer is unquestionably yes, but not as a deliberate task or formal undertaking; after all I am only a team of one!

This book is indeed designed to be a new product that delivers to customer needs for information and inspiration (and perhaps also entertainment) through excellent quality. As far as I know, at the time of writing there are no other works specifically on DFSS as such, so this is certainly very new and both a product as well as a service. Marketing and customer research has been completed and a strategy for commercialization set out with the publishers. Trials and pilots have been undertaken by speaking on Six Sigma and DFSS at international conferences, and customer needs matched to the new product offering. Much note taking and conceptualization has taken place over many months and a full project plan for execution is now in hand. I have a timetable for writing, and monitor progress by counting the daily production of words, a key metric for project success! However, customer-measured success does not always increase with the number of words written – short, focused chapters full of value are far more important. Automation and technology by way of a word processor certainly helps, particularly with spelling and formatting. The hard reality, of course, is that the actual content is still very much up to the author/designer, and there is no substitute for the highly creative activity of setting one word after another according to a master plan. Computers can do many things, but they cannot yet write books that inspire. Design – the peculiar art and craft of creating the *new* by plan – is unquestionably hard work but very rewarding.

My father was certainly the inspiration for my keen involvement in design and engineering, and his wide interest in chemistry, astronomy, and electrical, mechanical and civil engineering provided many rich childhood experiences that continue to underpin much of what I know and do. Since my youth the achievements of the notable engineers and designers of the Victorian period have been a constant source of wonder and inspiration. In particular I have great admiration for Isambard

Kingdom Brunel, who was one of the all-time giants in the design of bold new products and services. Brunel did more than just design the Great Western Railway; he inspired a whole new approach that changed the limits of what was capable, and had his broad-gauge track survived to today it would no doubt still outperform in terms of speed and stability as well as passenger comfort. With a distinctive pedigree, the GWR was affectionately known as 'God's Wonderful Railway'; there are few designs and products that have inspired such loyalty from staff and customers alike.

Since this book is intended as a practical guide to deploying DFSS in an organization, the exercises at the end of each chapter are provided as an aid for the more studious reader to consolidate learning and understanding through practical engagement. Each exercise will generally build on previous work as well as the current chapter, and may also be used in a group to promote further discussion. Model answers are not provided – it is hoped that the questions are broad enough to challenge any reader from any background and organization, and engagement is more appropriate than 'correctness'.

In passing, I would like to thank Randal Gilbert at Northern Ireland Electricity for providing fresh insight with his discussions and alternative ideas on the use of FMEA. I would also like to thank Joann Neuroth of On Purpose Associates for the challenging ideas on chaos – where change is indeed a way of life. Continual growth and creative development, a part of the composite whole of the Six Sigma approach, needs to be nurtured and actively encouraged to retain the leading and cutting edge to change. With so many new organizations turning to a Six Sigma methodology, I acknowledge the fresh inspiration and impetus provided by the growing band of companies adopting and championing Six Sigma. Naturally the extension of Six Sigma to the whole field of the design of new products and services is a very real challenge but one with outstanding return for those who apply the tools and principles with success.

GEOFF TENNANT

Introduction

In application, Six Sigma is clearly one of today's most powerful and most effective management strategy programmes for cultural and process change, ultimately leading to world-class customer quality. Although originally conceived as long ago as the early 1980s, the application of Six Sigma is still very much a novelty and long overdue in playing its dynamic part on the world stage of customer-focused quality.

Six Sigma in its entirety is many things including a philosophy, a methodology, a goal and a metric, and is certainly broad enough to work in both pure manufacturing as well as wholly transactional and service industries, and anything in between. At the very heart of the application of Six Sigma lies a process improvement methodology of immense power and utilization, but ultimately extremely limited in its scope. The currently accepted best practice for process improvement methodology emanating from GE Capital is the DMAIC model – *define, measure, analyse, improve* and *control*. However, where Six Sigma has been in serious use in an organization for more than 18 months, it gradually becomes apparent that the DMAIC approach fails to solve all ills. Six Sigma – as a *process improvement methodology* – knows almost no boundaries to attaining success, but typically fails to deal effectively with the improvement or introduction of *new* products and services. Six Sigma improves the existing and failing process, but does little to help with the successful design of the *new*, and the Six Sigma methodology has a real need to evolve further to counter this deficiency.

It is this weakness that has spurred a majority of the scarce few organizations with long-standing Six Sigma initiatives to devote time and effort to developing methodology add-ons and adaptations, targeted to deal with all the issues drawn to the surface in the wake of the design of new products and services. Perhaps since Six Sigma is so large an undertaking, and typically entrenched in a corporate-wide and all-encompassing drive for customer quality, there exists the temptation to bolt 'design' onto the side of Six Sigma 'improve', with the result that some implementations may tend to look a little ragged at the edges. Many companies have adopted and adapted a prominent methodology, commonly known as DMADV – *define, measure, analyse, design, verify* – which attempts to retain much of the DMAIC model and in so doing often confuses rather than simplifies. Certainly this variant has not had the universal appeal outside such organizations as is enjoyed by DMAIC.

Design For Six Sigma is a more generalist term covering a basket of individual approaches for introducing entirely new products and services and for coping with the inherent limitations of the DMAIC Six Sigma model. As such, these DFSS frameworks have each evolved out of earlier Six Sigma improvement methodologies, rather than from an altruistic desire to derive a better 'design' process, or perhaps to better deliver new products and services. 'Design For Six Sigma' naturally evolves from, and is an extension to, the simpler 'Improve For Six Sigma', but it is time for a comprehensive reconsideration of all that Six Sigma attempts to achieve, and all the frustration encountered within the commercial launch and design of the 'new'. No single DFSS model currently deals adequately with all the issues, and there is a very real danger in the multitude of adaptations and adjustments to Six Sigma that the real and ultimate customer need will be missed.

Six Sigma process improvements can achieve outstanding reductions in the defect and error rate commonly accepted in the typical commercial organization, and yet such improvements are in the end limited to a maximum return equal to the worst error rate. As organizations move slowly towards the Six Sigma goal of just 3.4 defects in one million opportunities, the hard returns from world-class quality diminish in favour of softer benefits, such as better-satisfied customers and proactive employees. However, far better returns are to be realized and gained in the realm of the entirely new product or service.

The writer of the Old Testament book Ecclesiastes (subtitled, incidentally, *The Quest for Wisdom*) confidently tells us that:

> . . . there is nothing new under the sun. Is there a thing of which it is said 'See, this is new'? It has been already in the ages before us.

There is indeed nothing new under the sun – and yet the *new*, like the poor, is always with us. It creeps in with the beginning of the dawn, and remains as a promise of tomorrow with the setting of the sun. No single individual or corporate group can exist in the commercial world of today without seeing and meeting the *new* at every turn. New is so very important for enterprise and organic growth, yet it is often either forgotten or taken for granted, the importance slipping into a distant memory as quickly as the newspapers of today become yesterday's news and thus tired and old. The new millennium replaces the old, the new year the old, the new technology the old, the new ways the old. Every company strives boldly to introduce the new at regular intervals – new foods, new clothes, new washing powders, new televisions, new computers and new mobile telephones. Surely 'new' (and 'improved') must be the most ill-used word next to 'quality', where several sectors of the marketplace, particularly information technology, attempt to sell simply on the status value gained from the 'new', without delivering the much-needed new performance, value or substance.

No company can ever begin life without a new product or service. Neither can that company continue to stay the course without repeated reinvention or major change – and in an ever-increasing pace of change, the replacement for yesterday's products must be bolder, increasingly different, and delivered with escalating rapidity. Yet, with such a need for new, better and bolder, the fact remains that the early stages of the launch of new products are often plagued with failure. Failure to deliver what was expected or required, failure to deliver on time, or simply failure to deliver at all. New services are far worse, and 'opening night' for many service organizations is the start, rather than the finish, of a long struggle to correct problems and defects in the service process. If incremental change and improvement is difficult, exponential or major change is far more so, and inextricably fraught with risk and issue. What is lacking in the commercial world today is an ability to confidently launch new products and services with speed and success, to exactly target customer needs and requirements and thus maximize investment and future return. Consider the staggering number of new items that fail, either in development, commercialization, or execution and delivery at the marketplace. Consider, too, the staggering potential for the organization that can replace the entire product/service portfolio each year with new products and services, each of which begins life with a performance better than 4.5 sigma – about one tenth of a 1 per cent error rate – in all that matters to the customer. If Six Sigma is powerful, DFSS is more powerful still. If Six Sigma is in need of application to any organization, DFSS is of greater need and worth. If Six Sigma is important and valid in any business today, DFSS is vital and a primary key to unlocking the real potential of commercial enterprise. If Six Sigma is expensive in application, DFSS is more so, and Design For Six Sigma is a real prize to be valued by any enterprising organization. If Six Sigma can hand back some 25 per cent of profits by process improvement, the rapid and successful launch of new products and services can often open up potentially double or triple markets, which places such simple process improvements (although highly important) very much in the shade.

Six Sigma, as an incremental process improvement methodology, deals only and slowly with that which *is*, and there is a fixed and real limit in the return on investment. DFSS in contrast achieves three things. First, it extends the application of 'basic' Six Sigma past simple 'improve' and as such can be considered as 'advanced Six Sigma', dealing successfully with the *new*. Second, it attacks the current and appallingly applied process of 'design of the new', which through poor practice often results in a failure to develop new products and services both rapidly and successfully. And third, but not in any way the least of these three, it empowers an organization to deliver better products and services, targeted specifically against the Six Sigma metric, to satisfy and perhaps even excite the customer. There may be many who fail to see the difference between the last two points; however, it is important to separate the value and appropriateness of the offered product or service from the design and commercialization process by which it is delivered. To date many evolving DFSS approaches rush to improve one part or the other, but never both.

The aim of this book is to provide a detailed resource of both guidance and inspiration, describing all the aspects of business strategy, design, project management, and practical execution and methodology necessary for the successful introduction of new products and services, under the auspices of a customer-focused Six Sigma approach. This work can be read at several levels and it is hoped that it will appeal to a wide cross-section in any organization. Students of Six Sigma will find it essential reading when the realization arrives, as it surely will, that 'improve' does not always work, and something more is needed. DFSS is very much an advanced branch of Six Sigma, although for this book the view will be that DFSS is a methodology in its own right, and not something to be squashed into DMAIC. Business leaders will find this work of value in being able to better understand and control both the strategy and process of launching new products and services, and thus gain confidence to champion, and become more involved in, the development of new entities for their organization. Designers of all walks of life will certainly find this work challenging and illuminating, as will development managers and engineers!

To be of use, such a book must equally consider services and products, as well as the design and implementation process itself. Looked at with care, it becomes evident that no product exists without a service process, and most services also deliver a product of some form or another. Design is a process too, with a product delivered and usually handed on to a secondary process of commercial instantiation. Success in the composite whole can only be achieved by drawing together all the separate processes of marketing, invention, design, delivery, and ongoing support and commercial gain. If a work such as this can promote and facilitate a reduction of just 1 per cent in the failures commonly experienced in launching new products and services, then it will return a benefit far in excess of that experienced with the already proven Six Sigma quality methodology.

Design For Six Sigma is an extensive topic, and this book has been divided into three sections to aid the reader. Part One is perhaps more theoretical and philosophical, dealing with a Six Sigma approach for the development of the 'new', the fundamental issues of good design, as well as considering a strategy for organic commercial growth. Part Two deals comprehensively with describing and unfurling a framework and a more detailed methodology for DFSS, as well as exploring the critical areas of advanced customer analysis, concept-solution development and failure- or error-proofing. It can be frustrating to begin a book wanting to know 'how', and then having to wade through a great deal of 'what' and 'why'; the reader with a more urgent need may progress more directly to Part Two! Part Three deals with some of the more practical and often difficult issues involved with the necessary in-house adoption and deployment of the chosen DFSS methodology.

PART ONE

Design and Six Sigma

CHAPTER ONE

Six Sigma overview

Design must be one of the most satisfying and creative activities known to mankind. Certainly it is a key faculty that separates us, even elevates us, from the remainder of 'intelligent life' on this planet. Our outstanding ability to design both physical objects and intangible concepts is unparalleled and should not be taken either lightly or for granted. There can be no better way to begin a consideration of Design For Six Sigma than with a fuller appreciation of all that constitutes both the art and practice of *design*, but first perhaps is a more pressing need to explain the basics of Six Sigma and customer-focused quality.

The importance and value of excellent design and of Six Sigma in commercial enterprise today is immense. If the reader has any doubt of either, a quick review of all the products immediately to hand will soon reveal that many are new, either in relation to the reader, or in absolute sense to the commercial marketplace. This book is certainly new, and in 'developed' society, so too will be clothing, computers, mobile cell-phones, motorcars and many domestic products. Indeed, the more 'developed' society becomes, the shorter also the acceptable lifespan for our products and services. Nothing seems to last much longer than about seven years, either physically or in vogue! In services too, shops, offices and consumer service all seem to be reinvented or altered considerably at regular intervals. The new millennium brings, globally, increased use of the telephone and e-mail for communication and commerce, with e-commerce now closely followed by m-commerce (m for mobile, shop from your cell-phone). The all-purpose call centre dealing with voice- and e-mail is now king!

Yet, with such aggressive reinvention and frequent introduction of the *new*, failure seems also largely to predominate. Grand and embarrassing failures hit the headlines from time to time, but for every London Millennium Dome, or Millennium Bridge, there exist many products and services that quietly struggle to see the light of day. Success is never guaranteed – delay, disappointment, even disaster wait to counter the undeniable benefit from dynamic commercial enterprise. How much better to design, deliver and execute new products and services with confidence and assured success, and above all targeted to meet customer needs and expectations precisely.

SIX SIGMA DESCRIBED

Whilst it is not intended that this work should deal in any depth with the basics of a Six Sigma application to quality, it is expected that many readers will approach DFSS directly rather than via 'improvement' Six Sigma and so a short explanation is in order. The value of a basic understanding and practical experience of Six Sigma in action cannot be understated, and if the reader is wholly new to the subject then preparatory reading is certainly suggested as a minimum. My earlier work, *Six Sigma: SPC and TQM in Manufacturing and Services*, covers the application of Six Sigma to process improvement, without excessive detail, and it was always intended that this book would follow the earlier work almost as a sequel.

Experience has shown that considerable interest in DFSS arises from practitioners of design and product/service development, all seeking a better methodology for the launch of new products and services. The drawback in arriving at DFSS via this route must surely be the real risk that the vision and philosophy of excellent customer quality is side-stepped in favour of rigour and structure. Whilst rigour, structure and method are valuable to any process, DFSS must engage the essential ingredients of Six Sigma quality in order to reap the full benefits. The target is to deliver excellent new products or services and the only way that this can be fully achieved is through the use and application of the Six Sigma metric.

Six Sigma is many things, but most appropriately for this discussion it is a common metric of quality, applied across an entire organization for the better measurement, and thus improvement, of customer-focused quality. In simple terms, every activity is a process, to which can be applied measures of one class or another. These measurements, taken over time, will be seen to fluctuate as every process exhibits variation, and it is this variation that can be associated with poor quality – uncontrolled variation is indeed the enemy of excellent customer quality! Variation is, however, quite natural in our world, and such factors as height and weight will alter from person to person. Basic variation is natural or common and arises from the inherent irregularities in each process. Make 100 cups of coffee, and each cup will be slightly different from the rest. Quantity, temperature, strength, time taken to make, are all metrics that can be measured for the process of making a cup of coffee and each will vary. For the vast majority of metrics that can be taken from such processes, the variation will always follow that of the *normal distribution* to some extent. The classic diagram showing this particular frequency distribution is well known; Figure 1.1 shows one such example. From the plotted basic histogram, the frequency of occurrences for the quantity of coffee in each cup can be estimated. Such a frequency distribution shows both the historical performance of the process and the projected future performance to be expected. Here we can see that, with no special cause and only natural cause variation, each cup of coffee will have a slightly different quantity of liquid, with the most likely outcome being the average value.

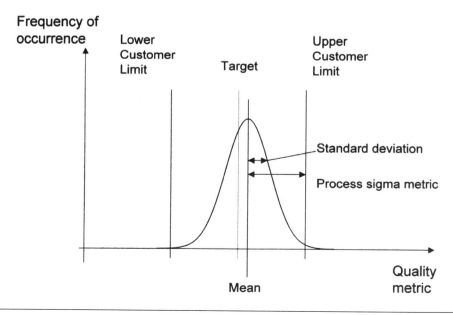

Figure 1.1   Distribution of a critical to quality metric

Traditionally the average, or arithmetic mean, has been the sole measurement of interest, if measurement is considered at all. If anyone has been interested in finding out what customers expected from a cup of coffee, and then actually measuring the outcome, then the arithmetic mean is usually presented in comparison to one target or perhaps one or two performance limits. The foundation, and success, of the Six Sigma approach is threefold. First, processes important to the customer are identified and key metrics of these processes accurately tracked over time. Second, acceptable limits to process performance are set, based entirely on what would deliver satisfactory quality to the real customer. Third, the process capability to deliver to customer expectation is measured using the sigma metric, and then, it is hoped, improved! The sigma metric is based on the standard deviation, which is usually described by the Greek letter s, sigma or σ. This sigma value of a process is a measure related to the amount of inherent *variation* in the process, whereas the *process capability* is defined as the number of sigma that fit between the average value and the (nearest) customer limit. In Figure 1.1, the quantity of coffee in each cup is classically normally distributed, and the average is close to, but not exactly on, the target quantity. The distance between the average or mean and the upper customer limit is about three sigma, making this a *three-sigma process*. Although in many cases the average performance is well within limits, the issue at stake is the potential for the process to deliver outside of the customer requirements. Figure 1.2 shows more clearly the, perhaps more likely, situation to be encountered if the process of making a cup of coffee by machine were to be studied. The machine has been set up to deliver a precise amount of coffee to each cup, but suffers from variation, and the shape of the distribution might indicate that special cause variation is affecting the process, since the shape is not quite a classic normal curve. The average quantity is off target from the desired setting, but within limits. The limits are, of course, what the customer requires, not what the manufacturer or process owner decides. For many organizations with automatic coffee dispensers, making and dispensing the coffee is a core process and one critical to the customer. The

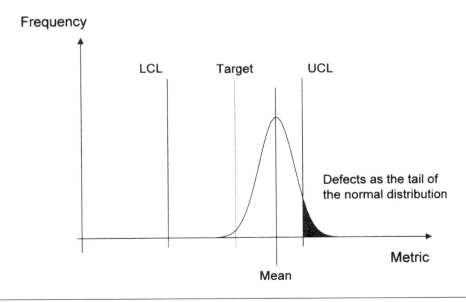

Figure 1.2   Defects as the tail of a normal distribution

critical, actionable and measurable factors about this process could indeed be many, including strength, flavour, temperature and certainly quantity. We can be sure that one certain CTQ (critical to quality) metric is the quantity of liquid in the cup. Too little, and the customer will feel 'short-changed'; too much and they are likely to spill the coffee, and even scald themselves or others. The lower customer limit, set from the voice of the customer analysis as much as anything, will perhaps be some 85 per cent of the volume of the cup. The upper customer limit, set also from customer research, but perhaps also too from observation, will possibly be 95 per cent, allowing at least a little room for manoeuvre. The target, which the machine aims to hit each and every time, will be somewhere between the two.

What would be seen in actuality when quantity is measured could be a distribution with part of the curve falling outside of one or both of the customer limits. In fact, the way the normal curve is shaped ensures that it never, in theory at least, reaches zero, and so some part of the whole distribution will always be outside customer requirements. Some of the distribution will spill into being a defect and the process-sigma metric aims to quantify this part of the distribution as a precise number. This number can be directly attributed to the experienced customer quality, as well as the associated costs of delivering poor quality to the customer. In this example the (short-term) process capability is around two sigma, with perhaps some 2 per cent of the coffee cups being over-filled. Being able, and willing, to identify core processes and CTQ metrics and then to measure and calculate the process sigma is only one part of the Six Sigma approach. The next step is to work with the process and the data collected to identify the root causes for variation and failure (both special and common), identifying exactly what gives rise to defect and poor performance. In terms of the diagram, the statistical aim of Six Sigma quality would now be to change the process such that the distribution has the mean at the process target and that as much of the distribution as possible is within the customer limits. Naturally, should this be achieved, the opportunities for the customer to experience poor quality of the product or service are very small indeed.

Traditionally the application of quality control in manufacturing environments has operated on what could be described as a 'Three-Sigma' quality approach. The normal distribution is well understood and it is known that some 99.7 per cent of all outcomes sit within three standard deviations either side of the mean. With the process performing such that the mean is half-way between both customer limits, and the variation so small that three sigma can fit between each limit and the mean, only 0.3 per cent of all cups of coffee dispensed would be either too full or too empty. At least that is the theory; in reality life is a little bit more complex.

Motorola 'invented' Six Sigma, both as a metric and methodology, during the early 1980s and from their study of process performance over time it was noticed that process distributions shifted. From this work the empirical adjustment of 1.5 sigma has been introduced, not always with the agreement of every commentator! For our coffee machine, following commissioning it may well dispense coffee in quantities where the average is on target and the distribution has three sigma fitting nicely between the customer limits. This equates to a short-term process sigma of 'three'; however, over time the water pressure may change, the ambient temperature may alter, the machine pipework may become clogged or the measuring equipment may move away from optimum performance. The outcome is that, in the long term, the distribution shape will shift and/or be fatter, and hence fewer sigma will fit between average and limit. Three sigma short term as the best possible process *capability* is accepted as being equal to only 1.5 sigma long term as the typical process *performance*, particularly if you are the hapless customer taking cup after cup of coffee over the longer term.

In addition to measuring the process-sigma metric, performance is often quoted in terms of the defects per million opportunities (DPMO), which equates nicely with the fraction of the distribution falling outside the customer limits. At three sigma (short term), the long-term performance will allow some 66 800 cups in each million to have the wrong amount dispensed, simply because with long-term shift and spread some 7 per cent of the distribution will fall outside the limits. It is accepted practice to quote the quality performance of any process in terms of the short-term sigma, yet tied to the defect rate equivalent to the long-term proportion of the normal curve outside of specification. Further, it is usually taken as a one-sided limit, on the assumption that standard performance is both centred and at three sigma, and defects arise from a one-sided shift over time.

The power of Six Sigma to apply a metric to customer-experienced quality extends to service processes; however, the typical experience here is that no one measures anything close to customer-focused CTQs, let alone controls the process. Typically such processes show really nasty distributions that look nothing like a normal curve, and defects are to be found both on the left- and the right-hand sides. There is also often the very real question as to whether there are indeed both upper and lower customer limits, rather than just the upper limit. Further, the issue of short term and long term is very much more difficult to deal with, as most service processes are inherently long term in outcome. Short term for a coffee machine is easy – one day at constant water pressure. Short term for a tea-lady with a tea or coffee pot lasts about as far as one cup; beyond that, long-term shift and spread become important. Typically in the Six Sigma methodology some thirty data points as a minimum are necessary to measure and understand the process, so service processes are inevitably all long term, but again quoted as a short-term sigma metric. Measure a tea-lady dispensing coffee and you might expect 7 per cent failure in the quantity (adjusting cups that are too full or too low, with top-ups, count as rework and would still be a defect). Hence the tea-lady is a three-sigma process. The coffee machine might well be 4.5 sigma for a day, making just 1350 defects per million cups, but over time this could still amount to 66 800 defects per million, again three sigma. Table 1.1 shows how DPMO compares to process sigma – the short-term column should typically be used; the long-term column is only shown for comparison.

Whatever the arguments for short-term or long-term sigma, the fact is that any process operating at six sigma will deliver never more than 3.4 defects per million opportunities. This is the new

Table 1.1 DPMO against short- and long-term process sigma

Process sigma long term	Process sigma short term	DPMO
–	0.0	933 000
–	0.5	841 000
–	1.0	691 000
0.0	1.5	500 000
0.5	2.0	309 000
1.0	2.5	159 000
1.5	3.0	66 800
2.0	3.5	22 800
2.5	4.0	6 210
3.0	4.5	1 350
3.5	5.0	233
4.0	5.5	32
4.5	6.0	3.4

standard for quality – the goal and vision of Six Sigma. On the basis of 'three sigma', which has been in operation for some seventy years, the customer actually experiences a failure rate close to 7 per cent, which is perhaps not all that out of the ordinary, but highly unwelcome nevertheless.

The philosophy of Six Sigma is to identify what really matters to the customer(s) and to deliver at such a low level of error and defect that perfection close to zero defects is achieved in practice. Of course this means that an organization must both know and understand its customers, and one of the more difficult parts of Six Sigma is the identification and quantification of appropriate CTQs. The practical part of Six Sigma, the methodology, is an umbrella of tools and techniques for identifying, quantifying and then dealing with the root causes contributing to poor quality.

Six Sigma, as a process improvement methodology, typically follows the DMAIC approach. Once core processes have been well defined, with customer needs and expectations converted to good CTQs, each failing area can be dealt with by running a quality improvement project. *Define* everything – team, project scope, and process – by careful mapping. *Measure* with care; the key CTQ metric as well as anticipated contributory factors; plot and describe the data; calculate initial process performance. *Analyse*, using process map analysis, inferential statistics and root cause analysis. *Improve* the process, reducing defects through selective improvements shown to deal with the root causes. *Control* the process: re-measure the improved process, introduce new procedures and control charts, and then return the improved process to a process owner.

The highly statistical nature of Six Sigma in practice comes as much from the manufacturing need for advanced statistics to find the real root causes of the variation as from the theory of the normal curve. In use within service or transactional projects, much of the advanced statistics is either unnecessary or even unhelpful and many softer but equally effective TQM (total quality management) tools are used to great effect.

Of course, Six Sigma is also about change, and this can be as much about the culture of the organization as about processes. In application, the introduction of Six Sigma to an organization will typically require an approach aimed at changing attitudes and practices, as well as improving processes. Change from the top down takes a long time to get to where it is needed, and change from the bottom up always seems to end in strangulation. To introduce Six Sigma successfully requires change at every level, and all at once, which is certainly a tough objective. If all the above reads as being perhaps quirky but not difficult, it should be well understood that in reality the hard part is in successfully introducing Six Sigma as a *philosophy and practice* into an organization.

Organizations are well aware of the need for excellent customer quality, and clearly the accepted standard is as close to zero defects as can be achieved. The question has to be asked, 'why do companies fail to deliver perfection as standard without the use of Six Sigma?' Or, perhaps to phrase it another way round, 'what is the real benefit of Six Sigma for my organization?' Clearly there is a balance between having no quality control or assurance, which costs nothing up front but hurts the customers and hence business long term, and driving for total perfection, which always delivers what the customer wants but costs a great deal to operate. The impetus injected through a Six Sigma quality initiative brings to an organization a much better understanding of current performance, as well as the ability to shift the equilibrium point further towards perfection, for the same cost. Dealing with issues by resolving the root cause rather than fixing symptoms, focusing on the critical areas rather than making do across the board, measuring and understanding (often for the first time) and taking every aspect of the cost of delivering poor quality into account, are all part of the Six Sigma approach. The changes here are strategic, and often the term 'breakthrough' is used when describing a particular corporate Six Sigma implementation. Break through old limits, old ideas, old approaches, and the inevitable 'it works, why change' mentality, or more likely 'it's broken, but you'll never get it fixed here' attitude. Six Sigma, in part, only works if an organization gets excited about it, and it can be said that an important fraction of the power for success in Six Sigma comes from the name, and the expensive attention, lavished by companies.

To break through the *status quo*, to ensure engagement and excitement, and quite simply to ensure sufficient resources for success, the typical business will need to drive Six Sigma via strong leadership and a hierarchy of experts and promoters from within. It must be visibly led and championed from the very top, and then each project supported by champions from the senior management. Both full- and part-time leaders and practitioners (Black and Green Belts) actually exploit the power of the methodology, with the odd Master Black Belt around to elucidate the finer points. Use of project teams, with Black or Green Belts and a cross-functional group, ensure the methodology and approach first succeeds, and then soon spreads to become indigenous to the culture and practice of the organization.

Six Sigma must initially:

1 Identify every business function or process.
2 Know and understand the customers of the business.
3 Distinguish the core processes that add value for the customers.
4 For each core process, obtain specific customer requirements by survey and analysis.
5 Convert process customer requirements into a small number of well-specified, actionable and measurable critical to quality (CTQ) characteristics for the process.
6 Measure every CTQ process metric, and for each determine the equivalent normal distribution plot.
7 Overlay onto the plot the customer CTQ limits, and calculate the number of defects outside these limits.
8 Convert this to a process sigma metric.

And then, repeatedly:

1 Identify, at a business level, the particular process and CTQ to be improved.
2 Perform initial investigation work (and re-evaluate the choice of project).
3 Charter an improvement project team, and document the existing situation.
4 Gather measurements from the process.
5 Analyse the measurements, and look for the root causes of defects.
6 Generate solutions, implement improvements, and measure the change.
7 Return the improved process to the business and controlling ownership.

Since DFSS is commonly and perhaps successfully regarded as an *advanced* approach to 'design' using a Six Sigma philosophy and methodology, this book will not attempt further to explain or justify Six Sigma. If the reader remains unsure or unsatisfied on the subject of Six Sigma itself, then further reading or investigation should be undertaken elsewhere.

This, then, in brief detail, is Six Sigma; so how does 'Design For Six Sigma' fit into the picture?

THE NEED FOR DESIGN FOR SIX SIGMA

If 'Improve For Six Sigma' succeeds by measuring defective processes and then improving them, 'Design For Six Sigma' must overcome two major obstacles to this basic approach – the challenge of the *new*, and for *products* and *services*, not just processes.

From time to time, improvement projects are unexpectedly halted midstream during the analysis stage. Usually the first sign of trouble with Six Sigma (once the initial shock of the whole approach has subsided) is when a quality project team is heard wailing 'But there is no process to improve.' The methodology of Six Sigma is a comfortable list of process steps, executed in sequence to achieve the end goal of a reduction in the number of process defects. Continuous improvement is not often seen as a daily activity, and being able to provide employees at all levels with a tried and tested process or routine is an important element of making change and improvement both possible and an everyday part of the culture. Naturally, once the idea of DMAIC is well established and has proven itself, it is rather traumatic to discover that it does not always work.

Cycle time is an excellent measurement for process improvement, as it is often critical to the customer, easy to measure and analyse, and usually open to easy incremental change. Where a customer-facing and manual paperwork process takes an average of three hours, and the customer requirement is for only two hours, improvement is going to be easy. In such processes the real added value or even just the hands-on work can often take less than twenty minutes. The rest, amounting to as much as 95 per cent in the worst cases, is 'fresh air', with documents sitting in in-trays or out-trays for many minutes at a time. In such cases, simple and highly effective improvement often results when a Six Sigma team gets to work. In contrast are the processes that may take weeks, with a substantial mismatch to customer expectation (often measured in just days or hours), and where a large part of the process is believed to be, or really is, unalterable. Having a coffee-making machine, with a cycle time of one minute, is perhaps quite acceptable when placed in a rarely used front office. Require a cycle time of 50 seconds – then run a process improvement team. If, however, you were one of fifty delegates at a conference, each wanting coffee in a fifteen-minute break, clearly the 'get a cup of coffee' process is not going to perform satisfactorily with just one machine and a cycle time of even 40 seconds.

The failure of DMAIC is inherent in perhaps some 5 per cent of process improvement projects, and arises when the analyse stage fails clearly to identify potential incremental improvements to the process, which will alone achieve the desired effect. This may be because there is genuinely no process; however, almost everything has a process of sorts and the usual case here is that the *status quo* is so unsatisfactory that improvement is simply pointless – what is needed is a new process. Alternatively, the capability of the existing process is very limited and incremental change and improvement will not be enough to move forward – again, what is needed is a new process. Further, and typically in service projects rather than manufacturing ones, the team, having measured the process for the first time, may then realize that the 'product' on offer is wholly unacceptable to the customer. The common factor here is the requirement for, or at least the realization of, a need for something new, and this is where the problem lies.

The historic disjuncture between *theoretical capability* and *practical performance* in manufacturing is a root cause of the poor quality experienced by customers. Process capability and process performance are often two widely differing measurements – the performance is what the customer experiences, and the capability is what the process could achieve, under perfect operating conditions. Six Sigma, as a process improvement methodology, allows an organization to eliminate the defects, align these two metrics more closely, and thus provide the customer with an experience not far from continuous perfection. There is, however, always an upper ceiling to what can actually be delivered, as once the defect has been removed, perfection is no better than the theoretical capability under ideal conditions.

Pouring a cup of tea or coffee is a time-consuming process and the best manual performance would be no better than perhaps six cups per minute. The days when tea-ladies pushed trolleys around factories and offices in the UK have probably gone for good, but the legend of the three-spouted teapot still remains. Using this strange object, the dextrous could pour three cups of tea simultaneously. At best this could deliver fifteen or so cups per minute, and with two or three large pots repeated delivery would be brisk indeed. Alas, this is more myth than reality, and the steady march of progress now dictates the need for machines to dispense tea and coffee on demand. With speed and reliability the first priorities, the result has generally been fairly unpalatable, with dried tea being added to hot water in a plastic cup. Making tea, as a beverage, needs time if it is to be done well, and modern machines actually brew fresh tea with real tea-leaves, which adds considerably to the process cycle time. Standing in a line waiting for tea, coffee or just cash from an automatic machine does prompt the question why it takes so long to perform such a simple and repetitive task. There is a real need for machines to punch out tea or coffee at a sustainable ten cups per minute, which is perhaps a challenging target beyond current capabilities. Here is a customer need for someone to design and deliver something that is new with *considerably* better capability and performance. This is such a bold step forward that it no longer remains the improvement of what already exists, but rather becomes the challenge to invent the radically new.

There is a fine line between aggressive stretch targets on the one hand and the almost 'mission impossible' of unbelievable and unacceptable challenge on the other. To introduce the *new* is certainly an order of complexity higher than the improvement of the *existing*, and when the drive is to do so using the sigma metric, the problem is compounded. Here are the two obstacles to the continued use of tried and trusted 'improve for Six Sigma'. First, there is typically nothing to measure, the entity in question of course being *new*, and second, the matter in hand is often concentrated on a product or service and not on a process. Realizing the difficulties in applying DMAIC, and perhaps wanting just one omnipotent methodology, some organizations modify the improve stage to a dual-purpose role of either improve the existing or design/redesign the new. This detracts from the simplistic and neat Six Sigma approach and still leaves many questions unanswered, such as which route does each particular team take, improve or design? It also still leaves the issue of how to approach the design successfully, bearing in mind that the team now has to measure the new, even if the design is still often limited to the process and not the product or service.

Here we have a pressing need for 'design for Six Sigma' to address the areas where 'improve for Six Sigma' cannot reach, for a methodology that is quite at home with new products and services, and where the improvement anticipated is considerably more challenging than just 'improve'. It is the need for non-incremental change that separates Six Sigma and Design For Six Sigma. In application, DMAIC Six Sigma must be something that *everyone* does, day on day, as part of *incremental* improvement of *existing* processes. This is both the power and the place for incremental improvement, taking what exists and simply but methodically inching forward to almost zero defects. The alternative to incremental change is exponential change, which implies an almost explosive introduction of the radically new, sweeping away the existing and dramatically pushing forward the boundaries of what is both possible and achievable. If that is not breathtaking enough, the need is to do all this and yet deliver at a high performance close to four or five sigma from the very start.

Having evolved out of a need from within DMAIC, Design For Six Sigma has a very real home of its own, rather than being tucked back into a part of the parent methodology. In an attempt to clarify, DFSS should be:

> *the design of new products or services, with a six sigma capability and performance.*

Such an activity does have a role to play within the DMAIC methodology, but in contrast, it is much more likely to be something that only a few people do, and as a special event to make exponential improvements to performance against customer CTQs. It therefore has an important place in the involvement of the introduction of the *new* generally and should be used to develop entirely new products and services from scratch. This may be where either nothing existed before, or what did exist is being totally replaced by essentially new products, services and procedures, often heavily based on new technology.

The overarching aim of DFSS is twofold. First, it must be to propel any new product or service, together with the associated processes, to a commercial marketplace at a level of customer quality far in excess of what would be expected traditionally. Second, it must also undertake the stages of design and development to commercialization of such product, service and process with a rigour and efficiency, and above all speed, that better facilitate the commercial introduction of the new product or service with high market impact. Many attempts are now being made to deal with sloppy and unsuccessful design and commercialization processes and DFSS should indeed bring an element of rigour and standardization that may be sadly lacking. On its own 'rigour' is not always the answer; the key driver of the initial success of the new product or service is often excellence in terms of customer quality. However, the best way to enhance the commercial success of the *new* is to ensure a holistic approach to new product or service design that is embodied in a business strategy of new product introduction (NPI). A better definition of all that DFSS amounts to could be:

> *a rigorous approach to the design of a new product or service to reduce delivery time and development cost and to increase the effectiveness of the product or service and hence customer satisfaction.*

A look at the entire end-to-end process of getting a new product or service to the marketplace demonstrates the many areas over which the DFSS methodology and philosophy must achieve and deliver success. Traditional design starts within the 'design arena' and ends in the 'production arena', whereas Figure 1.3 shows that design should start in the 'business arena' and follow right through to the 'usage arena'. There is a requirement within commercial design for the entirety of astute business involvement, good product/service design, quality-controlled production and customer-focused delivery in the marketplace. No world-class product or service can be brought into use without a clear business and marketing strategy, without successful design, without defect-free production, and above all without a perfect delivery to the end customer. To achieve Six Sigma in one area alone will not facilitate success in the whole.

To accomplish all the above and yet take noticeably longer than the competition will gain no real commercial advantage. Being the best in class is often a second-level accolade to being the first to arrive. However, few organizations achieve market dominance from being first, and often not through perfection in the product alone. It is usually the first in the market with the 'right' product who wins, and 'right' is a complex blend of quality, delivery, technical advance and customer acceptance. The largest failure in business is that experienced with the failure to capture the market by introducing something new. Failure can arise from not taking part, from being late, arriving behind others, or simply from delivering something that is not wanted, does not work, is too expensive, or simply cannot be sustained over time. The rich rewards will go to those who can aggressively develop new products and services, rapidly and efficiently, and with guaranteed customer success from day one.

Design For Six Sigma therefore has to be many things, including:

- a way to extend the successful DMAIC framework beyond *improve* to *design*;
- a strategy to facilitate the appropriate introduction of new products and services;

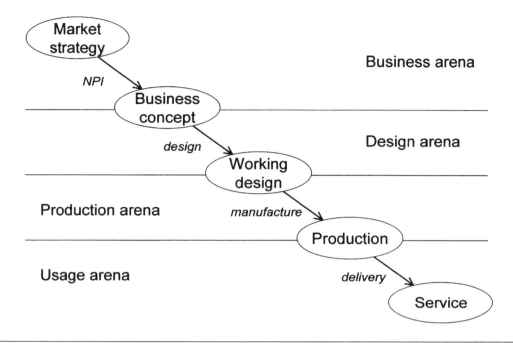

Figure 1.3   The entire design process

- a methodical, rigorous and yet creative framework for the design stage;
- a successful approach to achieving practical commercialization and launch; and
- an environment within which a customer-focused sigma metric predominates.

MANUFACTURING AND SERVICES

Historically design has been almost exclusively associated with physical entities, such as machines, buildings and consumer products. Even today, few people actively and consciously design services and transaction processes. Likewise Six Sigma, arising from a manufacturing need to deliver better-quality products, has been predominantly concerned with process improvement for the physical and corporeal within manufacturing. More and more organizations are now realizing that the artificial boundary between a product and a service, and that between manufacturing and non-manufacturing, is very thin indeed. A more enlightened approach is to consider that products and services are inextricably united both before and during the consumer encounter, and hence customers experience a level of quality dependent upon the ability of the combined product/service and process to meet their expectations and needs. Six Sigma applies perhaps even more appropriately, and often with greater opportunity for success and reward, to service organizations such as call centres, banks, retail outlets and the like, where levels of customer quality are inherently lower than those of product quality in manufacturing. Similarly, DFSS can bring outstanding success to the introduction of new services and transactional processes, where total customer-focused design has often been sadly missing. Figure 1.4 shows from general observation the disparity between manufacturing and service industry where levels of customer quality are between one and two sigma lower. The positioning of the sigma metric scale is arbitrary rather than absolute, as the targets for

Services	Process sigma	Manufacturing	Failure rate %
	6	World class	1/2941
World class	5	Excellent	1/43
	4	Good	0.7
Excellent	3	Average	7
Good			
	2	Poor	30
Average	1		70
Poor	0		93

Figure 1.4　Levels of quality in services versus manufacturing

success/failure are set through customer requirements, and it could indeed be argued that service processes should be measured more leniently or at least differently. The reality is that it is more likely to be the service element of any customer offering that demonstrates the worst level of quality and also offers the greatest area for improvement and gain. DFSS is a stretch to go beyond 'excellent' levels of quality to 'world-class'; failure rates for service-based processes below 1 per cent are often a considerable challenge. Should Six Sigma over time bring about a similar effect within the service area as has been seen over the past fifty years in manufacturing, it is to be expected that the contrast between these two sides of the same coin will gradually diminish.

Figure 1.3 hinted at the fact that a new object, taken from a strategic business need to delivery in the marketplace, emerges via a complex process during which it is not always either just a product or a service. Everything we do is a process, and processes almost without exception deliver both a product and a service, where increasingly the two are inseparable. It is folly indeed to look at the product alone, without seeking out the service by which it is delivered, or to look at the service delivered, without due consideration of what is being produced. It is an appalling tragedy for any commercial enterprise today to regard products and services as wholly separate entities. Whilst appreciation and consideration individually may be both appropriate and necessary for the simpler improvement of processes, the design of the new must involve due consideration of nothing less than the holistic union of product, service and process. In practice, the overarching methodology of DFSS contrasts considerably with DMAIC, in that DFSS has to consider not just one but multiple CTQs, and to create one or more instances of a unified product, service and process.

To better understand what constitutes the *new product and service*, it is worth considering first the 'typical' product and service individually. Perhaps the easier to understand of the two, a product is normally something tangible, physical, with material substance and value. Manufactured products range widely from bricks and widgets to light bulbs, motorcars and spaceships. In contrast, service-related products are often intangible, ethereal, and yet still hold real substance and value. Products associated with, for example, the financial services industry might include loan accounts, current cheque accounts, savings accounts, mortgages, pension and life assurance assets. The key elements of distinction are that a product is an *object*, which possesses physically measurable characteristics, and can be transferred in ownership between individuals.

Product

An entity of significant value, which could be placed into a container and labelled. Packaged and static, the value comes from *having*.

Transactions and services are in truth two distinct things; however, they are almost indistinguishable in practice. All services execute one or more transactions at core, and it is only for the hidden and automatic transaction, such as electronic transfer of monetary funds (direct debits), that the 'service' shell around the transaction becomes purely nominal. Whether called a service or a transaction (this book predominantly uses the former), the key element to distinguish the service from a product is *time*. Services are temporal and less substantial in embodiment than products, in that services occur as a sequence of events over time, and add value to the end customer primarily through their execution.

Service

Execution of a potentially repeatable time-related sequence of events, which add value. Executed and dynamic, the value comes through *performing*.

The financial product of a mortgage or the lending of monies against security can be seen as a product even if the tangible shrinks to a simple piece of paper signed by both parties followed by the almost invisible transfer of funds. Ownership of the product is held by the customer and can be transferred to another, wherein the value of the product is also transferred. The services associated with opening, updating through interest payment or redemption of the mortgage are acts of service transactions where often no product is exchanged but value is imparted, usually with an associated charge. The act of opening a mortgage account is not, however, something that can be completed simply by purchasing an inert object. There are no instant mortgages in boxes on supermarket shelves, and the hopeful house owner often has to endure both the purchase of the product as well as the execution of one or more lengthy service transactions before the product – the loan finance – arrives where it is required.

To understand better the *conjoint* product and service, we can consider as an example a modern and technically complex personal product, which both requires and facilitates many identifiable services. The mobile or cellular telephone has been around for over a decade, and yet only recently has it begun to achieve real market dominance. In the UK, as in Europe generally, more than half the population now owns 'mobiles'. These telephones are not simply products, but a more complex product/service that meets consumer needs, and (significantly) only when both constituent parts of the product/service function correctly and in unison.

Table 1.2 shows how certain aspects of a modern mobile phone can be seen as 'product' and other aspects as 'service', with particular aspects more appropriate to a 'product/service' duality. The phone is a physical product, as is the case, the charger and the 'image' sold through careful marketing. These are all things of value, the amount of value perhaps differing from customer to customer, but all obtained through *purchase*. The purchase process, billing process and repair process are all services, the value of which is gained through *execution*. The process often referred to as 'upgrade', where either phone or contract-related services are exchanged after a period of time, is likewise much more

Table 1.2   Products and services

Product	Product/service	Service
Phone	Phone call	Purchase
Case	Phone number list	Billing
Charger	Charge battery	Repair
'Image'	'Status symbol'	'Upgrade'

of a service than a product. The middle ground can be seen in such things as a telephone call, the use of a personal list of numbers stored in the phone, the charging of the battery and in the 'status value' attached to the 'image' of the phone.

If this concept of a middle-ground product/service is difficult to appreciate, consider the phone battery, without which the phone will simply not operate. The battery is a product, as it is a physical object which hands value to the customer through purchase and ownership. The battery is, however, only half of the story, as it is the electrical charge stored in the battery that really holds the value for the user. The stored charge is in itself a product, but one that is obtained only through the visible service of 'charging the battery'. This 'service' is a time-related sequence of events, where value is obtained through the execution of the sequence, and the totality of value occurs for the customer only when both product and service combine. In contrast, it is today possible to purchase dry-cell (non-rechargeable) batteries, for use when abroad on business or holiday; such an item is clearly a product only for use where the normal charging process will not work.

The status value of a mobile phone, still a key selling point for a considerable part of the market, is both product and service. Status is something that is purchased along with a product, and many manufacturers work hard to build status into mobile phones using 'newness' and fashionable interchangeable covers as well as image branding and marketing. Status, however, is not achieved simply by *having* the object; the value of status is gained, and gained repeatedly, by execution, that is by *using* the product. First buy the most expensive, flashy new phone, and then use it in front of friends to impress!

A more complex product/service example exists where a telephone call is made using a (mobile) phone. Here the product is a point-to-point communication link, set up by the telephone companies, the value of which is given to both callers when it is 'purchased' ('rented' perhaps might be a better word). The value of such a link comes not only from its existence and ownership, but also from such features as stability, correctness and speed of connection, availability (world-wide roaming), cost-effectiveness and others. The service provided comes through a sequence of events, typically prepare the phone, dial a number, use the connection, and terminate the call, followed by billing and payment. Here the value to the user comes through the execution of these services, and also such features as speed, ease, accuracy and accessibility. Now we can begin to see the benefit gained from merging manufacturing and services and in considering the combined product/service from a customer-focused viewpoint. In making a call to a friend on a 'pre-pay' mobile telephone the customer will use both product and service in a joint manner that cannot be separated without utterly destroying our better understanding of experienced quality. To make a call requires the product together with a number of services – turn on phone (easy and reliable), gain network signal (quickly), press just two buttons (easy-to-use stored number), make connection (first time), talk (with stable and clear connection), disconnect (controlled and informed), debit account (accurate and cost-effective). To design any new facet or component of this complex product/service requires due and fair consideration of every part. The model and approach of Design For Six Sigma must be applicable to any form of entity, and will be of considerably greater benefit when the full new product or service is viewed both in totality and from a customer-centric viewpoint.

SUMMARY

- Six Sigma stands for many things, including a metric, a philosophy and a methodology.
  - The philosophy of Six Sigma is total customer satisfaction.
  - The metric of Six Sigma is related to the proportion of a customer-critical process measurement falling outside of the customer requirements. This ties in well with the customer experience of quality, as well as the costs associated with delivering poor customer quality.
  - The methodology of Six Sigma brings together many tools and techniques to enable successful process improvement, through the (often incremental and repeated) identification and elimination of process defects.

- Design For Six Sigma evolves from and is an extension of the simpler 'Improve For Six Sigma'. There is a need for DFSS to extend the ability of Six Sigma to cope with both the *new* and *products* and *services*, and also to advance *exponentially* the inherent capability of each process. Further, DFSS must successfully embrace the entire process of developing, instigating and supporting the new in a more rigorous, efficient and yet creative manner.
- Six Sigma and design have predominated in the area of product manufacture, with service design and high-quality delivery traditionally remaining undervalued and isolated concepts. Products and services may be well defined as:
  - Product – an entity of significant value that could be placed into a container and labelled.
  - Service – execution of a potentially repeatable time-related sequence of events that add value.

The more complex and technical market offerings of today present a more conjoint application of a product/service, and greater success will be achieved through the application of customer-focused design to such new product/services.

EXERCISES

1 Identify ten *new* products or services used or experienced within your immediate household – each should have been introduced to you or the household within the past year, and preferably also be generally new to the marketplace.
2 For each such item, identify the product/service components, and briefly describe the process through which you acquired, experience or use the product/service. Where possible also note the added value brought by the product/service.
3 Identify ten failures or disappointments of each product/service, and rank in order of both occurrence and impact on customer quality. For a chosen top failure, calculate a rudimentary process sigma metric, using DPMO (identify and count opportunities for defect, count or estimate the defects, then use the formula and table in the Appendix).
4 'Many of the failures of new products/services to deliver to customer expectation are entirely due to the original design of the product or service.' Discuss.

CHAPTER TWO

Design considered

Three key elements are required for a successful Design For Six Sigma methodology and approach: first, a customer focus and the ability to measure quality, using the sigma metric and philosophy from Six Sigma, as has been described in Chapter One; second, appropriate design that delivers excitement without failure, and does so to budget and expectation; third, an overarching business strategy and management that brings out the very best for organic growth, through the repeated and regular launch and successful development of new products and services. Strategy and management will be discussed in Chapter Three, but for a fuller understanding of the need and working of DFSS it is essential first to fully understand 'design' *per se.*

Design is perhaps the key activity that humans undertake which sets us apart from the rest of the animal kingdom and may very well be the one thing that computers will neither truly mimic nor replicate. The use of tools by chimpanzees, birds and other creatures is well known and studied; however, design is much more proactive and involves a higher level of thought. It has been said that the arch, a vault of brick or stone, is the key differentiator between mankind and 'lower' levels of life. The argument states that only man has the ability to build the arch and some debate has raged over this statement alone. Termites are known to build arches too, as part of their extraordinary ability to construct a home many metres high. However, this ability is regarded as simply an inherited and autonomous sequence of events, much as follows:

- The colony becomes overcrowded, which is a trigger for some termites to start heaping new material in a pile.
- After a time, check your immediate neighbour's pile, and switch to working on their pile if it is higher.
- At a certain height above the floor, begin to bring two adjacent piles together and thus form an arch.

A visit to a few buildings and bridges will show that the arch is very much in evidence in the field of human endeavour, and mankind has taken many steps forward to both understand and become master of this elemental building structure. Advancement has progressed far, for example in turning the arch upside-down to form the suspension bridge; this provides a hint about the nature of design. Design is mankind's unique ability to solve problems and deliver a fresh answer through the power of thought and planning alone. Arches do not simply grow from an autonomous need for more space, but are carefully devised, conceived and constructed in a form and place that meet the many requirements of that particular time and situation. It is the unique ability to *design* an arch, rather than simply construct one, that sets man apart.

THE NATURE OF DESIGN

Design is often regarded as just a problem-solving exercise – a process and procedure by which a plan is conceived or constructed and which in execution will solve the problem at hand. This can promote a rather shortsighted view that the end goal is simply to identify and implement a solution, which can all too easily be shortened to first finding the solution and second looking for a problem for it to solve. Design often springs from a need for a solution, but that is by no means the entirety of the nature of design.

Many varied definitions of *design* exist, such as 'moulding the environment to suit material and spiritual needs' or alternatively 'initiating change in man-made things'. The idea of 'moulding the environment' is an incomplete definition, since mankind has been doing this without any real plan or thought for thousands of years and little of this could be called conscious design. We light fires to warm our environment, but this is not design, just the application of a known solution to a known problem. Similarly the idea of 'initiating change' is a poor definition, since war and bombs make speedy change: the bigger the bomb, the bigger the alteration. Nero had a plan, and Rome burnt as a result, which was a change but perhaps more a wild reaction than a well-conceived design. What is required is a definition that encompasses the concepts of problem solving, of changing and creating the new, and yet doing so in a way that is measurably better. I suggest that design be described as:

> *The assembly of known entities or concepts into a composite whole, leading to a new entity of value and so as to maximize such value across a wide range of criteria.*

Design is a conceptual activity, in which we take what we already know and convene a new thing that is, we hope, a better solution to a given need. It is important to separate this from the invention or discovery that may precede design, and from the execution of the plan that usually follows it. Design is neither invention nor discovery, but rather the better use and application of already known ideas and practices to create a new composite entity of better value. Figure 2.1 helps to position design against such concepts as *discovery, technology, engineering* and *new products*. As it can be seen that fields of *endeavour* lead to new *concepts*, which through *application* lead to new *entities*, then design is part of the activity that takes a 'concept through an application to a new entity'. The other part of this journey is the less conceptual activity of engineering, craftsmanship and commerce that takes a worked design and transforms it into hard and often commercial reality. We probably see design as a blend of these many elements, for practical design often requires some invention as well as practical execution to complete. Design takes place in very many fields, from literature and music, the visual

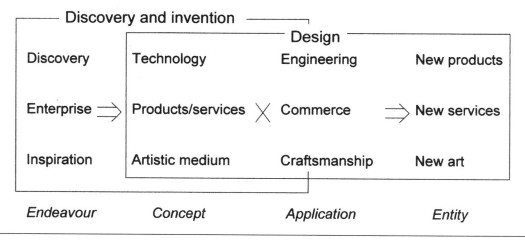

Figure 2.1 The positioning of design

and performing arts, to engineering and manufacture, to name but a few. From inspection, the entire range of human endeavour can be divided into three broad categories – the sciences, the arts, and trade and commerce. Each area propagates the new through its own field of endeavour, expressed most often as scientific discovery, artistic inspiration and commercial enterprise. Such endeavours lead to new technology, new artistic media and new commercial products and services, and it is the application of engineering, craftsmanship or commerce that actually turns such ideas into new products, services or expressions of art. On the one side we have discovery and invention, a purely creative and inspired activity, and on the other side design with implementation, the practical conversion of high-order concepts and ideas into the hard reality of pragmatic and commercial use. Areas such as scientific discovery lead only to new technology, just as artistic inspiration leads only to a new medium in which to practise. It is the application of design and the associated skills that transform both existing and new things into the furtherance of new products and services. These skills may include the full range, from engineering, craftsmanship and commerce, which in their totality enshrine the ideals of design.

As products and services become more and more complex, the requirements of effective design now include many skills from the broad range of technology, art and commerce. In contrast, the elemental activities pursued are often segregated into particular jobs, and the very large multinational of today will often have researchers in an R&D department, designers in a design department and production engineers somewhere else. The artist who was inspired to use plastic sheeting as a new medium required craftsmanship to develop the use of this material, and then had to work to solve problems to wrap a chosen rocky outcrop in plastic. It is quite typical to find artists such as these actively involved in the entire 'inspiration, design and execution' of their work, but not so in other walks of life. What, then, makes for good and successful design?

The development of the railway locomotive is an excellent example of the interplay between discovery, design, technology, engineering and commerce. Many labour under the mistaken impression that George Stephenson invented the railway locomotive. In reality, steam was discovered shortly after fire, and several historical figures dabbled with the properties of steam, realizing simple turbines or cylinder-piston mechanics. It was Thomas Newcomen in the first half of the eighteenth century who was the first commercially to harness the power of steam, or more correctly the power of the atmosphere. Using low-pressure steam from a rudimentary haystack boiler, a large cylinder would be filled with steam to exclude as much air as possible and then condensed with a jet of water. This created a partial vacuum and the air pressure drove the piston downwards. These engines were slow and very inefficient, but practical, robust and far more effective than water or horse power, and were normally found being used as pumping and lifting engines for deep mines and the like. James Watt was responsible for most of the improvements to steam-engine design during the second half of the eighteenth century and took good care to patent every idea and change he devised. His principal alteration was to introduce a separate condenser, which dispensed with the need to repeatedly chill and warm the working cylinder, and Watt sold his engines according to the savings in coal for the work obtained against a similar size of Newcomen engine. Measurement was facilitated using counters (an early improvement project and 'cost of poor quality', perhaps) and Watt has passed into history as the name now associated with the unit of work.

Watt, with his partner Matthew Boulton, made a comfortable business and was not overly keen or in any real need to extend the abilities of the steam engine with higher pressures. Patents are wonderful for protecting the laudable rights of an inventor to profit from their labour and achievement; however, they have a tendency to stifle proactive development for a considerable period of time. As high-pressure steam was also only really practical when boiler design and construction improved, not much changed for many years. It was Richard Trevithick who endeavoured the hardest both to raise pressure beyond the 5–10 lb per square inch then in use and to further improve the design by applying steam rather than air to the outside of the piston. With his own steam engines gradually reducing in size yet growing in power, in 1804 Trevithick accepted a wager to build and run the world's first steam locomotive over the recently built 9½-mile Penydaren Tramway. The engine used for the wager was in fact designed and intended for a sawmill and was modified to drive the normally stationary wheels it was to be moved around on. The attempt worked after a fashion, and once proven, others gradually followed to improve the design. By the time Stephenson came to build the now famous *Rocket* for the Rainhill trials at the Liverpool and Manchester Railway in 1829, steam locomotive design had quite rapidly progressed through many stages and perhaps some two dozen working designs.

Here we begin to see in reality the very nature of design, where a designer/engineer struggles to overcome practical difficulties to achieve a new device or plan of commercial worth. Newcomen was a great inventor, but did not progress his design once he had a working machine. Watt was a great inventor and businessman, but did not progress his work either, once he held the dominant market. Trevithick was a great inventor and improver, but made no long-term gain or commercial success out of his work; he started more things in life than he ever finished. Stephenson is regarded as a very conservative engineer for his day, but was highly successful in taking what was available and fashioning it into something new and of usable and commercial value. Isambard Kingdom Brunel entered the railway engineering fray a few years after Stephenson, but is today noted as one of the greatest designers and engineers of the Victorian period. Brunel's bold and grand schemes often ran into many difficulties, both financial and practical, but it is noted that for many of his designs he returned to basic principles to fully evaluate what would be the *best possible design*.

The 'battle of the gauges' that marked the early years of railway mania in Britain was as much a battle over good design as it was a fight for market territory. In designing the new mainline railways Stephenson and his contemporaries had to rework almost every aspect of the basic precedent provided by early tramways. In essence every component of the undertaking was redesigned to bring together both new objects as well as new ways of putting the plan together, track and steam locomotion being two key areas for much-needed improvement. Stephenson had simply adopted the then typical gauge of the track used by tramways and plateways of the northern coalmines, and this gauge itself probably dated to Roman occupation. The Romans standardized and mass-produced long before Henry Ford, and all fort and city gateways were of a similar size, with carts and wagons having a standard width between the wheels. Over centuries this produced marked ruts in the roads at these gateways and after the Romans had gone it was far easier to continue with the same size than to change. In due course the prevailing carts and wagons were adapted for use on early tramways and hence the 'standard' gauge of 4 ft 8½ in came into being across many parts of the country. Why should Stephenson use anything different for the early railways? After all it worked. Brunel in contrast stopped to wonder if this gauge was indeed the best to use, and at a critical point in time designed and engineered the formative Great Western Railway (GWR) from London to Bristol using a gauge of seven feet.

Brunel was often far more adventurous than others, and certainly had a grounding in invention gained from his father, Marc Brunel. It was Marc who had invented the tunnelling shield, inspired apparently by the tough head of the ship-worm that eats its way through timber, that was used to build the world's first sub-aquatic tunnel under the Thames at Rotherhithe. Both father and son had laboured to invent a 'gaz engine', but without any real success. In changing the gauge Brunel instigated a major alteration to the fundamental design of his railway, which Stephenson had avoided but was thus constrained to smaller, less stable and slower locomotives and wagons. The simple question as to the width between the rails was a key facet in the design, which thus affected the building, functioning, and ultimately the future and success of the GWR.

The true nature of design is a battle waged between many conflicting aspects within the creation of a plan for the new. Boundaries between invention, design and execution are certainly not clear, but it is true to say that the nature of proactive and advanced design touches on creative invention and is often realized only through skilled practical interpretation. Such questions as to what constitutes good design, and how design actually takes place, have still to be answered.

ELEMENTS OF DESIGN

Having realized that design by its very nature is a complex mix of skills and abilities, often instrumental in creating a plan for the new, the next logical consideration must be to centre on the key elements leading to a definition and practice of *good* design. Design may range from conservative and bland through to visionary and challenging, but the outcome of the design activity must be measurable on a scale at least from 'bad' to 'good', depending upon the experience and approval or otherwise of the many involved. Even today the argument continues as to whether Brunel's broad gauge was a better design for a railway. How can this be judged, unless there is first an understanding of the key ingredients for success? The broad gauge was more expensive to build and rapidly suffered from becoming the non-standard for the British Isles, which was ultimately to prove its downfall. In contrast the larger gauge paved the way for the GWR to provide bigger locomotives and larger carriages, which were faster and more comfortable to ride in, as well as slightly more economic to run and maintain.

It might seem that design success comes from a list of positive and negative points achieved in practical execution, although this is only part of the visible accomplishment of good design. More fundamental, perhaps, is the need for design to achieve positively in seven critical areas:

● Foundation – a primary necessity
● Form – aesthetic appeal
● Function – practical benefit in use
● Formation – ease of instantiation
● Facilitation – ease of maintenance
● Flexibility – future adaptation and change
● Favour – satisfaction and approval.

To consider the importance of each element, and what happens when an element is lacking in the design offering, we can turn to the activity of bridge building. The railway age from 1830 to 1900 in Great Britain did much to accelerate best practice in a number of fields, and the building of bridges and bridge design generally was one such notable area. Before the canal age bridges were typically only built where roads needed to cross rivers, and the basic design had evolved gradually from just two primary forms. Many civilizations had built crossings using lintels of stone (the Greeks) or arches, again of stone or brick (the Romans). Flat stone bridges still exist, but are prone to failure, as stone is not the best material to use under tension. Wood and rope are excellent materials for many situations, but tend not to last well, and certainly not when in contact with water. Predominantly bridge design and construction was based on the arch and, as for large buildings, this was very much part of the stonemasons' art and craft. With the advent of canal building there was a greater need for many more over-bridges and a few aqueducts. When railways came to the landscape, the need for progressive and radical change completely outstripped the slow and sure pace of evolutionary design, principally since railway tracks were initially challenged to be as level as possible.

If we consider new bridges of today, for example the London Millennium Bridge over the river Thames, we can begin to see the importance of each element in contributing towards good design.

FOUNDATION

The primary element of successful design requires a need for a basic problem to be solved in the first place. This may seem too obvious for words, but nevertheless many people design either without need, or for the wrong reason, particularly so in the service industry. It can be said that 'design a better mousetrap and the world will beat a path to your door'; however, this must have been written by an inventor rather than an accountant. The need for mousetraps today is sparse, and the available models have no real fault or lack of performance. Across the UK several millennium projects came to fruition during 2000, and almost every one is receiving acclaim for achievement in design. Several footbridges have been constructed, and each has a foundation in meeting a need to journey between two points hitherto distanced by difficult or impossible terrain. The London Millennium Bridge opens a new access from the City of London to the new Tate Modern. In contrast, the Millennium Dome has proven to be without foundation and was perhaps constructed just for the sake of building something to celebrate the year 2000. Whilst the building is a world-class example of design and technical achievement in creating space, there is almost no provable need for the building as a visitor attraction and it has notably underperformed as a commercial success. The Dome was designed and built out of a need to achieve for the millennium, and then something was sought to fill the space. Far better, maybe, to have designed the visitor attraction, firmly based on a real need, and then put a building around it.

FORM

Perhaps this is the most typically overworked and overstated part of design today. Since many professional designers (those who design for a living) have a real and pressing need to sell their abilities and skills, the visual aspect of the solution is often taken out of proportion. The perceptible and demonstrable appearance of a design is both a short-term sell and often the only realization of the composite solution before execution. It also has a long-term appeal in many cases where distanced users only have contact with the design by sight, and Victorian engineers were well aware of the impact this could have.

Since sight is the dominant of our five senses, visual design is often lauded over practicality and mechanical design. The London Millennium Bridge epitomizes the folly of vision over practice, in that the design aims were to produce a very flat bridge with visual appeal and sleek lines. There is no doubt that this bridge looks quite outstanding, particularly when illuminated at night. However, in striving for flatness over function, the bridge as built suffers from excessive oscillation and wobble in use. After a cost of over £18 million and 18 months in building, the bridge was closed after only four days of public use, and it will require perhaps £5 million and 12 months to make alterations to reduce or dampen this fault. The question has to be asked why a modern bridge with such a long tradition of design could be constructed and yet be so unacceptable in use. In balance of course it must be noted that visual appeal is sometimes critical in obtaining public acceptance, and many mobile phones are today designed and purchased in sole consequence of the appeal of the visual form.

FUNCTION

Fighting for a righteous first place, and yet often relegated to second or even third position, is the need for functional success: if the design delivers something that does not work either in part of whole, it will soon be deemed a failure. This is the counterpoise to *form* for the Millennium Bridge, as the real users are those who walk across it, not those who see it from afar; it was the general public who experienced the immediate design failure after opening. Historically it is the *function* element that has, if anything, failed in the vast majority of bridge designs. Collapse is due to poor material use, poor construction or maintenance, or inappropriate design generally. The railway bridge over the river Dee in Chester was designed almost as a flat lintel construction and used the available cast iron of the day. Regrettably, while fine in many situations, cast iron is brittle and little stronger than stone under tension, and the bridge collapsed under a train in 1847. The film of the *Tacoma Narrows* suspension bridge collapse of 1940 is a classic to rival *Gone with the Wind* and that particular bridge has probably been seen oscillating itself to destruction by more people than have seen the latter film!

Although failure of function tends to be catastrophic with bridges, they generally only have the one function, which either succeeds or fails. Oddly enough, with more complex and multifunctional objects it is perhaps failure or diminution of function that the customer accepts above all other elemental failures. Many products and services disappoint, and yet still remain stoically in use.

FORMATION

A far more esoteric element of good design, the ability to complete the plan as a practical instantiation is generally given less consideration than it requires and deserves. It is certainly a folly of almost monstrous proportions to design something that simply cannot be built, unless there was never any intention to execute the design. The final designs for some of the early railway bridges concentrated as much on how the bridge was going to be constructed as they did on how it was going to perform as a bridge. Brunel was a romantic engineer, but often accomplished some of his best work in the avid pursuit of practical execution. The Saltash railway bridge was of a variant construction type (the closed arch or modified suspension), a challenge enough in itself, but half of the challenge was getting the two large components floated out and raised into position. The launch of the *Great Eastern* steamship required the moving of some 12 000 tonnes, a major task which likewise had never been undertaken before. Design for manufacture is now realized as being essential and a critical factor for execution, quality and cost.

FACILITATION

Once designed and built, the entity must be maintained in working order, but not everything is designed with this in mind. A key factor if a design is to remain usable over an extended period of time is the *facilitation* for maintenance and upkeep.

The Tay railway bridge, designed and built by Thomas Bouch in 1878, crossed the Firth of Tay as part of the east-coast main line in Scotland. Badly designed, built and maintained, it fell down in a storm a year later during the passage of a train, and has passed into history as perhaps the most famous railway accident of all time. Certainly the design did not take sufficient account of wind pressure, and the on-site casting of the iron support piers was below an acceptable standard. The inquiry did note, however, that no provision had been made for regular inspection and maintenance. Buildings are still designed and built today where there is no easy way of cleaning the windows without abseiling down the sides!

The Forth railway bridge, crossing the Firth of Forth in Scotland, followed the failure of the Tay Bridge, and owes much of its over-engineered design to public reaction from the preceding disaster.

A fine design based on the cantilever principle, and well executed, the bridge is now almost a national monument for Scotland, and a real problem to paint. Start at one end, and by the time painting is done it is time to start all over again.

The modern motorcar has benefited from more time and expense lavished on the design stage than almost any other object of our time, and yet how long does it take to perform a routine service? Often it is the maintenance engineers who learn the hard way the good and bad aspects of 'design for maintenance'.

FLEXIBILITY

Flexibility, though perhaps not in the literal sense, is the ability of a design to be adaptable to a future and changing environment. The success of early railway bridges in remaining in use 150 years later is due more to grandeur (the visible sell) and the over-tall funnels on early locomotives. When Stephenson and Brunel designed early bridges they needed to support a locomotive and train of some 30 tonnes, travelling at 20 to 40 miles per hour. Today the same bridges support loads of ten- or twenty-fold, at considerable speeds, and in most cases without major alteration over the years. The loading gauge (the space around locomotives and carriages) was set high by the need for a tall chimney to draw the fire in inefficient boilers, and without this need many more bridges would have long since been rebuilt. When overhead electrification was introduced on many lines, bridge after bridge had to be replaced to provide the extra clearance needed for the wires, at considerable cost. There is a need for a certain amount of hindsight as well as foresight in design, and a balance between extension of the design for the future and the added cost and inconvenience today.

FAVOUR

Last, *favour* is the acceptance of the design, or of its instantiation, by peers, customers and the general public. The customer for a product or service often has the last word, and sometimes the most damning. In the example of bridge design, urban road schemes in the UK have left a legacy of footbridges dotted about large towns now only used to hang publicity banners from, although this may have more to do with lack of foundation and real need than public favour. Even where there is a real need, lack of public approval or even acceptance can deal a fatal blow, as with the notorious Sinclair C5 electric 'car' and as indeed still happens with some motorcars today.

DESIGN AS AN ACTIVITY

Before the Industrial Revolution activities commonly associated with design were generally restricted to major buildings, landscaped gardens and instruments of war. Interestingly enough, the words 'engine' and 'engineer' come from the military siege engines of Roman and later medieval times. It was perhaps the Roman Empire that first propagated the best skills in design and engineering execution. The Romans had brilliant technology (much of which came from the Greeks) but failed to innovate, and the basic application and principles first adopted were still in use almost unchanged some four centuries later when their empire collapsed.

Design as a process had altered little until the pace of change and demands of the Industrial Age forced a more radical approach. A few individuals held the critical knowledge of the way things had been done in the past, and this was replicated time after time without much alteration. Any new advances were slow and often insubstantial, with the way forward being tested wholly by experience. The basic design of a stone cathedral worked, and if the next one to be built was bigger or different, it either fell down or stayed put, and where it fell down the master craftsmen were generally able to reason why and not to make the same error twice. Naturally such design only worked where the knowledge and experience base was passed from generation to generation, and often the master at his art would travel extensively from country to country supervising any new building work. With accelerated discovery and invention, the religious, political and business growth strategy of Europe, and the bland climate of Great Britain, the Industrial Revolution rapidly swept aside almost every aspect of centuries of rural farming existence and paved the way for the technological and commercial society of today. The *new* has prevailed for over three hundred years, and it is the need to design or redesign regularly, repeatedly and at will that has brought the activity of design to the fore.

To be successful design requires five key enablers:

1   A principal discovery or invention to underpin the potential for a new solution
2   The wherewithal in technology, resource and expertise to produce and deliver
3   Commercial need and support together with leadership to promote and execute the design
4   Several loops of a *design cycle* to acquire skills and understanding and to attain perfection
5   Early success to engender favour commercially, publicly and with employees, together with a noted lack of any critical failure.

The first three points are really triggers that start the design cycle and ensure that it can complete at least one loop. To begin any successful design activity, an *invention*, the *technology* and ready *commerce* are all required, but not necessarily in that order. Perhaps most typically the invention comes first, followed by the technology and then commercial backing, such as for the steam locomotive. Less common is the situation where the invention is followed by commercial backing looking for the technology to exploit the idea. Large organizations today often run R&D establishments funded to take existing patented ideas and find a way of making them work for commercial gain. In wartime such ideas as nuclear capability, well understood in theory before 1940, were accelerated to practical use under an extreme pace of technological development. In other situations the technology may come first, with inspiration seeking a new way of using it to solve a problem. Very rarely does commerce precede both discovery and technology. In healthcare, for example, large-scale funded research into cancer and the like begin with commercial backing, look for the discovery, and then find the technology to make it happen.

Whatever the nature of design, and however the success of design is measured, design is basically an activity completed through a process. The basic design loop is about *selection* and *making choices*, then about *communication* and *implementation*, and finally about *assessment*, *evaluation* and *commercialization*. Figure 2.2 shows the most basic design process, which has its origins with a *plan – do – check – act* loop. There are perhaps many paths through such a design process, depending upon the freshness of the invention and technology, as well as the number of times the loop has to be executed before success is deemed to be attained. In the extreme case design can range from *minor* to *major design*. Major design takes place where the invention is new, the technology uncertain and the commercial risk high. Here it would be expected that several loops of *design – build – use – evaluate* will be necessary, and the inevitable risk is that far too many loops are required before commercial success is assured. Minor design, in contrast, might be seen where the invention and technology are already well established and all that is being undertaken is one single loop. As design is now a well-established activity, minor design is very common and takes place whenever something like a new house is designed, or a new factory using a 'design and build package'. The domestic design of a new kitchen, for example, uses no new ideas or technology but simply makes a fresh selection of options to effectively rearrange what already exists. There is a real risk that major design is treated as minor by assumption and thus not properly executed. The London Millennium Bridge might be

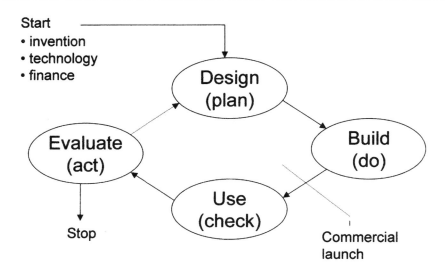

Figure 2.2   A poor design cycle

considered as an example: typical suspension bridges work with a span to cable-dip ratio of 10:1, which has changed very little in almost any design. In this new footbridge, with a view to obtaining outstanding visual flatness, there are no cable towers and the span to cable-dip ratio has been increased to 63:1, far in excess of standard practice. This is sufficient to constitute major design; however, it is interesting to note that the bridge was not tested under dynamic load, as this was not deemed necessary.

In many architectural, typographical or couture establishments, design activity is part of the everyday work, and is mostly minor. This does not in any way diminish the importance of successfully completing one, and perhaps only one, loop of the design cycle. It does, however, heighten the importance of major design, as perhaps can be seen in the development of the steam locomotive. When George Stephenson came to build the *Rocket* for the Rainhill trials, he had behind him the invention of the steam engine, which had led to high-pressure steam and engines that were then powerful and light enough to become mobile. Stephenson had some fifteen years of experience in locomotive development, much of which he had gained personally, and the backing of some very powerful figures in the north of England industrial arena. The Liverpool and Manchester Railway (L & M) had been constructed, much as canals and tramways of that age were, on a plateau and incline basis, and was anticipating the use of stationary engines to run cable inclines. Stephenson suggested the use of steam locomotives and the financial choice for the railway company was quite simple. They required some 48 stationary engines to run the line, but a trial of only two or three new locomotives would cost much less and would not compromise a later reversion to stationary engines if the trial failed. Stephenson had the invention, the commercial backing, and was able to overcome the technical difficulties and exploit the potential of steam. The Rainhill trials were successful in many ways, not least in that they proved the better solution (of four entrants) and visibly generated supportive public interest. The line opened shortly after the trials using a small fleet of *Rocket*-type locomotives and from the very beginning passengers unexpectedly became a major part of traffic on the line. The locomotive option was accepted by the business, it was a commercial success, it worked in practice, and there were no major failures for the L & M. It was thus that in 1830 the Liverpool and Manchester Railway entered the history books, as the first commercial and publicly accessible major railway on specialized track to run a service intentionally using steam locomotives.

This might seem a fairly simple example of the design activity, although it does show that Stephenson did not begin with a blank sheet of paper, and it must be noted that locomotive design in the UK continued to evolve for more than one hundred years after Rainhill. It is also worth noting that the L & M were fortunate, as all earlier and several later railways experienced considerable failures with steam locomotives in their early years. In contrast to the apparently neat design activity for steam locomotives, the rail track used in early railways in England went through a protracted period of design and development before the present-day approach was adopted. Early use of track originated in deep mining for coal and ore, where small tubs or *drams* were in use underground to move material around. These were difficult to manoeuvre, and the use of planks of wood to run the wheels on was soon augmented by a dowel on the dram running between the planks and acting as a guide, forming the early dramway. Over time this evolved into a wood track system with running rails cross-tied by dormant rails or sleepers to which they were pegged. Wooden tracks went from single pieces of hard wood, sometimes six inches square, to hard wood facings on soft wood. When iron became more available the wood was faced by cast iron, and finally the wood was omitted altogether as water often accumulated at the join, rotting the timber and rusting the metal. In moving to metal running rails or tramways, two distinct and regional variations appeared, one being a plateway with a guide lip on the rail and flat wheels, and the other an edgeway with a flat running surface on the rail and the guide on the wheel. Unless covered in ballast, wooden sleepers were very prone to damage and wear from the hoofs of horses and donkeys used to pull carts on larger tramways. As it was expected that rigidity would be needed to deal with the many rail breakages seen, the rails were fixed to large stone or granite blocks set well into the ground, and wooden sleepers were universally omitted. This measure was expensive, actually increased the number of broken rails, and removed altogether the action of the cross-tie to hold the two rails together. When Stephenson and his contemporaries began to construct larger railways, not only did they use an existing and typical gauge, but they also adopted the typical rail and block system from the edgeway, albeit with modified and larger rails. It was only Brunel who questioned the entire approach, and set about designing the perfect rail-bed from scratch. The design was radical and new in almost every aspect and, in a style typical of Brunel, it was he who sold it to the railway company rather than being asked for it. The need for a better track was for Brunel self-evident, as he had travelled on Stephenson's track on the L & M, and noticed the unevenness and slow speed. Brunel wanted a smooth and fast journey and rightly reasoned that the track was a critical limiting factor. His solution was for a new type of rail on a wider gauge, fully supported on timber rails and tied together by cross-ties, with the entire track held down by vast piles of wood some ten inches square and driven seven feet into the ground. Brunel had noted that heavy and faster-moving locomotives had a tendency to push the plateway rails apart and reasoned that a completely rigid track was required. Hindsight is a wonderful tool, particularly compared to foresight; today it is realized that a degree of flexibility is required in rail track. Brunel's track soon became a very real source of trouble, as over time the ballasting under the rails settled or was washed away, leaving the piles holding the track up instead of holding it down. This was almost the greatest early problem encountered on the GWR, along with difficulties met from the poor performance of the early broad-gauge engines. Brunel almost lost his position as engineer to the railway – acceptance of the solution and early success are indeed important in any design. In contrast to the concept of careful design and planning, the solution to the track problem was found almost by accident. On certain sections of his line Stephenson had compromised on the standard rail and stone system by using wooden sleepers to support the track. Wood was used where the track passed over soft ground and the heavy stone blocks were liable to sink. Over time it was noticed that these sections of track performed very much better than elsewhere, and the use of wooden sleepers gradually replaced the original approach.

This is design at its worst commercially – an evolutionary hotchpotch of ideas and approaches without rhyme or reason and often losing sight of good ideas, going backwards and only learning by hard experience and failure. Although there was nothing radically new in either invention or technology, very many loops of the design cycle were performed without real success at any one time. Although George Stephenson was noted as being uncooperative and unimaginative, and Brunel perhaps too grand and fanciful, both Brunel and Robert Stephenson (son of George) are noted for moving design on to a more scientific activity, based on observation, measurement and considered experimentation. Robert Stephenson needed to construct bridges both at Conway and Menai, close to where Telford had advanced the use of the suspension bridge several decades earlier when building the A5 London to Holyhead road. Suspension bridges are generally not used for railways, being less than stable with live loads and very prone to collapse (a fact which still seems to escape designers, perhaps because suspension bridges *look* too good). Stephenson came up with a radical new bridge construction using metal tube girders and running the train through the tubes themselves. Together with an associate and a consultant mathematician, he designed, built and tested a one-sixth-scale model to test and observe deflection, and then constructed the smaller of the two bridges at Conway. The larger Britannia Bridge over the Menai, like Brunel's bridge at Saltash, remains a striking example of how successful and progressive the design activity can be.

FAILURES IN DESIGN

Historically design has been an evolutionary activity pursued through the passage of many circular loops, where failure was primarily encountered in the inability of the final design to meet and solve the primary need. With greater pressure on the design activity to make radical and rapid advances, failure is as much about lack of timely delivery as it is about failure of the product so designed. In the highly commercial pressure of today, design needs to be radical, speedy, effective, efficient and thorough.

Failure in design in manufacturing is endemic, since the design process usually takes some five or six attempts to get the product right and the users generally do not have either the time or the patience to wait. Failure in services seems almost to be taken for granted, as any new service will typically evolve through failure and adjustment in the marketplace rather than any conscious up-front design. The contradiction is this: to be commercially effective, design must be major, bold and revolutionary, and yet to be successful it must be minor, incremental and evolutionary. Observation and experience from the field clearly shows that the *new* must become acceptable and 'catch on' during the first two or at most three loops of the design activity, and yet it often requires longer. It is therefore worth stating quite clearly:

New products (and services) are almost guaranteed to fail.

Failure in design comes from either failure in the delivered output, or failure in the design process, leading usually to delay and overrun on budget. Elimination of the reasons for failure, with appropriate risk analysis, is vital to design generally, and essential for a DFSS approach. Poor design activity generates:

- products or services that no one needs or wants;
- products or services that are ugly, both physically as well as practically;
- products and services that fail, degrade rapidly, or deliver below expectation;
- products that are hard to produce, maintain or change over time; and
- services that are inefficient, cannot be sustained, and lack the flexibility to adapt.

It is worth asking just how much of the typical product failure is applicable either directly or indirectly to the original design. I have a new mobile telephone that is also very new to the marketplace and is one of the first commercial WAP offerings (Wireless Application Protocol, a form of mobile Internet). The phone is made by a well-respected company (which is using Six Sigma in the manufacturing processes) but in only four months' use it has demonstrated a considerable number of disappointments. The product itself is very well made, nice to use, robust and reliable and typical of the excellent level of well-designed and well-made manufacturing output in the field of telecommunications. The typical user, however, does not purchase the phone simply as an icon of modern manufacture, but rather to use as an all-purpose communication tool. Failures noted by the user are those experienced from the poor quality of the product/service and its inability to deliver reliably to expectation. This will be viewed in totality, even though an altogether independent telecommunication company provides the communication service. Here is my list of the failures and disappointments experienced in using this product/service to date:

1   The spring-loaded cover has broken and no longer works.
2   The 'ear piece' is difficult to locate at the ear without audio feedback.
3   The phone takes too long to initialize when switched on.
4   The SIM card memory cannot be accessed quickly when first switched on.
5   The backlight goes off sooner than expected, and cannot easily be turned on when required.
6   The network connection is unreliable even in good signal areas.
7   The signal strength is too low to use the phone indoors at home.
8   Voice (and text) messages, once left, can take hours to be notified on the phone.
9   The voice message service is sometimes activated even when the phone is on and working.
10 The 'vibrate' setting is not easy to turn off, and still operates even when off.
11 The data modem can become 'confused', requiring the phone to be switched off and on to reset.
12 The WAP information service only works about 40 per cent of the time.
13 The auto-menu customer support service only works about 80 per cent of the time.
14 Failure of either service is not explained, but attempts at use are still charged to the customer.
15 Account call charges via the information service can be four to five days out of date.
16 Calls while roaming abroad do not perform as described in the roaming documentation.
17 Many of the more commonly used options in the large and complex menu are difficult to get to.
18 The phone is already obsolete, and change or upgrade is difficult and expensive.

And the list continues to grow! It could indeed be argued that the majority of items on this list are ultimately an outward expression of poor design in either the product or service provision. The new WAP service is a classic example of a commercial drive to deliver a new product/service without good overall design. Very few mobile phone users suffer any real want without WAP, and the current WAP offering is very much below user expectation. The delivery of the service is currently demonstrably bad, with a process sigma for access to any particular page of just one or two at best (ten measured and successive attempts failed on seven occasions). Even where failure occurs in the execution of the service components of the product/service, the original design activity can be quite capable of ensuring that failure is designed out of both product and service. If the cover is likely to break or fail, then it should be designed not to break, to be easily repaired or replaced by the user at very low cost and inconvenience, and/or to have a lower profile in the user experience of the product.

Going back to Figure 1.3, it can be seen that design failure can occur when:

- the business selects an inappropriate strategy for the design need;
- the design process fails to deliver a suitable solution;
- the design cannot be manufactured with ease and reliability; or
- the product performs badly, cannot be maintained or fails to excite and gain favour.

The current WAP offering probably scores a valid hit on every single one of the above points. In contrast, successful design must achieve two objectives. First, the design cycle must be shortened by any means possible, perhaps in terms of the length of time between commencement and the attainment of a successful design, rather than the start-to-stop single loop cycle, as even good design may take too many circuits around the loop. Second, the designed product or service must deliver successfully in each and every element: it must be wanted, effective, aesthetically pleasing, easy to deliver, maintain and evolve, and above all gain favour in use.

Figure 2.3 shows the basic improved design cycle that provides the necessary rigour for DFSS. To deal with the failures in use of both product and service it is important to learn from the past and to learn from experience in use through testing. To deal with the failures of inappropriate strategy, lack of favour and poor performance, it is important to learn through exposing the design to business and customer requirements early on in the cycle. By shifting the starting point to first learning by example, then testing a concept against business and customer needs, evaluating the design against quality metrics, and then piloting prototypes, by the time the design is launched commercially it will be guaranteed a greater degree of success. Success in design comes from a rigorous approach, a customer focus, and in ensuring that hindsight becomes foresight:

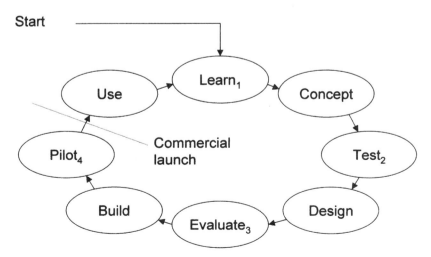

Learn – by example$_1$, by exposure$_2$, by examination$_3$, by experience$_4$

Figure 2.3 Improved design cycle

- learn by example from both the present and the past;
- learn by exposure to business scrutiny;
- learn by examination against customer requirements; and
- learn by experience in test and prototype.

Failure of the design activity can ultimately be measured in terms of hard costs. There are real costs associated with an inefficient design process where effort is wasted or the process generates much rework. There are ongoing costs associated with the full life cycle of the product or service in use. Any extra work or material that could have been avoided in production, maintenance or future evolution of the product is waste and might as well have been designed out of the equation. Figure 2.4 shows how the costs associated with any change in product or service design across the full design cycle grow exponentially. Where the cost for conceptualization and associated changes can be measured in terms of 'one', the costs at the design stage are often measured as ten- and even a hundred-fold – the costs associated with changing and correcting design faults once in production and commercial use can measure 10 000-fold. One hour of extra work and thought at the concept stage could save 10 hours in design, 100 hours in prototype, 1000 hours in production and over 10 000 hours when the product is in commercial use! There are also very real costs associated with the failure to capture or dominate a market segment through failure to design appropriately, design well, design for the customer and design efficiently and timely.

DFSS must provide a better design process, a better-designed product and service, with inherently higher capability to deliver better value to both the company and the customer:

- lower design costs through a shorter and more effective cycle;
- lower production costs (design for production);
- lower maintenance costs (design for maintenance);
- lower future adaptation or removal costs (design for the future);

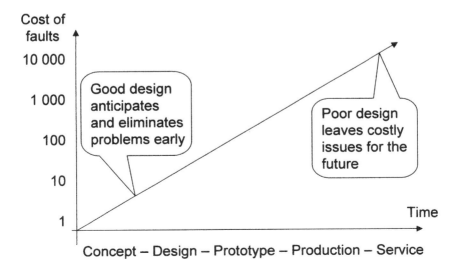

Figure 2.4   Cost impact of poor design

- higher end-user acceptance (targeted customer needs and wants);
- higher intrinsic value, leading to greater commercial worth; and
- higher strategic value, through future growth, market penetration and consolidation.

Of course there is a very marked conflict between the needs of the customer and those of the company. To design well from the customer perspective often takes a long time and much work, and to design well from the company perspective often requires an acceptable commercial offering 'yesterday'. This conflict of interest can be a primary contributor to design failure, but the solution is not to be found within the design process itself. Often the question of 'price', or just what is charged to the end customer, is quietly ignored from the process and left to marketing. Price is very much part of the conflict of interest between customer and company, and all of this is a question of corporate strategy.

SUMMARY

- Design is the assembly of known ideas and objects to form a new composite plan to add value in solving a problem. It is a separate activity from *invention and discovery*, and also the *execution* of the design, but often requires input from both to succeed in practice.
- The seven critical elements of good design are:

  1 Foundation, a need
  2 Form, the visual appeal
  3 Function, success in action
  4 Formation, design for manufacture
  5 Facilitation, design for maintenance
  6 Flexibility, design for future change
  7 Favour, approval and acceptance by the customers.

- Design requires five key ingredients for successful completion:

  1 A principal discovery or invention
  2 Supportive technology, resource and expertise
  3 Commercial need and backing
  4 Several loops of the design cycle – *design, build, use, and evaluate*
  5 Early success and favour, without failure.

- Design can be *minor* or *major*, where major design springs from new invention and uses new technology for a first-time commercial application and may require many circuits of the basic design loop. Minor design uses existing and established inventions and technology, with perhaps just a reselection of existing alternatives.
- Traditionally design as an activity has been a circular and evolutionary path, where progress is made through slow advancement based on experience and intuition. Often today more rapid and radical design is required, applying considerable pressure to the design process to perform faster if not better. Failure in major design often comes from an inability to get the product/service right for the customers in the smallest possible number of design cycles.
- The failure of design to achieve success in a new product/service can be seen in:

  - products or services without want or need;
  - products or services lacking aesthetic appeal;
  - products and services that fail, degrade or deliver below expectation;

- products that are difficult to produce, maintain or adapt over time; and
- services that are inefficient, lack sustainability or flexibility to accommodate change.

- The design activity can make a very significant contribution towards product and service success at all stages of the life cycle, and can add value to both company and consumer, through:

  - reduced design costs with a shorter and more effective design cycle;
  - reduced production costs at manufacture or delivery;
  - reduced maintenance costs during the product/service life;
  - reduced future costs as and when the product or service evolves;
  - increased end-user acceptance and sales volumes;
  - increased intrinsic value, promoting greater commercial worth; and
  - increased strategic value, promoting market growth, penetration and consolidation.

EXERCISES

Take a common domestic product close to hand, such as a kettle, toaster, coffee maker, hoover, refrigerator, television, telephone or similar.

1 For this product identify and describe the particular design elements involved, their importance and any interplay between them. Roughly quantify how well your chosen product meets your expectations for each element, and decide where the greatest failings lie.
2 Trace the evolutionary design of this product from the first invention, initial technology and first commercial introduction, identifying at least five complete circuits of the basic design loop.
3 Note particularly when significant advances have been made to this product over time, and whether these have been instigated by new discoveries, new technologies, materials or techniques, or by a fresh commercial undertaking.
4 Through a simple poll of colleagues, associates and family, identify the primary weakness in the product today.

Identify a commonly experienced service process, such as queuing in a shop, bank or similar.

1 Does this service exhibit any evidence of a design in either the service or the service delivery process?
2 Identify the 'product' offered to the customer as part of the service, and again look for evidence of design in the service/product.
3 Select one major failure of the service to deliver to customer needs and identify the main reason for failure.

Select either your product or service, and devise a revolutionary new approach or solution to overcome the failure.

1 How real is the consumer need for your solution?
2 Is your solution commercially viable?
3 What are the technical difficulties to be overcome?

CHAPTER THREE

Business strategy for growth

Where services and products are brought to the marketplace without any design, the result will range from at best inefficiency and lacklustre performance to at worst disaster and active customer hostility. Good design, the kind that seeks out the best possible solution to meet all customers' needs in every element, will certainly lead to excellent products and services. However, whilst bad design will almost certainly guarantee commercial difficulties, good design in itself will not always usher in a glowing commercial success.

Design is quite a limited activity that simply spans the gap between the decision to introduce a new commercial offering and the handover to commercial production and launch. This chapter will concentrate on the work that must go on either side of the basic design activity and which must be one of the main foundations for *commercial* design success. The interest of this book is not in pure academic design, but in robust and practical commercial design for profit and gain. The difference between the two is often not to be found within the design activity itself, but rather in the corporate strategy that both calls upon and enables design to facilitate a broader plan. Excellence in design is the handmaiden of strategic growth, and a corporate strategy with strong organic growth is the key to commercial success.

Design is an activity that can often be wholly divorced from business reality and a sound plan for growth. Six Sigma, as a customer-focused and process-improvement methodology, is also often divorced from aggressive and organic growth by remaining incremental in its approach. A careful balance is required between aggressive and perhaps overreaching development and a more conservative 'wait and see' attitude to follow in the wake of market leaders. Six Sigma *improvement* is part of a strategy for realizing the cost savings to be gained by eliminating failure and error in products and services. Six Sigma *design* must be part of a strategy both for realizing the cost savings from *preventing* failure and error in services and for *successfully* bringing the *new* product/service to market. To achieve this requires a corporate strategy that enshrines the highest understanding and execution of profit and commercial gain, long-term planning, strong customer focus, appropriate use of new technology and an excellent design methodology that meets both business and customer needs.

MAKING A PROFIT

Any organization selling any mixture of products and services makes a commercial profit based on the sales revenue generated. Far too often such profit is merely viewed as the amount left over when the expenditure has been taken away; a more revealing approach is to view profit as *customer-generated spending*. This can be described using a simple equation such as:

$$P = C \times (S - V) - F$$

where the *profit*, P, is equal to the number of *customers*, C, multiplied by the average *customer spend* less *variable costs* $(S - V)$, less the *fixed costs*, F. Perhaps it is the inclusion of these two cost elements, fixed and variable, that has traditionally directed focus away from income and towards cost saving and avoidance. Many businesses today strive to attain perfection by reducing and controlling costs – 'British boards of directors devote nine times as much attention to counting and spending their companies' wealth than in expanding the source of that wealth' (*Sunday Telegraph* Business File 20/8/00). In contrast, the above equation demonstrates clearly that profit is driven just as strongly by income as it is by expenditure. It also shows that two key elements constitute the make-up of this income: the *number of customers* and their *average spend*. To raise profit a company must increase the number of its customers and the average customer spend, as well as reducing costs. Quality initiatives have a very bold part to play in this area, as it is quality of product and service that directly affects the customer base of an organization. Here is the secret of profit and organic growth – successfully propel more products of better value and better quality to the marketplace more quickly and profit will rise substantially. Certainly costs must be controlled, and the application of incremental improvements with a Six Sigma approach can achieve outstanding success in this area. However, the big gains are to be made by proactively and rapidly launching and relaunching first-class products and services to a willing market.

The amount of profit against turnover for any one organization will vary considerably from market to market, but might typically be about one third of turnover, or 33 per cent. Six Sigma initiatives have demonstrated in practice that some 25 per cent of turnover can be lost to the 'hidden factory' of waste and inefficiency. The smaller gains can be achieved by removing the cost of poor quality and increasing profits by up to 75 per cent. The larger gains can be realized by doubling turnover, and then perhaps worrying about the cost of poor quality later. The happiest situation of all is to both double turnover and virtually eliminate the cost of poor quality, and often these must go hand in hand. Customers will buy more often and spend more when the products and services on offer are of excellent quality, and excellent quality comes from the experience of perfection and the satisfaction of needs well met. Certainly this is true in the customer's experience of new products and services, which are often considerably worse than more established offerings!

As in all cases, a careful and working balance between the conflicting arguments must be achieved. It would be folly indeed to suggest that Six Sigma improvements be ignored, and yet the latter-day drive for lean manufacturing and just-in-time operations does indicate the predominance of 'save' over 'invest'. Here is a striking example of the simple power of the *new* to eclipse the benefit of improvement of the old when driven to an almost illogical conclusion. The biro writing pen has done more to alter the field of communication than any other invention, perhaps even including the telephone. I am of the generation that went to a school where the desks still retained holes for ceramic inkwells, and where pens were typically filled each week from a bottle or with the new disposable cartridge. A review of my immediate working area reveals some seven writing pens, all of the biro type and all except one disposable and of very little intrinsic value. The biro is cheap, easy to use, disposable and quite an inappropriate device to promote good handwriting. It is also an excellent case study in lean manufacture, with the logical extension to reduction in complexity being perhaps just four or five parts. Repeated execution of Six Sigma quality, or lean manufacturing, or *kaizen* or whatever will reduce this further, with ever-diminishing return.

The question that has to be asked is what a biro is used for. The answer is note taking, doodles and sketches and suchlike, certainly not letter writing, as handwriting has often given way to word-processing. The recent introduction of the personal digital assistant (PDA) has opened up a new way to note, doodle and sketch using a stylus or plastic 'pen'. The typical pen here is a single piece of plastic, nothing more. Such 'pens' have evolved in an explosive leap of design from being the active element in writing to being the inactive element. Now the intelligence is in the PDA and the screen rather than the pen, in contrast to the active biro and inactive piece of paper. True, the biro and paper may be more reliable, certainly cheaper and potentially more adaptable, but consider the profit and gain from the sale of the new 'pen' stylus. Whereas a modern biro may cost as little as 10 pence to make and then sells at 20 pence, replacement plastic styli for a PDA typically cost £3 to purchase, and even if the market volume today is small, they must still cost only pence to make.

Profits, and customer sales, are related to the added value extended to the customer within the goods and services provided. The simple fact remains that profit is generated at core by being able to provide some form of product or service at a cost that is significantly lower than the overall added value for the customer. Reducing costs and also increasing either the real or the perceived added value can widen the gap between production costs and the sale price. Regularly reconsidering what the company offers in terms of added value can lead to new territory and the launch of the *new* is very much a part of this strategy. The *new*, on its own, carries a premium simply because it is new, fashionable, avant-garde, fresh, unexpected and welcomed. Certainly in the field of fashion, the designer label has recently captured the broader market as well as the exclusive elite. Designer clothes are sought after, partly because they are unique or exclusive (although looking at the fashion stars attending a major event will show that this is not always the case) and partly because they are *designed* and well thought out. However, designer clothes are generally *newer* and more up to date, simply because in the world of fashion 'you are only as good as your last design offering'. Keeping up with the Joneses is about having the *new* in one's life.

Every product, and perhaps also every service, has a typical market life cycle of development, growth, plateau and then decline. The big gains are always made at the front and by the dominant market leaders. The new product and service will catch both the early and rich pickings and also have the best opportunity to acquire a stake in the market. Naturally the risk here is higher, and if this risk can be mitigated and controlled, even eliminated, then rich and fertile ground awaits the bold and entrepreneurial.

SHORT TERM AND LONG TERM

A key component in successful corporate strategy, and also by implication product/service design, is the ability to balance the needs of the short term against those of the long term. A definition of short and long term is difficult without considering the needs and circumstances of each particular industry. The manufacture of building materials is certainly long term and will change very little over time. In contrast, the leading-edge industry involved in the manufacture of hard drives for computers will have a product life cycle of only months. Where the requirement for data storage capacity increases twofold each quarter and the production methods have to follow suit, long term will often mean months rather than years.

It is worth considering the typical life cycle for products, as shown in Figure 3.1. Sales growth will be slow during the development and introduction stage, and it must be noted that every product will have, or has had, an introduction period at some point in time. Once early success has been assured and hesitancy, resistance and lack of familiarity and product awareness are no longer holding back sales, a period of growth should follow, with maturity and eventual decline as the product moves towards redundancy. This pattern will repeat in one form or another for every kind of product and service, but perhaps with very many variations. The building brick was invented long ago and used in specific localities in England for the well-to-do houses of the Middle Ages. With the advent of the railways, brick production was of necessity increased and bricks were used for almost every building project. As a consequence they became more widely available and also more fashionable through

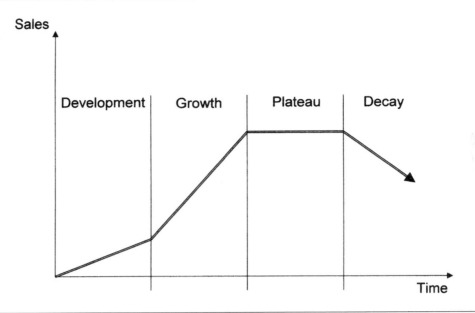

Figure 3.1   The product life cycle

both use and better transport by rail. In modern times brick use has been challenged by the introduction of the concrete block and alternative building forms, but has been revived in commercial building in a more recent swing in fashion away from plain concrete. Long term the use of brick will not change much, as they remain versatile, easy to make and handle, and have an enduring appeal both domestically and commercially. The same cannot be said of domestic television sets, where the immediate future holds a picture of wider screens, high-definition reception, loss of terrestrial signals in favour of satellite and cable and advancing use of new technology enabling flatter screens. The day of the flat wall-sized TV may not be that far away and long term for current production may be only a handful of years.

Neither Six Sigma quality nor design has intrinsically much to say about corporate strategy and planning. It is the domain and responsibility of each organization to identify its own mission and aims, to identify exactly where it wishes to be in the marketplace generally, and its placement within the product life cycle specifically. For some market segments 'new' may mean advanced technology at the cutting edge and yet for others 'new' may mean the re-release of last year's model with a new colour and trim. Being leading edge has considerable advantages as well as major drawbacks; good reward can be gleaned with new introduction and the domination of the market, but the cost of failure is also high. The transition from a commercial to a domestic market opens up new and larger markets, but 'Joe Public' is more fickle than the average business. Taking video recording from commercial models and practices to domestic models and use, as an example, introduced a customer expectation of ease of use and a price tag that kept such a move as a flight of fancy for many years. It was not always the early leaders who gained from such a move, and the struggle and rivalry between the differing formats did little to help. The Phillips offering was probably technically superior, with Betamax a good and highly practical second; however, long term it is the VHS format that has captured the market share. In contrast, the mass market for domestic sound recording only took hold when Phillips introduced the now legendary audiotape cassette and their highly portable tape recorder, many years after the first commercial reel-to-reel machines had first become available. Table 3.1 shows in general terms the passage of new ideas from the 'sharp end' of development through to general use.

It is generally agreed that there are five contributing factors to the early success and consumer uptake of new market products:

- quality
- price
- advertising
- R&D
- service.

Reward and payback for the entrepreneurial company comes from a rapid rise in sales early on following launch, and then the retention of a large slice of the market, together with a long and sustained period of maturity with slow decline. Note the importance of quality and customer satisfaction in the short-term life of the new product or service. Quality and service speak for themselves, but advertising is also dependent upon early acceptance and good encounters. The satisfied customer will tell several others of a good experience, but the dissatisfied will express discontent to a far wider audience! There is only one better advertisement than a really happy customer, and that is a really happy customer with a new toy. R&D must be adventurous, bold and highly capable of meeting customer requirements, and there is a very real need for a corporate strategy that actively promotes rapid and ambitious R&D at all times, since this is where the next good product will often come from. Price, of course, is the other element that can often be omitted from the picture, perhaps relegated to early market testing and pre-launch guesswork. Price is a key element for the customer and, as has already been pointed out, customers expect added value as fair equivalence to the price they pay. Price should be part of the entire strategy and design activity, to ensure both short-term and long-term success by maximizing the overall return.

Product and service *generation planning* is highly important to achieve a balance over the longer term. The London Millennium Dome was the most successful visitor attraction in the UK during 2000, with over six million visitors. Commercially it has been a failure, as some twelve million visitors were expected and required to balance the books. In real terms it took almost the full year for the attraction to settle in, deal with problems and overcome the early negative publicity to gain acceptance, if not approval. With the 'big bang' approach and a fixed one-year window to succeed, the Dome has failed, just like many other 'all at once' approaches, although given more time it might well have turned the financial corner. In contrast to a single launch with all the bells and whistles is the repeatable launch

Table 3.1 Market positioning for technological development

Position	Players	Example
Focal point	Applied science and technology	UV stable plastic
Cutting edge	One institute, company or group	Military use for radar covers
Leading edge	One market sector	Outdoor covers and shields
Following edge	Spin-off sectors	Domestic windows and doors
Support edge	Allied fields	Building and construction
Distanced	Indirect fields	Electronic piano manufacture

to the market of something new but smaller during the growth through to maturity segments of the product life cycle, to help sustain the duration of the maturity period. The short-term 'big bang' requires everything to go right from day one and is in direct contradiction to the observable fact that new design often takes time to get right. Being leading or cutting edge may be far too arduous for all but the largest corporations, and being trailing edge during decay is a diminishing market in which few companies will make a living. Design excellence is vital to leading-edge and has little place in trailing-edge markets; however, active *redesign* during the product sales plateau will help sustain the market in many ways. As part of a corporate strategy for new product/service placement, such generation planning and a phased introduction seek to rationalize and limit the immediate design requirements to something that can be delivered to the marketplace quickly and effectively, and yet pave the way for future product/service adaptation and commercial marketing.

STRATEGY APPLIED TO DESIGN

Whilst for the most part the practice of design exhibits a reasonably well-structured approach, the aspect frequently missing is a holistic corporate strategy into which the design activity fits comfortably. The design stage itself may be both fully appropriate and well conducted, but unless there is a strategic plan for the long-term development, the newly designed products and services run a major risk of failing to excite the market.

The key strategy for any organization must be one of organic growth through the regular and phased introduction of new products and services to meet customer needs. How design achieves success in meeting customer needs and without failure is the domain of the design stage; however, corporate strategy must bridge the gap between the visionary high ground and the potential cliff-face of launching the new product or service. Many corporate models of quality exist, each attempting to identify and position essential elements and pointing a way towards 'excellence'. The primary focus here is towards design and excellence in customer quality, and to support the challenge of world-class quality such models must consider *processes* and *customers*. However, to be applicable at the highest level and to ensure success throughout, any model of excellence must be *strategic* in its view. In seeking out a corporate strategy into which design of the new can easily fit, it can be seen that there are really only three core elements to any organization:

- Customers – buying products and services:

  - engaged, loyal and actively participating;
  - articulate, listened to and focused on; and
  - excited, experiencing world-class quality.

- Processes – delivering products and services:

  - effective, delivering results;
  - appropriate, acceptable to customer, employee, organization and society; and
  - efficient, zero waste and error.

- Employees – supporting processes, products and services:

  - enabled, fully trained and backed by adequate resource;
  - active, performing well, both monitored and mentored; and
  - enthusiastic, rewarded and recognized.

Figure 3.2 shows such a strategy-centric model, positioning the three core elements of customer,

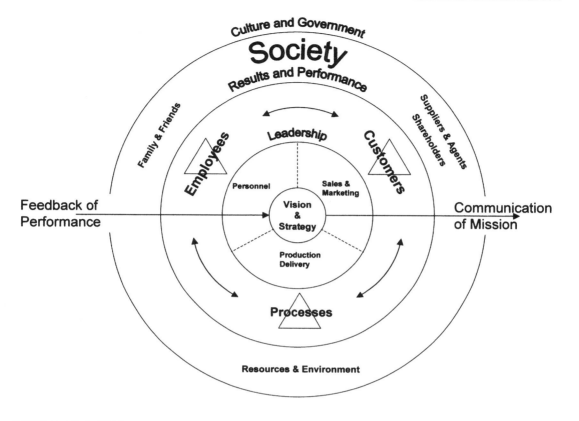

Figure 3.2 Strategy-centric model of excellence

process and employee around the corporate mission and objectives. The aims and vision of the organization are central to the model, and the executive leadership ensures that communication of the company mission is propagated outwards, whilst feedback on the company performance is propagated inwards. The three core elements interact with each other around the corporate leadership and within the encircling band of society as a whole.

Within such a model the placement of the value and importance of products and services, particularly for the *new*, is often solely held within the corporate aims and vision. To translate what is a fairly abstract ideal into a more actionable process, many organizations utilize some form of new product introduction (NPI) approach or strategy. Figure 3.3 shows how design, and specifically DFSS, is strategically positioned within a typical NPI process, and shows the relationship between DFSS and the contribution from marketing, R&D and other specialist input. It is the responsibility of the *entire* NPI to ensure success in every aspect of any new product/service, and clearly what amounts to the sub-section of 'design' does not intrinsically deal with price, marketing, advertising, R&D and corporate strategy. Failure in design may be a foregone conclusion where the marketing department targets the wrong customer segment, R&D devises an inappropriate invention or discovery, sales and marketing arrive at the wrong price, or management actions the wrong overall strategic plan. Effective and appropriate strategy must be seen in both the short-term and low-level view (the detail in the physical design) and in the long-term and high-level view (the business and commercial plan).

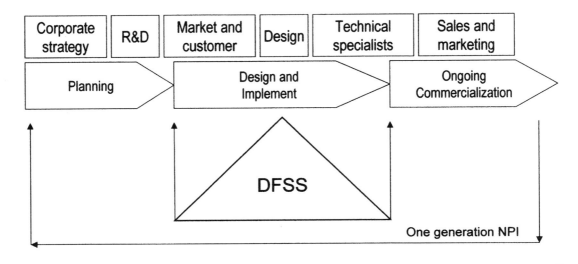

Figure 3.3   DFSS as part of the NPI process

A key strategic approach at the low level will be to shift the focus of the effort expended in the design and launch of the new to the earlier stages. The cost of conceptualizing a new product is generally small, but increases exponentially through design, prototyping, production and commercial service. Good design not only returns strategic benefit in the long term; it also returns real cost benefits in the short term, but only if the entire approach is driven with a view to anticipating and eliminating problems at the earliest possible stage. Improvement For Six Sigma targets the cost of poor quality, seen as anything where waste or inefficiency lurks. The cost of not getting it right first time is whatever is actually expended in a comparison between perfection and reality. For Six Sigma *design*, the costs of getting it right or wrong can be astronomical. One or two individuals have become millionaires as a result of introducing and marketing a good idea. Very many organizations have lost millions through failing to accomplish hindsight as foresight. The big mistakes completely wipe out a product for generations, or even for ever. Where are the atmospheric railways, the airships, the electric cars and the talking photocopiers today? Figure 3.4 shows a picture that many people talk about in DFSS without really giving it much thought. This diagram shows how the effort in DFSS is very much more up-front than for traditionally directed and executed design projects. The concept is all well and good and quite acceptable; however, this graph hides a key issue. To make DFSS work, or even perhaps to *allow* DFSS to work, it is necessary or even essential to change the *strategy* adopted. This is certainly about how to run DFSS and how to eliminate defects in the design and commercial launch, but it is more about the attitudes and the corporate NPI approach adopted in any organization. DFSS needs more time at the beginning, to save time and money later. The greatest failure in DFSS is not to use the methodology at all, usually as a result of a rush to get to the product launch in time. This is not about resources, effort or practice. This is simply about the strategy adopted by any organization with regard to developing and launching new products and services. Look at many large and visible projects today and you will see the majority slipping past a deadline date. The many millennium projects were quite literally the test of the millennium, as the deadline date was not going to move for anyone! Rush and things go wrong; slip and budgets go awry. What is required at the basic level is a strategy of starting on time, estimating well, tackling the achievable,

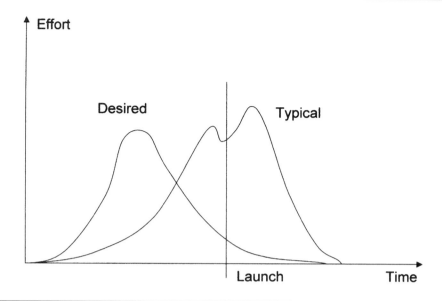

Figure 3.4 Expended effort in design projects

resourcing appropriately, and monitoring carefully. All of this is strategic and the foundation for later success.

The best corporate strategy at the high level is one where regular corporate review, supported by active and ongoing market analysis, competitor strengths and positioning studies, R&D and technological advancement together with an understanding of shifting customer needs, direct a long-term plan for product and service renewal and revitalization. Such a strategy will support a pool of conceptual products and services that can be released for active development, through a well-structured NPI process, and at exactly the right time and pace. Success will be attained when the entire NPI process is well monitored, and if the conceptual products and services can be accelerated, retarded or even cancelled during their passage as required. Clearly the greatest effort will be expended at the commercialization stage and also the preceding design and implementation stage, and it is important to cancel or change the inappropriate at the earliest opportunity. There is clearly a vital need for a good set of metrics that can be applied to both the NPI process and the new product/service to ensure the best overall performance. What better strategy-focused metric to use than something that is directly related to the customer, and every proactive organization should certainly and regularly identify and count customers, record customer spend, and measure customer satisfaction.

CUSTOMER FOCUS

Six Sigma as a philosophy, and certainly as a methodology, emphasizes the vital importance and value of a strong customer focus. This is unquestionably a key area in which the design of the new can really benefit and the entire corporate strategy for both the *new* and the *existing* should foster a strong customer-centric vision. Since the end customer for any product or service is often the most eloquent and effective critic, design processes where the customer is either excluded or paid only lip service will engender considerable risk of missing the mark.

The concept of 'customer' in the broadest perspective naturally includes employees and anyone who touches in any way either the process or the product/service. Figure 3.2 shows that 'customers', through end customers, employees and those who come into contact with the process, can indeed range over a very wide spectrum, from end users, shareholders, directors, internal and external agents, as well as suppliers, employees, family and friends and also society in general. The company that manufactures bricks for a living has customers who buy the bricks and also customers who see or experience the bricks, as well as builders, architects, merchants and hauliers and the people who live close to the factory. Organizations such as waste sites, nuclear power plants, chemical factories, ammunition works, pig or sewerage farms should spend more time considering the customer in relation to their view, smell, noise or fallout!

The list of customers for something simple like a large hotel is quite staggering. Apart from the people who actually come to sleep in the rooms, there are chambermaids, porters, laundry companies, bed manufacturers, decorators, builders and maintenance contract companies, tourist agencies, room booking firms, as well as anyone who simply walks past the front door. Rather than risk being drowned in the vast pool of people to consider, a better approach is to segment customers into typical groups. For the hotel, much like almost any other service industry, there are perhaps four primary segment groups:

- consuming customers, who sleep in the rooms;
- supplying customers, who provide laundry, electricity, food and so on;
- process customers or employees, who service the rooms and greet the guests; and
- indirect customers – shareholders, tourist agencies, taxi drivers and so on.

In setting out to design a brand-new hotel, typical approaches might only concentrate on some segments and then only for partial needs. Room size and layout might be designed, but room service access and lifts forgotten. Lobbies and stairways are designed, but how to find the hotel from the airport in the dark is omitted. To even begin to get design right requires a view of each and every need of each and every customer segment. Particularly in service processes, it only takes a little failure in one small element in one small customer segment to lead to dissatisfaction and disloyalty.

Being nice to the customer is not charity, but just good common sense. Failure to deliver what the customer expects will always lead to some form of complaint, even if it may appear to be silent on the surface. Customer goodwill pays, perhaps not quite in hard currency that can be banked, but in continued loyalty and patronage. What is often missing is due consideration of the extension of the process, past the point at which the customer has paid and the organization metaphorically waves goodbye. There are tales of hotel managers who spend one night at a time in each and every room in the hotel, just to experience what the rooms are actually like. Consignia (the UK Royal Mail), in a recent survey, suggests that only 10 per cent of respondents cited price as the main reason for discontinuing a supplier, and yet almost half did so because of missed deadlines, shoddy products and unhelpful staff. In the past, to engender good customer service many organizations stated that 'the customer is always right'. This may have been vaguely true up to a point; however, as life becomes more complex, organizations are finding that customers are increasingly wrong, confused, or at the very least much more inclined to approach the customer–company interface actively seeking advice or support. The customer today asks questions rather than stating requirements, and this hides a greater vulnerability on the part of the customer, as well as greater responsibility and opportunity on the part of the company. The typical DMAIC Six Sigma improvement methodology shows how important the customer is. Projects must be selected on the basis of what matters to the customer (as well as the business, which is also a 'customer'). Customers must be surveyed to hear what they are saying, and to turn customer requirements into actionable, critical and measurable characteristics. Process mapping must be conducted, and root cause analysis undertaken from a customer perspective. Solutions must be identified that deal with the real problem, for the customer, and piloting and testing must be carried out in conjunction with real customers. Above all, metrics and process management must be carried out from a customer point of view, and with satisfaction of the customer clearly in mind.

Without a balanced view of the importance of the customer, Six Sigma initiatives run the risk of becoming just another internally focused process improvement programme, and will certainly fail to excite. In designing a new product/service, which will be marketed directly to customers and must gain early and strong approval and acceptance from them, failure to place the customer within the design focus will without doubt end in commercial frustration.

> Q. Why is the customer so important?
> A. Because they buy the product and use the service!
> Q. When is the customer important?
> A. Right from the very start of the NPI strategy to the very end of the product life!
> Q. How can we involve the customer?
> A. Stand on the customer's side of the fence. Go and talk to the customer, listen to the customer, become a customer!

What does it take to achieve a customer focus? Count the number of times each day you act out the role of a customer of one process or another. Then ask yourself why it is that so few organizations ask *you*, the customer, what it is *you* want. The people who design for us often put things in the wrong place, use the wrong colours, fail to think of everything, incorrectly anticipate our whims and fancies, and often overstate our ability or understate our needs. There is a strong undercurrent of desire for many people to design their own kitchens or houses or offices. The ground-swell of the customized or the bespoke, even on the mass-produced scale, is indicative of the basic need for each person to make their environment work, and work for them. To misquote the familiar: democratic commerce is design by the customer, for the customer, and of the customer.

NEW TECHNOLOGY

New technology is undoubtedly the most powerful driving force for the introduction of bold and adventurous new products and services. As was noted in Chapter Two, introduction of the *new* is dependent on the input from each and all of invention, technology and commerce; however, technology is often the major initiator or trigger for change. Certainly the reintroduction and advancement of existing products or services is frequently dependent only upon new technology, which time and again pushes back the boundaries of what is both possible and achievable in practice. Technology is a wide subject when viewed in the broadest sense, and covers materials, machinery, equipment, tools and techniques, but is mainly the availability of specialist knowledge and expertise. It is such specialist expertise that contributes significantly to the successful execution of the design process, but technology is also a key factor in enabling and empowering, and perhaps even suggesting and promoting, a fresh approach that can in itself radically push back the boundaries of current performance and expectation.

Looking back over history, it is possible to identify periods for a *lead technology*, where cutting-edge technological improvements promote and facilitate a wider and major impact of social and economic change. The lead technology of the day will both introduce and use the very latest invention and application in such a way as to alter, widely and radically, the accepted level of what is both achievable and possible. The railway age had perhaps one of the most influential of the lead technologies of all time, and is perhaps the most distinct period in which virtually all new technology developed, advanced, and was applied in consequence of just one field. If the concept of a lead technology is extended across time, the following list can be seen as a reasoned attempt to attribute leading-edge technological change to a root cause of the period:

Early	Religious beliefs (temples and monuments)
Year 0–400	Roman military and civil engineering
Dark Ages	War and siege engines
Middle Ages	Stonemasonry
Late Middle Ages	Deep mining
Year 1800–1900	Railways
Year 1900–1930	Air flight
Year 1930–1955	Atomic capability
Year 1955–1970	Space flight
Year 1970–1995	Electronics and computers
Year 1995–	Mobile communication?

Almost everyone knows of at least one spin-off from the space age, namely non-stick frying pans. The invention of the transistor was a fairly minor event; however, the development and application of the technology involved has revolutionized the world today. Each period, in its own way, has driven back the frontiers of what we, the general public, expect as possible.

The railway age both required and facilitated tremendous advances in technology. This included areas such as steam locomotive development, rail track and civil engineering, bridge design and construction, tunnelling, passenger and freight handling, signalling and control and many others. The social impact of the railway age was outstanding. Two examples are the effects on employment and on time. Before the railway age people generally worked in the immediate locality, which meant that cities were overcrowded. People did travel, but only the wealthy and well-to-do could repeatedly and reliably cover any distance. Following the introduction of the railways, people were able to move more freely and easily, which promoted greater diversity of skill amongst craftsmen, allowed the more well-to-do to move home outwards from the cities, and allowed larger factories to be constructed away from population centres and the commercial markets they fed. Goods had been shipped over distance, but generally rather slowly by ship or canal, and thus only non-perishable materials would survive such journeys. With railways providing an evolutionary leap in accessibility, fresh farm produce could be brought daily to the city centre, along with workers and traders. Time had always been measured locally, with noon being the time at which the sun was at its highest point. Since there is a significant difference at which this point occurs even across the British Isles, time in Bristol was ten minutes later than that of London, and the London to Bristol coachman had to adjust his timepiece along the route. Railways, with a more regimented timetable, were not able to accommodate this difference, and for many years 'railway time' was based on London time and was quite distinct from the many local variations. Indeed, for many years the town clock in the centre of Oxford had two differently coloured minute hands, one for local time and the other for railway time!

Two things happen at the cutting edge of leading technology. First, the technology requires a new way of thinking about and approaching problems, and second, the development of solutions to solve these problems radically alters the platform against which existing capability is measured. The platform from which railway technology had to spring was very thin indeed. Bridges from the canal age were typically over-bridges, of stone, and only measured tens of feet in length of span. The railways at their peak in Great Britain in 1927 had some 62 000 bridges, of which about 39 000 were underline. Many new bridges were required, and what was required had generally never been attempted before. Until relatively recently the Simplon Tunnel under the Swiss Alps was, at $12\frac{1}{4}$ miles, the longest railway tunnel in the world. Built during the 1890s and part opened in 1906, this was one of the greatest civil engineering challenges of its time. The problems that were overcome in construction led to many new approaches and techniques, subsequently used elsewhere. In surveying for the route, during three consecutive summers, new methods were developed to overcome the effect on the instruments of the gravitational pull of the mountains. Over the length of the tunnel the curvature of the earth becomes important, and in the very depth of the Alps temperatures of 49 °C were experienced, along with incredible pressure from the rock above and vast quantities of water entering through fissures. Compressed-air tools were developed for use in this tunnel, delivering both power and fresh air to the working face from well outside the tunnel itself. A tunnel such as this, like many major tunnels both before and since, could simply not be built without new technology. Once invented, devised and put into use, such technology often radically alters practices generally, although success is not guaranteed.

Although Brunel was certainly *inventive*, he was not really an *inventor* as such, and one of his most noted disappointments was the atmospheric railway. Brunel had as many failures as did the less imaginative and more intuitive engineers such as the Stephensons, but he spent more time ensuring that his mistakes did not become public. Indeed, Brunel had many outstanding strengths, including the ability to conduct research, measure and observe, and work hard with both public and companies to ensure that his ideas and strategies were presented in the best possible light. In the very early days of railway track-bed design, the primary aim was to ensure as close to a perfect level as could possibly be obtained, and Brunel was a master in this work. The Great Western Railway (GWR) is known as 'Brunel's billiard table' with a ruling (or steepest) gradient of about 1 in 1000 over most of the line, rising gradually over the route from Paddington to the Cotswold limestone escarpment. Brunel concentrated almost all the descent required for the final stage to Bath and Bristol at a gradient of 1 in 100 within the two-mile-long Box Tunnel. With exceptionally smooth curves and the broad gauge, this line remains perhaps one of the finest ever built. Yet within twenty years Brunel was at work with the new technology of the atmospheric railway. Invented and first used in France, this operated by means of a travelling piston within a large pipe resting on the track between the rails. The air in the pipe was partially evacuated ahead of the piston using stationary steam engines, and it was the greater air pressure following the piston that pushed it, and the attached train, along at speed. Brunel seized upon this new idea, and began to build railways to use the new technology. With no heavy locomotive engine to run, he was able to ease considerably both gradients and curves on the new lines, making major cost savings in the expensive civil engineering required. The South Devon railway from Exeter to Plymouth in particular was a bold step forward, even for Brunel. Alas, the system failed to retain the reliability experienced in the shorter trial lines used in France, and several factors led to the complete abandonment of the idea within two years. Naturally this left the newly constructed railways with major problems in working existing locomotives over these lines.

The failure of the atmospheric system, often quoted as being due to rats eating the leather air seals along the pipes, was more due to the inherent difficulties of the system and local climatic conditions. The vacuum pipe began and ended well clear of the stations, since it prohibited any form of track switch or point, and all handling had to be completed manually, including braking and stopping the train at the correct point at stations. The pipe had a slot at the top, for the attachments between piston and train, which was sealed with a leather-covered metal flap. This suffered a great deal from the salty air so close to the coast, and the special closures at the ends of the pipe were not able reliably to withstand the impact of the piston, often travelling at 60 miles per hour.

Like much of new technology even today, when it worked it worked very well indeed, and when it failed, as it did all too often, it was the direct cause of major problems. The principle behind the use of the atmospheric approach was very well founded, and had outstanding potential to break free from the constraints imposed by the steam locomotives of the day. Until the commercial use of electric motors became reality, power sources (ignoring animals) were simply water wheels and steam engines. The Stephenson approach was for mobile steam engines, taking both fuel and power delivery with them as they went. Brunel realized the potential of having more efficient and easier-to-run stationary engines delivering the motive power in another way. This idea of course was not new, and was the basic principle behind many earlier tramways using cable haulage to pull trucks up steep inclines. The first public railway to be built in London was cable-hauled, with a relatively short run and some six stations. There was one carriage for each station, and they all left at the same time with an individual guard disconnecting each carriage from the cable as required. The return journey involved starting the cable engine only when every station was ready, and new technology in the form of the recently invented electric telegraph in this case proved very reliable and very necessary!

Cable railways are very limited, literally tied to a piece of rope. The new technology of the steam locomotive opened up great new possibilities, and in turn a fresh alternative to the transmission of the motive power by vacuum showed further promise. Perhaps today, with better materials and compressed air, the potential for atmospheric railways could be realized, although electric traction achieves the same principle in a variant form. Whilst technology does indeed rewrite the script of what is possible, the scope for disappointment is considerable. This is the conundrum: leading technology can be both expensive and risky, but it can also be an explosive liberator and shaper for change. Adopting any new technology could be a path leading to failure, or just as easily to market dominance, and the very real risk is of a competitor obtaining significant technological advantage with devastating effect. Nuclear capability, rocket science, radar and cryptography are all technologies that provided extraordinary advantage during World War II, and in some respects even fifty years later they remain fairly exclusive 'clubs' to which entry is moderated and controlled. Even without government control, technology is a subject rather alien to the majority, and often left to the corporate specialist. Certainly the skills required often separate the technocrat from the technophobe in business life generally, and this was often seen where Brunel had to spend time and effort overcoming resistance to his bold schemes. Where business conservatism sits on one side, and unfettered enthusiasm for the rash and bold sits on the other, both sides lose out. Many civilizations of the past have developed and retained quite advanced technologies; however, the key to success for both commerce and fundamental growth and development is the ability to embrace and innovate. Nothing much happens without technology; the very real question is how to moderate and yet excite the design activity that must arrive at new and better solutions, without overt or serious business risk either way.

DESIGN CONSTRAINT METHODOLOGY

Design by its very nature is highly creative, and when the design activity is entirely unconstrained it is frequently a chaotic affair with considerable lack of certainty in the outcome. Give two young children a large piece of paper, some crayons or paint, ask them to design a house, and the result will be interesting but of little real use! To make 'design' more palatable within any strategic business activity, it must be appropriately constrained to ensure that the outcome is indeed satisfactory from the commercial point of view.

Take one ebullient but thoughtful and comprehensive design engineer such as Brunel and great schemes will be hatched. Bigger, bolder and certainly each one increasingly potentially rewarding and yet riskier than the last. The question is, how can design deliver its best? The answer is not in the design activity *per se*, but lies in the way in which the design activity is constrained to operate. Two factors are important – the capacity for highly creative and unfettered generation of alternatives to the *status quo*, and a set of constraining targeted deliverables to ensure appropriateness in the final outcome. Design is like the sagely oracle, in that it will reply to any question that might be asked of it, but the real importance of achieving enlightenment is found in framing the question to be asked. A commercial design strategy needs first to work backwards, from a set of answers towards the question, and then and only then allow the design to proceed.

It is the business that comes to *design* and *technology* to ask 'Can we have a new railway?', and design will always answer well, particularly if the designer is highly skilled and knowledgeable. However, only if we ask the right question will the answer be *exactly* to our liking and appropriate to our needs. The question has to be 'Can I have a new railway that does not cost more than this one, and yet gives a smoother and faster ride?', that is, a question with conditions or constraints attached. True, any good designer will self-apply constraints to the question/answer process, but it is not for the designer to decide what these constraints should be. Far too often designers in all walks of life are expected to design first, and be judged later; hence they apply their own invented constraints, which may or may not suit either business or customer. Successful design can only work if the designer is free to be radical and omnipotent in considering change, and if the agreed criteria are set well outside of this activity and set in advance by the business in conjunction with the customer.

A traditional design–implement approach will look like the simple plan – do – check – act cycle:

- constrain
- design
- make
- ship and fix.

For an improved approach, the initial concept must be better developed against business strategy, the constraints must be better developed against customer and business requirements, and the design and implementation must proceed freely while being repeatedly tested and evaluated against these constraints.

An improved approach will take the form of:

- concept development and refinement
- constraints based on business concept and customer requirements
- careful design to constraints
- testing and evaluation against constraints
- pilot and commercial launch
- much reduced post-launch fixing.

For example, the London Millennium Dome is now seen in hindsight as perhaps a poor concept to begin with, and had perhaps only one overriding constraint – to get it built by 31 December 1999. Once built, much work had to be carried out to refine the commercial offering, and whilst successful in attracting six million visitors, the original commercial target had been for twelve million visitors. It would have been far better to thrash out the concept first – is it a building or a visitor attraction or something to mark the millennium? What need does it address, and how important or critical will visitor numbers be? Again, it would have been better to devise constraints on the design that related firmly to the customer – value for money, ease of use, effort and reward – and far better to have tested the progressing design against the customer during the design process rather than wait until commercial launch! How wonderful is hindsight, which in DFSS projects *must* be turned into foresight!

After the strategic development of the concept solution, a practical DFSS process must identify the customers, explore customer product/service issues, clarify needs, translate needs to requirements, convert requirements to CTQs (critical to quality), and finally convert these to CTPs (critical to process). It is the application of such CTP metrics that bridges the gap between customer needs and design constraints. If customers will attend an attraction only if it is within four hours' travel, then a CTP is 'site within four hours of customer base', which implies an upper limit for any attraction in London, and might suggest that Birmingham in the Midlands is a more appropriate site. Of course, in this instance the primary CTP was that the attraction was situated on the prime meridian to celebrate the millennium. Typically in any design there are conflicts between contrasting requirements, and DFSS must bring powerful tools to deal effectively with each and every conflicting business and customer requirement.

In designing a new washing machine, mobile telephone, customer call centre or retail outlet, the need is to identify a potential and strategic solution acceptable to the business, and then to flush out all the issues the customers have or will have with the product/service. From this will come the design constraints needed to design creatively with commercial success.

Successful Design For Six Sigma has much to achieve, and must deal with the difficulties and pitfalls through a methodology that is both applicable and effective. There are perhaps just three key elements required for the successful DFSS approach:

- **Strategy** – a corporate framework within which the entire NPI and design process sits to ensure maximum commercial benefit and alignment to corporate direction and vision.
- **Rigour** – use of a tollgate methodology and a customer-focused Six Sigma quality approach, with business approval at each stage of the project.
- **Structure** – a basis of tools and techniques to derive appropriate design constraints (CTPs) and to promote effective design, as well as sound implementation and future commercialization.

Having fully explored the process, weakness, potential and requirement for success in design, it is now appropriate to consider a practical methodology in more detail.

SUMMARY

- Profit is acquired by adding value to goods and services and selling to a customer base with the income revenue generated as far above costs as possible. Profit can often be increased by reducing costs, but more effectively by increasing the customer base, perceived added value as well as customer spend, especially through the regular and repeated introduction of bold and new products and services. Customers often pay a premium for *new* in general, but design of the new can also lead to better added value and significant reduction in many cost areas.

- Design plays a key role in a corporate strategy for aggressive organic growth, and both short- and long-term planning of product launch, continued development and phasing are essential to make the best market gains from new products and services. Early success is critical, followed by a long-term approach to maintaining market share.
- Organic growth is dependent upon a successful strategy plan, incorporating a wide-based new product introduction (NPI) approach that focuses on the customer and appropriate use of new ideas and technologies, where greater effort is applied at the early stages of the NPI sequence to eliminate waste, error and failure over the longer term.
- Customer focus is a key element to a successful Six Sigma approach, and has a particularly strong part to play within any Design For Six Sigma methodology. Failure of the new product or service is often the result of an early inadequacy to excite customers or to deliver to expectation, and design without a strong end-customer focus has a considerable risk of commercial disappointment.
- Technology is a key element in the fight to develop new products and services that significantly push back the boundaries of performance and delivery. New and leading technology, developed at the cutting edge of the day, is often the trigger for new products or services, as well as an enabler of the refreshment of existing products and services to achieve new levels of performance. Considerable risks are inherent in the exploitation of untried new technology; however, the commercial gains can be dramatic and the prize in successful subjugation and competitive dominance based on technology often drives inappropriate commercial use. A seemly balance needs to be achieved between exponential technological advance and incremental conservative commercialism.
- The design constraint methodology is a way of allowing and even encouraging dramatic creative design, and yet ensuring delivery of new products and services with guaranteed commercial application. By building into the constraints all the necessary aspects of a strategic NPI and customer focus, the very best creative use of new technology can be applied to the design problem and yet deliver a controlled outcome.
- Design For Six Sigma brings *strategy*, *rigour* and *structure* to design, and must sit within a strategic NPI targeted for organic growth, with a strong customer focus, making the best use of new technology, and yet remaining well controlled through constrained design. The DFSS methodology is therefore primarily an approach to devise, evaluate and apply customer-focused and business-strategic design constraints to the primary design activity.

EXERCISES

Make a quick survey of the ten most recent purchases of products you have made.

1   Are these completely new products (and services) or do they replace and possibly upgrade existing ones?
2   To what extent does a new technology or technological advance facilitate or play a part in the introduction of these examples of new items?
3   What is the key commercial strategy for profit adopted by the manufacturer/supplier of these products/services?

You are required to develop and launch a new variation on an existing domestic product, such as a toaster, kettle or coffee maker. Elaborate a strategy for achieving this aim, encompassing marketing, product development, launch and commercial production.

1   What is the key new feature that you will offer the customer?

2   Identify a lead technology of today, and investigate whether there are new advances in this field that could be applied to your chosen product.

3   What constraints will you apply to the design stage to ensure commercial success, practical achievement and customer acceptance? How can you evaluate the appropriateness of these constraints, and their eventual success in use?

PART TWO

A DFSS Methodology

CHAPTER FOUR

DFSS framework and overview

The commercial design and implementation of a new product or service is in itself a process with inputs, outputs and process steps. It is appropriate for a better corporate strategy, and also for both rigour and control, that a good design methodology be used and preferably one that ties in well with customers and the Six Sigma approach. The standard Six Sigma methodology should be a good starting point to work from; however, there is a real difficulty in that Six Sigma is principally about process improvement and not design. There is a considerable difference between *improve* and *design* as fundamental activities, and the DMAIC methodology is highly selective in that it is almost exclusively optimized for the improvement of processes. The stages of *measure, analyse* and even *improve* are often complicated by the almost total lack of any existing process to measure, analyse and then incrementally improve! Every organization currently extending Six Sigma into the field of design for the new is generating an alternative methodology and nomenclature, and there are certainly many varieties of approach from which to choose. The GE Capital approach, which is perhaps far better optimized than any other for general *service* offerings, has the advantage of being developed from best practice and experience in use. This will certainly deal well with the difficult and uncharted area of service design that is becoming so critical in launching new products today.

In attempting to retain a tight link to DMAIC – define, measure, analyse, improve, control – the DFSS approach is commonly named DMADV, that is, define, measure, analyse, *design, verify* (which includes implementation and control). In theoretical physics the 'grand unification' of all elemental forces into just one force (there are four – gravity, electrostatic, weak nuclear and strong nuclear) is proving very hard to achieve. The desire to unite both Six Sigma DMAIC and Six Sigma DFSS in one simple approach is likewise proving more idealistic than realistic. DFSS teams often react to the naming of the measure and analyse stages in DMADV, particularly when there is clearly nothing to either measure or analyse. It is much more appropriate to develop a DFSS methodology with a pedigree of its own.

Just as it has been said 'healer, heal thyself', so it can be said of DFSS 'design methodology, design yourself', and there is some truth in this almost bizarre concept. Any good design methodology must be capable of designing anything, including methodologies and ethereal concepts, and therefore design itself. A good DFSS approach can be used to design *ad hoc*, and also to become the basis or integral part of any commercial design process, and could in theory at least be used to design a new design process *per se*. This may be a concept belonging more to the philosophical realm than to the realm of practical use; however, the more adventurous will be able to use the DFSS framework for real gain in extending its propagation of the *new* to any new idea or concept, as well as any new product or service. Naturally the question that follows must be 'Which comes first, chicken or egg?' Using an existing process on which to improve is typically a DMAIC improvement approach, and much of the proposed DFSS methodology that follows in this part of the book is axiomatic in that it is devised or contrived somewhere else. If this methodology is really capable of designing new things, then it certainly should be capable of application to itself; however, this is a quite mind-numbing concept and definitely left as an exercise for the advanced student!

It should be realized early on that, whilst DMAIC is usually broadly applicable to the improvement of *any* process, there is much less scope for such generality of application using just one DFSS methodology. DFSS is much more than just design, and each utilization of the methodology will be strongly flavoured both by the environment and by the demands of the particular design involved. What is required in a first step towards DFSS is an outline methodology or framework, which includes all the prerequisites for excellence in design, but still allows adaptation, moulding and fine-tuning for use in real-life situations. This chapter, and indeed this entire part of the book, will work towards such a framework methodology for DFSS. Later chapters will discuss aspects relating to its practical application and adaptation.

AN OUTLINE METHODOLOGY

In the preceding chapters it was shown that there are many factors vital for the promotion of excellence in commercial design and implementation of a new product/service. Every approach to designing the *new* encapsulates a necessity to deliver success in each and all of the following areas:

- a business strategy for growth with a sound development plan for both the short term and the long term;
- the phased and timely launch of new products, services and supporting processes with strong added value;
- bold and creative design limited only by an appropriately devised constraint model;
- design constraints built from highly perceptive VOC, VOB and VOE analysis (voice of customer, business and employee);
- rigorous tollgate methodology with time and cost budget control and sound business governance, together with excellent overall project management;
- proactive use of the sigma metric to focus on a set of core CTQs and CTPs (critical to quality and process) and using simulation and pilot trials to pre-evaluate and thus guarantee customer-experienced quality performance;
- perceptive FMEA/EMEA (failure/error mode effect analysis) and piloting together with a sympathetic commercial launch to eliminate all causes of failure;
- overall product and service design with a view to achieving excellence in the seven key elements of design; and
- appropriate use of new technology for risk-controlled innovation balanced against future and current incremental improvement.

There is a great deal to aspire to in this list, and a first step must be to distil the essential points from the above and to identify the critical focus for attention. Certainly there will be many areas of interaction and overlap between the above points, and the following simplified list of five focal points is far more concise but still catholic in its scope for encouraging excellence in the design of the new:

1 Total business ownership from start to finish
2 Cost- and risk-effective, yet exciting, use of new technology
3 Customer focused for added value and satisfaction targeted for an assured Six Sigma performance of four to five sigma in all the metrics critical to customer satisfaction
4 Design that is creative, demonstrates excellence in the seven key elements of design, yet remains well controlled by effective and suitable constraints
5 A well-managed project, with sound implementation and commercialization free from failure.

This is still a well-defined yet ethereal list of goals to aspire to, rather than a methodology or approach to execute in practice. Certainly the best methodologies are those that can be accomplished in performance as a very simple and neat sequence of steps, preferably few in number and each easy to remember! What is required is something that progresses in neat stages from the business strategy, through the customer needs and the actual design, and lastly to implementation and a final return or handover to the business. All of this needs to be in a neat sequence, yet enabling each of the above five points to be soundly accomplished. Allowing for the pre-work and project set-up, and for a handover stage to return the project to business ownership, the following is a suitable basic DFSS methodology:

Initiate – **Define** – **Customer** – **Concept** – **Design** – **Implement** – *Handover*

Called DCCDI, this has much in common with the DMADV mnemonic, but names the 'measure' as *customer*, and 'analyse' as *conceptualize*, which perhaps far better describes these particular stages. 'Verify' is, in truth, a separate justify, implementation and control, and many today feel that the DMAIC approach should be DMAIIC, the second 'I' representing implement, since without actual implementation many projects often achieve little more than a fat report. Control, too, can often be the stage skipped or poorly executed, and moving this out of the design project and over to the business is one way of resolving this problem.

As a more formal list of individual stages, the basic methodology now becomes:

1   Initiate project (hand over from corporate strategy planning)
2   Definition stage
3   Customer analysis
4   Concept development and business/customer approval
5   Design – formal and technical together with evaluation
6   Implementation to commercialization (including trials and pilot studies)
7   Handover to business ownership (control stage).

The mnemonic form is popular as a general *aide-mémoire*; however, as such it can often be taken to extremes. In the bold scheme of Six Sigma, the DMADV project is often seen as conceding the 'verify' stage to a complete further cycle of MAIC for much-needed process improvement following the 'design' project. This then becomes DMAD–MAIC, which is certainly rather a mouthful! Although DMADV has not much in its favour as a mnemonic, DCCDI must have even less, and if the reader has a passion for neatness there may well be many alternatives, particularly in languages other than English. Modification and adaptation for local use does require customization, and a little more thought might yield an alternative (but not necessarily more useful) naming convention, such as:

Charter – **Commence** – **Customer** – **Conceptualize** – **Convene** – **Create** – *Commission*

There is always an element of uncertainty in devising any new methodology, and the tendency is often to add more and more steps rather than to focus on the critical stages. In very large projects the design stage itself will have to be subdivided into smaller parts, perhaps conceptual design, specification development, technical design, practical design and even sub-specialist design work. The highest level for DFSS will be the inclusive NPI strategy as shown in Figure 3.3:

● business strategy planning
● design project
● marketing and commercialization.

The DCCDI approach is perhaps one or even two levels below this and will be adequate for the vast majority of commercial design projects, although in more complex projects the design stage will have to expand further. Figure 4.1 shows the outline methodology in more detail and indicates the ownership at various stages, as well as defining the entities passed from stage to stage. It also shows how a tollgate approach will limit each stage and ensure full evaluation of each part before moving on to the next stage. Clearly the objective is to divide up the entire ownership and responsibility between the *business*, the *customer* and the (design) *project team*. With a rigid tollgate approach and the project both beginning and ending firmly rooted within business ownership, there is little room for slap-dash corporate governance and misinformed project management. The principal stages of the DCCDI are as follows.

BUSINESS INITIATION (HANDOVER FROM NPI PROJECT STRATEGY)

The beginning of the project for real will often be rather a grey area and more of a managed transition between the business ownership and project team ownership. This is the initiation of the DFSS project by the business, under controlled governance, and handover of the prime business needs for the design of the new product/service. This stage may require marketing and R&D input as well as early prototyping and the like, but all of this work should be carried out without either consequence for or impact on the eventual DFSS project team. The aim of this stage is for the business leaders to be comfortable with the project that they are about to endorse and champion, and to select the scope and make-up of both project and team.

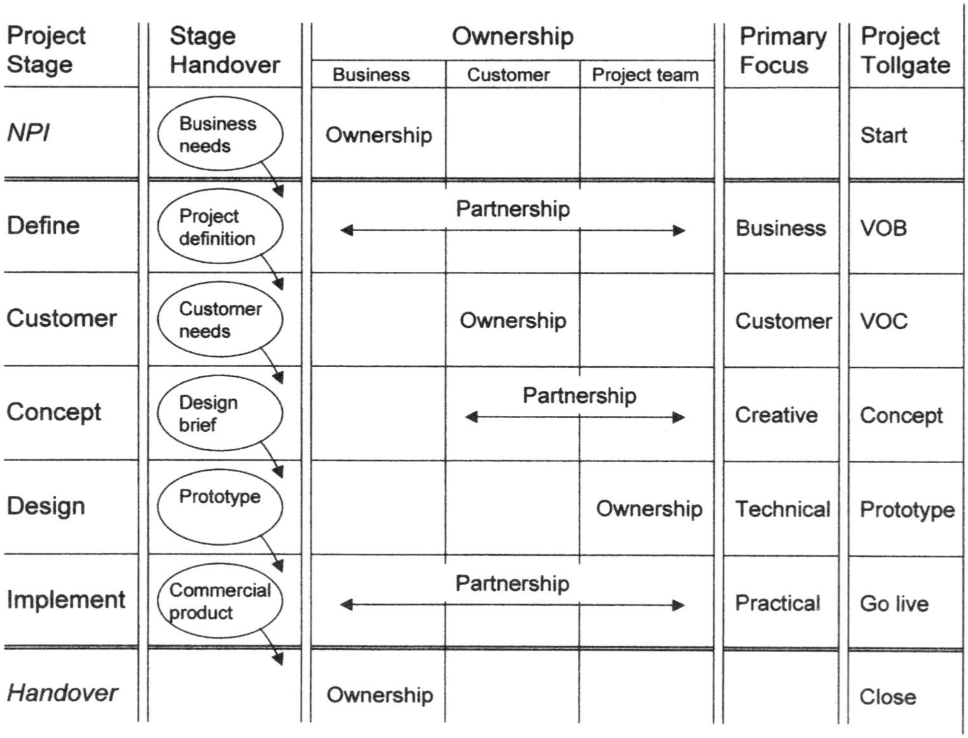

Project Stage	Stage Handover	Ownership			Primary Focus	Project Tollgate
		Business	Customer	Project team		
NPI	Business needs	Ownership				Start
Define	Project definition	◄——— Partnership ———►			Business	VOB
Customer	Customer needs		Ownership		Customer	VOC
Concept	Design brief		◄—— Partnership ——►		Creative	Concept
Design	Prototype			Ownership	Technical	Prototype
Implement	Commercial product	◄——— Partnership ———►			Practical	Go live
Handover		Ownership				Close

Figure 4.1 DFSS project stages

DEFINE

The outcome from the define stage must be a comprehensive project team charter. This is a working and living document, setting out the axioms and rules of engagement for the team to operate against. It will also clearly set deliverables and budgets, as well as expectations and resources for the team. This stage is also a partnership between the business and the team, and should if possible include the customer or at the very least the voice of the customer. This stage may well continue some of the NPI work, as the team begin to take ownership of the project scope and define more precisely what should and could be achieved.

CUSTOMER

This is probably the stage least likely to be familiar to many organizations, and often not practised by service providers at all – certainly not as a *discrete* stage within a commercial design programme. This stage is critical to the Six Sigma approach in identifying customers, their needs of both product and service, and in converting these needs to a set of key critical metrics which relate well to customer-experienced satisfaction and thus quality. Much work will need to be completed during this stage to pull together what will ultimately become the base metrics that provide the constraints for the design, and this may well be the part of DFSS projects omitted by teams under business-imposed time and budget constraints. Only if this stage is fully evident, operational and endorsed can the project be called Design For Six Sigma, for without the customer it may just as well be called Design For The Business!

CONCEPT

In this stage the project team pulls together all the disparate parts of the work conducted to date. Here the original business concept for a solution will be fleshed out and tested against the customer metrics, as well as the business needs and plain common sense. This stage is one of conceptual design, rather than technical or even practical design, and the aim here is to arrive at a working paper model that, in concept at least, will completely satisfy both business and customer. This model must ideally retain sufficient laxity for the design proper still to operate creatively and yet be rigid enough now to propose a set of design constraints – the design brief to be handed to the designers.

DESIGN

Exactly how the design is carried out in practice will depend on both the magnitude of the design work and the technical skills required. For small projects it should be possible for the quality project team to complete the design themselves, perhaps with the help of a member of the team with specialist skills and knowledge. In larger and more complex projects the work will certainly shift from the business-led and customer-focused team to an entirely different team, populated by experts and designers with a design lead and technical focus.

The power of DFSS will be seen in that the technical design can now only (but freely) operate within the boundary constraints set by the business and customer, with a target of delivery to both. Given a precise solution framework, as well as the critical to quality (CTQ) and critical to process (CTP) metrics, the technical design solution must be shown to achieve success against these metrics, or be firmly rejected. The design must therefore continue to evolve and be evaluated or tested against the CTPs, until finally the business, the customer and the technical designers are sufficiently contented to proceed to commercial production. What comes out of this stage is a fully evaluated and proven prototype for commercial launch, which only needs final implementation.

IMPLEMENT

Implementation for real does not mean selling the new product or service to the market immediately, but rather implies a need for some form of pilot or trial, followed by re-evaluation and adjustment before a phased roll-out is undertaken. Even though the design is assured to meet business and customer expectations, the risk of failure in implementation must be reduced to a minimum and the final commercialization undertaken with due care and attention. The project team will also need to ensure that plans for ongoing control and product/service support are developed and put in place. Again, in the larger projects, the implementation team may be different to the design team; any continuity from the earlier work will certainly benefit the project.

HANDOVER

However large the business or technical desire to make the design of any new product or service an idealized single and explosive event in time, design in reality still remains inherently an often-repeated circle of incremental improvement over an extended time period. If the organization is to gain the very best return for the effort invested, then the office of business ownership must be correctly and properly undertaken. It is the long-term requirements for continued maintenance, customer support, employee training and empowerment, process monitoring, ongoing incremental improvement, market positioning and feedback, and strategic business development that dictate a corporate responsibility for the parenting of the new child prodigy. This is certainly more an ongoing responsibility than a well-defined and unique stage in time, and must encompass a real shift in management attitudes towards the Six Sigma and customer-focused philosophy.

FLAVOURS OF DFSS

Not only will any DFSS methodology have many levels of practical approach, it will also have many variations or flavours between two quite distinct extremes. On the one hand are the very large new design projects, where the aim is to deliver something complex, often radically new involving a mix of both product and service. On the other hand and in contrast are the much smaller design projects that originate from a typical Six Sigma DMAIC project team. Such cases are often seen following the measure or analyse stage when it becomes evident that simple process improvements will either not work or are very difficult to engineer in practice, and what is required is an element of design of a new process, product or service.

To help clarify the distinction between a major DFSS project and perhaps a more minor DMAIC project either using or borrowing design (for Six Sigma), consider Table 4.1, which lists many of the tangible differences between *improve* Six Sigma and *design* Six Sigma.

Although the two sides of this table represent the extremities of a very wide spectrum, the message is clear that DFSS comes from a fundamentally different stable to DMAIC and will thus require different tools, attitudes and management. The typical Six Sigma improve project starts with a business requirement to deal with one, perhaps quite isolated, customer problem. Often a small team of four to six people will be formed and will look at the issue as an isolated case, considering no more than one customer CTQ, and running for perhaps no more than 90 or so days. The resultant change will be an improvement to the process, with perhaps a one-sigma increment in the performance of the one CTQ considered. Often such projects are run in relatively large numbers, and may even be repeated sequentially two or three times in the same area to move the one CTQ forward by repeated incremental change. In contrast, DFSS projects arise from a business need to deliver something *new*, often radically or exponentially different, and the business must first furnish the design project team

Table 4.1 Differences between *improve* and *design* Six Sigma

Improve	Design
Start with a customer problem	Start with a business solution concept
Process improvement	Product/service design
Customer focused	Business focused
Isolated undertaking	Part of a bigger picture in NPI
One or two CTQs considered	Every CTQ considered
Small team of 4–6	Large team of 40+
99-day timescale	999-day timescale
+1 sigma increment	Launch at 4 to 5 sigma
Many projects (19 in 20)	Few projects (1 in 20)
Small impact and focus	Big impact and focus

with an outline conceptual solution rather than a problem to solve. This is not an isolated undertaking, and will certainly be part of a larger picture within the corporate NPI process, will require more people and will definitely take much longer to execute. The project scope will range over many, if not all, of the CTQs affecting the customers, and should deliver a new product/service that can begin commercial life with performance somewhere between four and five sigma for all the CTQs involved.

Figure 4.2 shows more graphically the fundamental difference between the various kinds of Six Sigma projects. For any process there exists a measure of both the process *capability* and the process *performance*. Capability is the theoretical delivery of performance that the process can achieve at the very best, with actual performance being that which it delivers in practice. For example, the customer ordering process may have a time-to-complete capability of three hours, and actually be achieving this without any defect or deficiency. Providing that the customer of the process regards three hours as both an acceptable and high-quality delivery, this could indeed be a 'six sigma' process. A 'six sigma' process is one that is in control (no special cause and only common cause variation) and delivers less than four defects in every one million opportunities, where the opportunities and defects are measured against customer-defined limits.

The situation where the process capability is indeed three hours, but performance fails to reach this for perhaps 30 per cent of delivery instances, is represented by case 'A' in the figure. Here Six Sigma would be used as a process improvement methodology or approach to improve performance while (generally) leaving capability well alone. Typically a failure of 30 per cent relates to a process metric of just 'two sigma', and one round of a DMAIC project might improve performance and reduce defects to just 7 per cent, or about 'three sigma'.

Case 'C' in the figure is a situation where process capability is three hours and process performance is good, with no defects over three hours, and yet customer expectation has significantly shifted to perhaps just two hours. If the process is therefore inherently incapable of delivery at the two-hour target, improvement of the capability through redesign is required, rather than improvement of process performance. Case 'B' can be regarded as the most serious situation, where both performance and capability are below customer expectation. If the customer requires two hours, and the process can only manage three hours at best and is actually performing at five hours, there is a real need to consider application of both process performance improvement and redesign for better process capability. In designing the totally new, where nothing currently exists, the expectation must

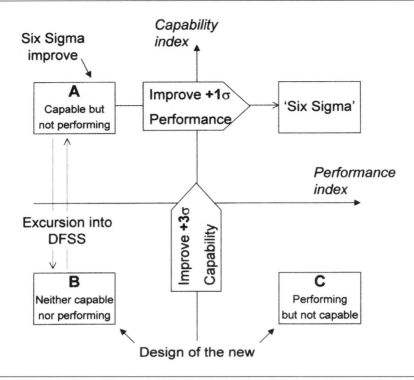

Figure 4.2   Flavours of DFSS

be that at the beginning of commercialization both capability *and* performance are likely to be compromised. Here DFSS has a powerful role to play in helping to ensure that both inherent process capability *and* immediate process performance meet customer requirements. This would be a real-life situation where the business needs a new 'customer order process' that is capable of a two-hour delivery and indeed does achieve two hours in reality, right from the launch date. In other cases, where performance is satisfactory but the customer targets have shifted and some redesign is required, then it must be assumed that any design or redesign is likely only to increase capability, and either not significantly improve or fail to guarantee performance. Often adding new technology or the like to help radically improve process capability has a detrimental impact on short-term performance. There is always the tendency for the 'C' situation to be transformed into the 'A' situation by new design, which is often why even good DFSS projects need to follow on with an application of the Six Sigma improvement methodology.

   Six Sigma improvement projects generally begin at the 'A' situation, and aim to shift to perfection through incremental process improvement. New design projects generally begin at either 'C' or 'B', and the assumption must be that the totally new begins at 'B'. The difficulty for a significant number of DMAIC projects is that, beginning at 'A', the team shows during the project that some redesign is required and that the project should have started at 'B'.

EXCURSION INTO DFSS

As Table 4.1 shows, the very nature of the DFSS project is quite distinct from that of a typical DMAIC project. Although there is a tendency to regard the improve stage of DMAIC as an either/or step where the process is either improved or redesigned, this is by no means an ideal situation. The reality of the difficulties often faced is seen when the quality teams themselves meet many obstacles to smooth progress. There is a need for a cut-down version of DFSS to provide a much-needed helping hand to overcome design issues in DMAIC-related situations.

The paramount need for successful execution of DMAIC is for the team to follow the methodology in a well-paced and timely way and not to come to a halt midstream. When cross-functional teams begin a DMAIC project, particularly in non-manufacturing environments, the team in unison will often expect to step neatly from define to measure to analyse and then on to improve. In situations where either the measure or the analyse stage shows clearly that improve is not going to be simple and achievable, the team generally stop, almost in disarray. The theoretical answer is for the team now to undertake a DFSS-type project; however, two barriers are confronted in that first the team has already started the DMAIC approach, and second there are often neither the resources nor the business backing to undertake a proper execution of DFSS. What is needed is a short *excursion* into the DFSS approach, with a very smart and timely return to the DMAIC project, almost as if nothing untoward had happened. Critically, the excursion, or 'day-trip to design', must ensure that at least the customer, concept and design stages from DFSS are executed, but without extending the basic project from the one-CTQ focus. Practical changes are that the team must now find a solution and then redesign – often products and services rather than processes, and yet without the luxury of considering much outside of the original brief or charter.

The elements for success in this situation are:

● Retain as much of the existing project framework, team and team charter as possible.
● Repeat only as much of the customer analysis as is required to identify critical needs in the area of the product/service to be redesigned.
● Generate an acceptable solution concept as quickly as possible for the team to work on, and focus on redesign and the process by which it will be supported, rather than new design and the product or service itself.
● Get the team to focus on the one critical CTQ that was at issue originally, and only worry about major interactions with other potential CTQs.
● Encourage the team to get back to the DMAIC approach as quickly as possible, install the solution and work on successful implementation rather than in-depth statistical analysis.

Ideally the concept solution that will help the team solve the problem should be rapidly arrived at, and perhaps from outside of the team. The team must then be encouraged to use this solution idea as a tool to radically change the process that they were attempting to improve. Naturally this is likely to be a challenge and some degree of flexibility is required; however, the overriding issue is often one of time.

FULL DFSS AS PART OF NPI

A key to success in formal dancing is to step out on the right foot from the very beginning of the dance, and certainly this can be taken as an excellent motto for any team beginning a major DFSS project! Such a project will run for years, and again the overriding issue is often one of time. Here there will be pressure to short-circuit the early work required in the customer and concept development stages, particularly as the early stages of the business initiation of the project should have already devised a concept solution. Clearly such additional work is expensive, and any real benefit gained will only be seen downstream of the project. The business, having provided a solution, will be keen to see payback in an early launch to the commercial market. The customer viewpoint must be given at the very minimum a reasonable hearing and due consideration, and it is essential to ensure that every customer is covered, including shareholders, stakeholders and employees.

The large DFSS project will focus on every single CTQ that every single customer regards as important for product, service and process to deliver world-class quality. Just this fact alone implies that the team will need powerful and perhaps new tools for customer research, identification and balancing of the CTQs, together with a view of design that encompasses the tangible product as well as the ethereal service and process. The target for such projects must be to deliver excellence across a broad range of facets, which implies a wide range of skills and abilities in the team make-up. Perhaps it will be necessary to change the constitution of the team, from business to customer focused, and then to design and technical focus. However the DFSS project is completed in actuality, it must always be remembered that the aim of the team is the design of something new, to excite the customer and provide commercial success for the business.

PROJECT CASE STUDIES

Even in organizations that either have undertaken or will undertake many Six Sigma projects, the occurrence of true DFSS-required projects should still be a rarity. The most likely scenario is the requirement for an excursion into DFSS, based on the discovery of a poor process by a typical DMAIC project team, and then only for early projects working in new and uncharted areas. The typically large to very large DFSS project is likely to be exceedingly rare, and only sizeable corporations with a proactive new product launch programme will have many examples to hand for review. What follows are two fairly typical examples substantially based on cases from real life, which perhaps illustrate the two extremities of the wide range of typical DFSS projects.

NEW DOCUMENT PRODUCTION – AN EXCURSION INTO DFSS

For many service-based companies, the development of new products is often hidden away in a small corner of the organization and not given the necessary exposure and support it deserves. Although the major business concentration is frequently on service delivery, it is highly likely that real and tangible products are still being sold, and thus the successful development of new products is vital to the ongoing business strategy. The 'product' being offered in this situation was a finance package associated with third-party office equipment, and almost the only physical representation of the product was the documentation involved. This was quite a complex area, as the product for the end customer was a piece of equipment, financed through a leasing agreement, the execution of which was a service offering. The product for the vendor-customer was the documentation that allowed a salesperson to formalize the contract for a new client, again the execution of a service. The product, as far as the finance company was concerned, was a more ethereal concept held in the minds of the staff and often only substantiated in the office computer software and the contract documentation being considered here.

An existing process had evolved *ad hoc* over time to take new 'finance products' from an idea to a tangible contract document, without which the commercial launch of the finance product was almost impossible. The process began with a new concept somewhere in sales and marketing in conjunction with the equipment suppliers, who were the real customers of this particular process as opposed to the end users of the equipment. Documentation for the new finance product offering was first designed and then produced for each new product, and it was the failure of this process to operate efficiently and quickly that had first attracted the attention of the senior management and in due course a Six Sigma project team. It must be noted that the process under review was critical to the development of *new* products, and was therefore a *design* process (design of *products*) in its own right. There was no apparent need for DFSS at this stage, as the organization did not want either a *new* process or a new *product*, but wished to *improve* the existing *process* by which new documents were developed, and therefore DMAIC was seen as the tool to use.

- Process – development of new contract documents
- Start – supplier agrees new finance product offering with marketing
- Stop – supplier sales staff have documents to use
- Product – physical contract document
- Service – design, proofing, printing and distribution of documents.

A senior manager championed the team, which included the sole process executioner as well as a salesperson, a representative from the 'new business department' and someone from the contract underwriting department. This was assumed to be a fairly straightforward Six Sigma project and the team progressed through the define and measure stages. The measurement stage showed that the average time taken from commitment of concept to real documents available for general use was about fifteen weeks. The overall distribution of cycle times showed that this was certainly not well controlled and a number of cases were excessively delayed. Setting a target for the customer requirement was not easy, and eventually a limit of four weeks was arrived at, although it was accepted that the customer of the process really wanted no more than two weeks. The immediate issue was that the process clearly and visibly took five to six weeks at minimum, which was the time taken to progress the finished work through the external printers. Naturally the team was reluctant to set a lower target, and when the real figures for the process duration became available there were glum faces all round!

The team identified many things that were hitherto unknown. From the emerging picture it was seen that:

- the new document production process was critical to the early and successful launch of new products;
- failure of the process was due to many causes, in particular the number of repetitive proofs required;
- hand-offs between internal and external people and repeated authorization contributed substantial delays; and
- annually some seventy new documents were produced, with the vast majority replaced over a three-year cycle.

The key to the problem was certainly the number of proofs required. Each proof took about two weeks to process, from layout changes, print of proof, return to supplier and then gaining acceptance or approval. The costs involved were in the order of hundreds of pounds for each proof, and on average documents required five proofs each. Indeed, following the analyse stage it became possible to write a simple but highly effective equation for the time taken for any particular document:

$$\text{Process cycle time} = \text{five weeks} + (\text{number of proofs}) \times (\text{two weeks})$$

Although there were many other causes of delay, the primary need was to reduce the number of proofs to just one, and this in itself led to many other root causes for delay that were quite easy to identify. The goal for the team was then modified to producing each new document in seven weeks and with just one proof. Saving an average four proofs for each of seventy documents each year alone would save £70 000, and the additional benefits from launching documents to the market eight or nine weeks early had extraordinarily large potential. With such challenging targets, the team in unison, including the champion, felt that this was an impossible task and almost gave up on the project. It was realized that something new was required, almost a new process and one that bypassed the printers. Clearly the printing problem was not going to be solved unless in-house printing was adopted, something that the champion had ruled out early on and which made the challenge apparently insurmountable. The task remained to produce each document with just one proof, or 'get it right first time', which is perhaps the outward sign and demonstration of the whole Six Sigma philosophy! The process operator, who was quite used to not getting anything right first time, was easily able to lower morale and persuade the team of the Herculean task required. The team leader needed help, and it was at this point that the newly arrived DFSS methodology was considered as a potential way of both empowering and encouraging the team to develop a new process.

The team itself stopped the project, which in hindsight did not become a major issue. The team leader went on DFSS training, and, together with supporting members of the Six Sigma quality department, used some of the DFSS tools to restart the team using a reduced DFSS approach. The trigger for success was a concept for a solution that had the potential to solve the proofing issues; this was injected into the teamwork so neatly that the team believed that it was their own idea. With a definitive and positive restart a few weeks later, a strong customer focus and some new tools, together with the potential for a solution, the team was able to develop its own designed process that had the inherent capability to deliver a new document with just one proof. Early pilot trials showed that this new process did indeed work, with a cycle time of just seven weeks! Re-energized, the team fleshed out the solution and successfully implemented it across a wide range of the simpler product documents.

As an early project in the Six Sigma initiative, solving the obvious need for design within an existing DMAIC project was a challenge of a practical nature and required:

- the natural halt of the team to learn new tools and regroup;
- a provided concept solution for the team to work on;
- a stronger focus on the customer of the process than normal for DMAIC;
- the ability to design a new process with dynamically increased capability; and
- successful implementation of the new process and launch to the business.

Although a midstream halt and the additional training might have been avoided had the team started with a unified DMAIC/DFSS approach, it still required a noted shift in focus away from process improvement to process/product design. Certainly in this case the solution adopted was a new and designed approach to one-stop proofing rather than an improvement or redesign of something that already existed. The challenge for such an 'excursion into DFSS' remains one of quickly shifting focus to a customer-oriented design mode without excessively reworking the earlier stages, and then equally quickly returning to the DMAIC stages of implementation and control. Although successful in achieving a reduction in average time from fifteen to seven weeks, and reducing proofing requirements from five to very close to one, there was still much more that could have been done. A little-known fact discovered by the team was that each and every document was a multi-part make-up of carbon-less copies, which were all glued together by hand to ensure a professional image. This guaranteed that the cost of each document was never less than £5, and the team also found that for every used document arriving at new business, up to twenty documents had first been printed. The fact that it therefore cost the company, for each new customer proposal, almost £100 for the documents alone was a very strong argument for an alternative approach using a paper-less system!

NEW IT SYSTEM – A VERY LARGE DFSS PROJECT

As a 'cut-down' DFSS project, the team in the previous example:

- largely retained the DMAIC framework;
- concentrated on just one area of the process (document proofing);
- limited project scope to two customer CTQs (speed and number of proofs); and
- dealt mainly with practical team issues – problem solving, design and team training.

In direct contrast, the second project represented an almost classic archetype of all that DFSS stands for. Within the European platform of acquired and diverse businesses, some seven distinct computer systems were struggling to operate, and doing so on a wide range of ageing equipment. These were legacy systems, disparate and disjointed, failing the immediate needs of both business and customer and certainly hindering future adaptability and change. Multiple systems are expensive to maintain and from a business point of view the amalgamation of the entire and troublesome medley into one shiny new and up-to-date system would be both strategically and financially appealing. On the other hand, Europe is naturally a diverse place and 'one solution fits all' was not going to be achieved with ease. The decision to sweep everything away and replace it with one new system was not easy to take and followed many years of protracted debate on the way forward. It was a business decision, helped where possible by the technical experts and prompted by escalating customer and service/product delivery needs. At the same time that the decision was made to move forwards (in principle at least), the Six Sigma initiative had advanced to a working model for DFSS. Had this project moved forward more quickly, then DFSS might have been quietly ignored; however, the legitimate procrastination meant that in line with dictated policy it had to be run as a 'DFSS IT project' – or else! What this meant in practice, and what it should have meant in theory, were two very different things. It has been noted on occasions that the label DFSS can safely be applied to almost any project after it has been completed, particularly when DFSS is seen as the flavour of the month, as it then was. In other cases, what should have been DFSS projects were quietly conducted as traditional ones, mostly due to pressure on time or resources.

The proposed business solution was a complete replacement of all systems to provide one *new* system, on a *new* hardware and software platform, with a future life expectancy of perhaps fifteen years and the potential to support the *new* e-commerce of the future. This was a major *design* work and certainly required *new* processes and services; here the team had to:

- adopt the new DFSS project framework right from the start;
- adapt the DFSS methodology for use within IT systems development;
- concentrate in totality on every business process;
- work with a scope that encompassed every single customer CTQ; and
- deal mainly with cultural issues of attitude – customer focus, service design and a whole new approach.

The initial project team make-up was bipolar, with a core 'business' team of no more than ten who drove the DFSS project forwards, and a larger team from the IT field. Matters were complicated by the use of an external consultancy firm to support the IT development, and naturally a project of this size and budget had a senior management steering committee with representatives from IT, business and, for the first time, (Six Sigma) quality. The story of this project is a long one, and probably quite a good subject for a whole book in its own right, as the project has continued to run for almost four years. The critical points of note are that, from the very beginning, the nature of the DFSS approach gave rise to a real need for almost abrasive cultural change within the business management and IT divisions. Business leaders who were happy to offer 90 per cent service to customers had to be encouraged to think of failing the customer at less than four parts per million. IT managers, who were happy to dominate the design with the technical issues and requirements, had to be encouraged to subjugate their design parameters to customer CTQ constraints.

The business team went right back to the business fundamentals – the basic reason for the existence of the organization and the primary market in which it operated. From this was constructed a set of virtual products and then a complete set of new high-level process maps for every single product and service offering. Then began the long process of identifying customers and customer segments, and obtaining survey material from which to build identified issues, needs and requirements. Naturally much work had already been completed as part of the standard Six Sigma initiative, and core processes and CTQs were already well defined for most of the business. The team went a great deal further by removing any trace of the current solutions in use, and in identifying the basic processes in such a way as to allow for *any* technical solution for actual delivery. This then set up the basic constraints for the IT design team to work within and actively encouraged better e-commerce-type solutions to meet the new challenging customer targets. More work allowed precise allocation of CTQ targets and limits and the construction of firm CTPs for the design team. The newly devised processes were then modelled and simulated to test their ability to perform to the CTPs, well before any computer code had been written. The long-term strategy was to develop prototype computer code to fully evaluate against the customer requirements in a pilot or 'model office' environment. The business team had members from each and every business location across Europe and all of the early work, including team training and development, took about six months. Clearly the dominant nature of the project was IT, and thus all work was undertaken side by side with a core IT team. At one point the IT development methodology was integrated with the DFSS methodology to provide commonality and to better define the interfaces between the two streams – business/customer and technical. The IT approach was to use a rapid application development (RAD) methodology, which was clearly lacking in the areas of pre-design and customer/business need development, but excelled in the more technical areas required to design and implement a new information system. With a joint approach founded on DFSS, the business and customer work proceeded to a point where the design constraints were handed over to the technical team, which had developed in parallel a foundation system on which the final technical solution was to be built.

The successes for the project team were slow in coming, but eventually it could be seen that what might have been a technically dominated development was now more customer focused, and even aspects of the business and employee needs were being integrated as 'customers' of the process or product/service. Failures were also evident and are perhaps almost inevitable in such a large undertaking. Impartial leadership was difficult to ensure and no one person was seen to hold a good balance of governance between business, customer (often only represented by the quality department) and technical development. Over two years the focus of the project shifted and some three project leaders came and went, which certainly did nothing to help stability and continuity. The size of the project clearly required substantial buy-in from the business and many individuals, as well as a major investment in the DFSS methodology to achieve the up-front elimination of design failures. For a large DFSS project, success will often only be seen long term over a period of perhaps ten years or more. This implies that the change in attitude towards a customer-focused pre-design and the investment in a DFSS approach needs to be encouraged and substantiated through the more visible evidence and experience across a number of smaller projects, which here was not the case. The need for a radical change in attitudes is shown by an early comment from a member of the IT design team: 'I just want to get on and write code.' This was said at a point where no one could clearly identify either what was required of the code, or how to measure if the written code actually performed. It was not just the technical side of the project that suffered, as early work had clearly shown that customers had an issue with the flexibility of the *products* on offer. Rather than deal with this thorny issue directly, it became subtly diluted to a customer need for flexibility in the *processes and services* offered. However, this one aspect alone, the need for customer-focused flexibility, did positively affect the design process and ultimately led to a number of radical changes in both the new processes and the computer systems offered.

The holistic model for DFSS must be concerned with both *practical* and *cultural* issues, and success can only be assured when the two aspects are clearly brought together in a workable methodology. The larger the project, the greater the need for rigour, project management and a better design methodology, and often, too, a greater need for acute customer focus and empathy, and for time and effort to be expended during the earlier stages. The key points evident from such projects show a need for:

- appropriate adaptation of DFSS and tool use in terms of both project scale and design environment;
- strong and 'democratic' leadership that is prepared to champion all stakeholders and customers involved;
- foundations in 'improve' Six Sigma to facilitate better understanding of ideas, tools and a customer focus;
- strong team membership that is cross-functional, multi-skilled and involves 'ideas people'; and
- sympathetic benefit analysis by the business that is prepared to both invest in the project and delay short-term deliverables in favour of a larger long-term payback that can often be very difficult to define and measure.

SUMMARY

- A successful DFSS methodology needs to achieve:

  - total business ownership;
  - the risk-effective use of new technology;
  - customer focus to achieve a Six Sigma performance of four to five sigma;
  - creative, yet excellent and well-controlled, design; and
  - sound project management and commercial implementation without failure.

- A basic framework DFSS methodology is DCCDI:

  - Define
  - Customer
  - Concept
  - Design
  - Implement.

- The output from a process is limited both by performance and by capability. A limit in performance is a failure to deliver at the best capability possible and can be improved by incremental changes to process operation. A limit in capability is inherent within the process and often requires a redesign to change the process fundamentally.
- DMAIC and DFSS are two different methodologies. Six Sigma *improvement* applies to process performance; Six Sigma *design* applies to radically changing the inherent process capability. Fundamentally *improve* is different to *design*. Typically new products and services, often with new processes of manufacture and delivery, require an application of both design and improve.
- A range of 'flavours' of DFSS exists, the two extremes being:

  - the excursion into DFSS from a DMAIC project, a small diversion to generate the design of a new product, service or (more typically) a process; and
  - the large-scale launch of a major and entirely new product/service offering, which will embody significant business risk, effort and major design.

- Achievable DFSS is about overcoming practical issues of design and project management and also about cultural issues that prevent a good customer focus and the appropriate use of customer metrics against which to both design and evaluate.

EXERCISES

Identify a new product or service recently launched in either your own company or an organization closely related to your direct experience. Work backward to the process by which such a new product or service is introduced and map out how this process operates, identifying the key process stages.

1 How well does this process align with the framework methodology DCCDI as described above?
2 What are the principal elements missing from your example approach, or are elements missing from DCCDI?
3 Identify one or more real or potential failures of the newly designed product/service and attempt to attribute the root cause of this failure to a stage within the design process. To what extent would the DCCDI approach – particularly the customer and conceptualize stages – have reduced or eliminated such failures?

If you have direct experience of Six Sigma as a process improvement methodology in one form or another, evaluate a large number (thirty or more) of projects undertaken and identify which if any can be classified as DFSS. How do such projects vary from the simple (excursion into DFSS) to the complex (full DFSS projects)?

'The two approaches – DMAIC and DCCDI – are fundamentally different and cannot be combined.' Discuss.

CHAPTER FIVE

DFSS methodology in detail

The tools that DFSS brings in addition to those commonly used in both quality in general and Six Sigma in particular are relatively few in number, but rather large and complex in their execution. Figure 5.1 shows the DFSS approach as a much-simplified schematic, based around the principal design stage. To achieve better design, the business must promote both the concept solution needed to seed the design process, as well as the constraints and evaluation criteria against which the design will progress and be measured. This is the key to attaining excellence in customer-focused design, and what follows on from the design stage is concerned only with practical implementation and commercialization, important though this is. This chapter will deal only with the design project itself, and for many situations the implementation stage can be relegated either to a sub- or sequential team, or even back to the 'business' as part of an early handover. Previous chapters have discussed the need for a corporate strategy as a precursor to the project, and much of this undertaking must be excluded from the design project itself, although the define stage may well continue some of this work.

Figure 5.2 shows in more detail how the various stages and tools interact to focus on the design activity. In the diagram the principal tools used are indicated by rectangles, critical stage outputs are indicated by diamonds and the principal activities (perhaps also with associated outputs) are shown by circles or ovals. This is a complex diagram at first sight but neatly encapsulates all the stages, steps, tools and outputs of DFSS. The entire process begins with the design concept (or more correctly the

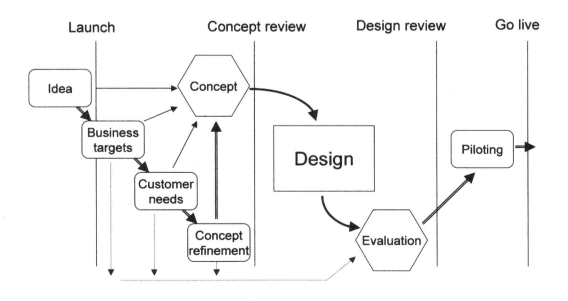

Figure 5.1   DFSS schematic overview

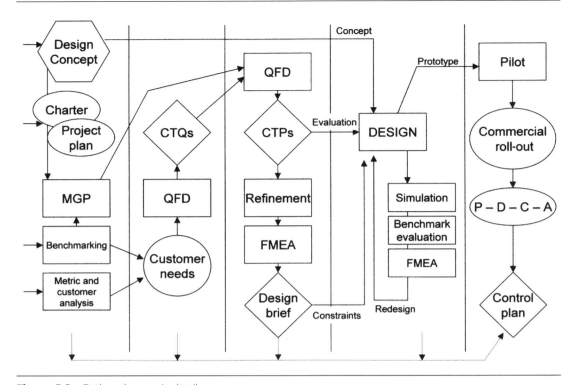

Figure 5.2   Tools and stages in detail

concept solution), which traditionally would pass directly to design itself. In DFSS the *concept* does indeed pass on to 'design'; much work is, however, completed before this. The first stage will start with the team developing a project plan and team charter with input and support from the business. General benchmarking needs to be undertaken together with specific quality metric and customer analysis. The team will also need to take the design concept, perhaps modified according to the initial charter and project plan, and further refine this using multi-generation planning (MGP). Once the first steps of customer survey and analysis are complete, the team can pass the first tollgate and move to the second stage. Here the information from benchmarking and customer and metric analysis come together in customer needs analysis and are the main inputs to the first use of the quality function deployment (QFD) tool. QFD is used to identify and refine the most appropriate critical to quality (CTQ) metrics, which will become the principal output from this stage. The second tollgate therefore requires validation of these customer-focused CTQs and, wherever possible, approval should be sought from both business and customers.

The third stage, design conceptualization, requires a second application of QFD, this time using the refined solution concept from the MGP tool in stage one together with the CTQs from stage two. Here the CTQs are mapped onto a set of critical to process (CTP) metrics that become one of the two principal outputs from this stage. The team will also use the CTPs to work on the solution concept by refining it to a working design concept that satisfies the CTPs, using its knowledge of the business and customer requirements. The team may also eliminate many potential design and product/service errors and failures using the failure mode effect analysis (FMEA) tool. This is a period of *non-technical* design, and the critical tollgate at the end of this stage divides the two fundamental halves of the DFSS project, bringing together all the work completed so far into one composite design brief. The entire design brief (containing the output from the CTPs and various design concepts, refinements and constraints) will often be more formally handed over to the design stage and (possibly separate) technical design team following this critical tollgate, which is treated as a joint review sponsored by the business and supported by the team and, again, representatives of the customer. Only when all parties are entirely happy that the proposed design brief is acceptable to the business and the customer, as well as to the design team, should this tollgate be passed.

The design stage itself will proceed much as any traditional design undertaking, although more simulation, testing and evaluation as well as failure elimination will be required. The ideal is for the design to progress as an iterative loop of design, simulate, evaluate and failure proofing, until the design fully satisfies the entire concept, constraint and evaluation criteria. The output of the design stage will normally be a prototype, which must pass a further 'go live' tollgate before going through a pilot and refining step. This will be followed by a commercial roll-out plan that is typically executed using a 'plan–do–check–act' activity. As well as dealing with all of the above, the team or teams involved will need to contribute at each stage towards the development of a control plan, which will generally be adopted and executed by the business following handover, although elements of the control plan will need to be embedded within the design concept and ultimate solution itself.

Clearly there is a great deal of flexibility in this arrangement, and the smaller project may be completed by the same team of people throughout and include more of the pre-work and handover work, whereas larger teams will certainly be divided into customer and conceptual design, followed by technical design. It is important, however, that the stages of define, customer and conceptualize are undertaken by the same team as a continuous and flowing process to ensure depth of application and continuity between the rather disparate tools used.

SELECTING AND STARTING PROJECTS

There can be no doubt that it is entirely the responsibility of the 'business' to both initiate and own any DFSS project, no matter what the size or scope. Failure to gain business ownership will almost certainly result in failure in either the process or in the final delivery of product/service and is guaranteed to be a costly error of judgement. If any DFSS project is worth undertaking, and it is to be hoped that DFSS is neither regarded nor used lightly in its application, then sponsorship, championing and ownership are critical factors for success and all of these must come from the business at the highest level.

Projects must begin by building a business case founded on both corporate strategy and end-customer need, preferably with a reasonably full case study undertaken first. The larger the project outcome, the more time and money are required up front, even before beginning the DFSS project for real. The first requirement of the project will be a team charter, a living document that sets out the objectives, scope, roles and responsibilities for the team. Developing the team charter before the start of the project is a valuable aid to clarifying the project objectives and in providing a speedy launch to the team. The charter can often be used to approve officially the start of the project at 'tollgate zero'. The business must *sponsor* the project, which implies time, money and effort, and a very good starting point is to write down what the project will require and then ensure that someone in authority has agreed and signed for this. The business must also *champion* the project, which is a subtle addition to sponsorship in that it implies a more active willingness to be seen leading, promoting and supporting the project and team. Someone must be the sole and ultimate champion of the project, upon whom falls the ultimate responsibility for success or failure, and to whom everyone can readily turn for leadership and guidance in crisis and for enthusiasm and support in the better times. This is a task for one person, not for a committee, and further highlights the need for business *ownership*. The larger DFSS projects are likely to operate only within the larger business or to run for much longer than typical Six Sigma projects. For small projects, sponsorship, championing and ownership may be vested in one person, but in the larger and longer projects these three elements of corporate responsibility may divide into several parts. The person who sponsors may be tempted to leave the money and depart, and the person who champions may be tempted to speak, enthuse and then depart also. Ownership in the legal sense implies both rights of decision, direction and disposal as well as liabilities and responsibilities, and often joint ownership leads to damaging dissent often divorced from practical issues. Many can sponsor and many can champion, but only one person should lead and own the project. Naturally this one person must show neutrality towards business, customer, team and technical issues, which is often a very tall order! This is particularly challenging if the project owner is also the future process owner, which is a good rule to apply for Six Sigma projects generally. Since DFSS is often used to develop new processes that may not yet exist, and since larger project scope and customer–business divisiveness can be very real issues, taking a disparate and disinterested party as the project owner may be far more appropriate.

What makes for a good DFSS project? There are many considerations of size, scope and fundamental objectives; however, a good guide is to dwell on the premise that nothing makes a good DFSS project, and then to see if in fact using DFSS would be a better idea. In organizations or subdivisions where design is part of the everyday activity, after a period of using DFSS in isolation for specific projects, the company may decide to integrate DFSS concepts and tools into the design process, or even to replace the existing design process with a modified DFSS methodology. However, this book is written as a general guide for any organization, and the vast majority will use the design of the new sparingly and as part of the Six Sigma approach. Application of DFSS is best suited for:

- large projects – in terms of time, budget and scope or impact;
- where exponential rather than incremental change is required;
- for active or major design rather than small improvement or minor design;
- where new or substantially new products, services or processes are needed;
- in cases where new or radical technology is being introduced;
- where meeting customer expectations (external and/or internal) is vital to the success of the project;
- when failure of business case, design or implementation and commercialization would be very damaging.

This should be regarded as a guide to identifying good DFSS projects rather than a definitive checklist. For the introduction of a new product to a new customer market, requiring design and new technology and costing millions of pounds, the answer is definitely DFSS. Where a small in-house design department turns out commercial prototypes day after day, each one a slight alteration of the last, then DFSS is perhaps overkill and maybe the blending of Six Sigma ideas for 'design *using* Six Sigma' might be more appropriate.

The trigger words for DFSS must be *customer, design, new, technology* and *change*.

Here are two examples of project statements:

- Our project is to redesign the layout of the post room to achieve better workflow.
- Our project is to design and launch a new web-based service to our customers to promote more business through on-line sales.

The first example is short-term minor design or incremental improvement, with a small customer impact, and is generally internally focused to save the company money. Six Sigma would certainly help; full DFSS would certainly add an overhead to the project that would cost more than it benefited, and perhaps an excursion into DFSS might be a good compromise. The second example, however, is a very good case for the use of DFSS. Here the design of several new products and services (where possibly nothing like this existed before) is needed, which require new technology and will affect a major section of the customer base. Probably too, like many 'dot com' offerings of the Internet revolution, a great deal of hope for the business future is at stake, and very little thought has gone into just why this is a good idea. It is astonishing how much that is both *new* and *designed* is in fact introduced to the customer without answering some very basic questions, particularly in the service sectors. Certainly a good proportion of the Internet web sites and portals are more than just a test or trial of the market, and yet many fail simply because no one has ruthlessly questioned the validity or substance of the idea. Hard questions for which DFSS forces an answer are:

● Why should this project be undertaken, and why now?
● What is the damage if it is *not* undertaken?
● How does this relate to the strategic plan for the company?
● What are the financial implications, costs and benefits?

A good point to ensure is that a projected business plan is produced using sound market research and conservative estimates. If the product/service is new, the first assumption must be that no one will want, need or use the product/service until proven (which is where the DFSS approach adds much value). Organizations that risk Internet-based ordering projections of 20 per cent of turnover on consumer markets largely populated by people without computers are in for a shock, and yet this attitude is seen all too often in retailing. A large and well-respected departmental store left Bristol city centre in the UK for an out-of-town retail park, where floor space was increased by 40 per cent and business flourished. The business market had been notably non-car-owners (parking was increasingly a problem) and office shoppers at lunchtime, with a wide range of goods at good value. A new owner, from well outside the area, took over the old store and spent £18 million on refurbishment, reducing the floor space by about 40 per cent and bringing in expensive and exclusive 'designer label' stock. The office workers did not like it – nothing small to shop for at lunchtime. The non-car-owners did not like it – far too expensive. The primary market, typically car-owners, moved custom to the out-of-town store with longer opening hours and no parking charges. The new store in the city was noted for having more sales assistants than customers, even during the lunch hour, and has now changed ownership.

   Another good question to ask of the project is whether the new offering is a product or a service. Often new technology is used for its own sake with little regard for the (end) customer. For many new web-based offerings the real answer is that such developments are seen as products, whereas in reality they need to be services. Design and development carried out by external or disparate in-house development teams will produce a 'web site', sold to the business as the new way forward. Being sold back to the requesting business like this makes the item, much like the emperor's new clothes, a product – 'Here is a new web site, buy it from us and sell it to your customers.' In fact, the web site is a new tool to replace the existing process of sales, ordering or whatever, and is clearly a core or enabling process providing a service. No external customer approaches a company wanting to buy a web page; they approach wanting to buy a real product or use a real service – the web page is merely the carrier of the service that provides or supports the product. Getting this one aspect of the new product/service into a correct business and customer perspective is indeed a major achievement!

What goes into the team charter? Certainly a written outline of the scope and range of the undertaking, showing what will be achieved and what will be committed to the project. This will also require objectives and a modified (more in-depth) Six Sigma problem statement and goal statement. The reason for the project will be outlined with the primary concept solution, target customer market and business needs, together with any case studies and projections. Project management is also important and will require a formal project plan and timeline, together with the team roles and responsibilities. Part of all this work must be an *a priori* solution to the business problem, and this can often be seen as a very strong test of both the relevance and feasibility of the project – no solution, no project!

THE SOLUTION COMES FIRST

In direct contrast to Six Sigma projects, where the work is firmly based on a customer or business problem, DFSS projects must start with a seed of a solution for the business need. DFSS in itself is not about finding or identifying a solution, but rather about refining and homing in on the most appropriate and final customer-focused solution. Any attempt to begin a DFSS project with just a blank sheet of paper will be interesting and protracted at best, and liable to miss the point or suffer total failure at worst. Failure in many design projects begins with a poor understanding or a poor definition of what the final design will look like and exactly what it should achieve. Failures, too, come from issues with the 'not invented here' syndrome and a great deal of hand-waving leading to 'Just build it and I will tell you if it is what I want.' A visit to any large consumer store will show that, where complex decisions are required of the purchaser, the store often actively promotes a range of demonstrations or suggestions as to how the product could be used. Whether the business especially commissions the first search for a solution, or utilizes existing and in-house R&D teams, the objective must be to ensure ownership, clarity and acceptance by the business. If the solution is clearly inappropriate, unwanted or unneeded, too expensive or just a knee-jerk reaction (everyone else is on the Internet, we must be too), then the business, not the project team, must see this, own it and deal with it.

How best can such 'concept solutions' be identified, and what do they look like? Clearly the basis for any work must begin with an inspection of the corporate or customer difficulty that gives rise to a need for a new design. This process is likely to be either so readily undertaken as to be almost ignored, or so infrequent as to be readily neglected. A good start is to ask the customer why they have issues with what they currently use or experience. Where new technology is on offer, 'dreaming sessions' can be interesting ways of promoting fresh ideas. Focus groups with customers, together with some input from a few dreams, can trigger novel ideas as the basis for potential solutions. The senior directors should also have a few ideas as to the future direction of the organization, and the corporate vision and mission should be used to influence and filter these ideas.

For example, the real problem with corporate invoices is that they arrive when you don't want them to, they are in the other company's format, not your own, they require handling and filing and often get lost, and they put you in debit and have to be paid. Put this together with a corporate cash-flow issue ('customers don't pay our invoices'), a corporate vision of being the easiest company to do business with (yes, this applies to invoices too), the latest technology ('I now operate my bank account on-line'), and potential solutions begin to arrive.

● Issue – prompt customer payment of our invoices
● Problem – we are not proactively supporting our customers in invoicing

- New technology – Internet systems and on-line banking
- Dream – our customers can manage their own accounts and pay on-line.

The concept solution then becomes quite a complex idea of creating Internet-accessible customer accounts and allowing customers to buy and self-invoice. Naturally this needs a great deal of refinement and clarification, and the real challenge is to bring the business needs and the technical design needs together, to avoid cries of 'that just can't be done' – from either side!

A powerful tool to aid both concept generation and concept clarification is benchmarking. Benchmarking is perhaps more a way of life than one particular tool, and has a place within DFSS at almost every stage. A benchmark is literally a mark, often in stone and used by surveyors to set a level point from which everything else is measured. Corporate benchmarking can be used internally, to gauge performance of products, services or processes, and externally to compare against one or more competitors and proactively to research alternatives. Any good Six Sigma initiative will have used internal benchmarking to define CTQ performances for the core and enabling processes across the entire business. Teams may also have already used external benchmarking to look for best practices elsewhere. How benchmarking is carried out depends to some extent on the immediate need, but more on the available resources to hand. Just like design, benchmarking will only provide answers to the questions asked, and at an early stage of a DFSS project the question must be centred on finding alternative solutions to the immediate problem. Here competitor benchmarking can be supplemented with cross-industry benchmarking. Finding out what the direct competitors are doing is always a good idea, but it must of course be carried out ethically. Asking questions of indirect or future competitors carries less risk, and probing indirect industries can throw up some interesting observations to fuel the search for a solution. There are many alternatives to the common 'purchase, get invoice, pay invoice' routine; for example, in the public utilities industry many who experience difficulties with credit invoicing pay on a pre-pay or token scheme.

Risk management is vital at this early stage, and it must be a joint corporate and design decision to rule in or out sections of the project. Clearly what should be attempted in DFSS are projects where there is significant gain to be achieved, a significant issue to be resolved (and only by the introduction of a new design) and significant benefit for this company to do it here and now. Scope-creep is a major problem and should be dealt with early on. A tool to aid both risk and scope management is multi-generation planning (MGP). This traditionally applies to products but also works very well with services (recall too that a serious question to be answered is whether the new offering is a product, a service, or both). Figure 5.3 demonstrates a completed MGP for our earlier example. Typically the generations of the product/service are divided into three steps or stages, where the first step is to 'stop the bleeding', or deal with the immediate big issue hurting the company. Step two moves towards taking the offensive, and step three is a leap to attaining market leadership through the new product/service. The important point is that the project to hand only deals with step one. The matrix allows for a clear understanding of what the project should achieve, and where the product/service is going in the future, which allows the project to underpin the next stages. In the overall plan one DFSS project might achieve step one, and then the MGP is revised, with step two becoming step one, step three becoming step two, and a new step three being created at the corporate planning level. Clearly many design projects get carried away and clear goal focus is a major benefit. As well as dividing the timescale or scope, the MGP can also clarify the vision, product/service generation and the necessary technology. The vision should be clearly understandable at the senior corporate level and must tie in with corporate strategy and mission. The product generation identifies the customer-focused critical areas required to deliver this vision, and the technology specifies in more detail what is used to make

	1 Step – stop the bleeding	2 Stretch – take the offensive	3 Leap – attain market leadership	
Vision	Static web site	Dynamic web site with ordering	Customer interactive web site	Where we want to be
Product generation	Access 16/5 Index 1000 page hits per month	Access 24/7 Index and published 5000 page hits per month	Access 24/7 Customer site updates 20 000 page hits per month	What we have to do to get there
Technology	Server, URL, page counters, indexing and authoring tools	Networked server and redundancy	Secure VPN Automatic database revisions	What this requires

Figure 5.3   Multi-generation planning

it happen. However this tool is used, it should bring together the corporate business and the technical design in agreement of what, how and when at the highest level. Use of such tools as MGP and benchmarking will begin before the DFSS project and perhaps spill into the project definition stage, but should certainly remain active long after the project has finished.

FOCUSING ON THE CUSTOMER

The customer stage of a DFSS project aims to fully understand and quantify the needs of the customer in order to generate the necessary CTQ metrics. The principal tool used here is quality function deployment (QFD), the basic form of which is shown in Figure 5.4. Because of the shape of this diagram, it is often referred to as a house of quality (HOQ), and there may well be several such QFD diagrams used in sequence in any one project. The basic aim of QFD is to map between needs or *wants* on the one side, and the potential solutions or *hows* across the top. Put simply, the team will construct a list of primary and important things that the business and the customer *want*, and also a list of suggestions for *how* this might best be achieved. The rest of the task undertaken in using the QFD tool is about finding the most appropriate 'how' to achieve the 'want' most effectively. Since this is such a vital part of the Six Sigma philosophy – giving the customers what they want – it will be covered in much more depth in Chapter Six. It is important to note, however, that such work can take months to complete and in large projects the QFD matrix can involve several hundred wants by several hundred hows. This is not a 'handle-turning' tool with a certain outcome, but rather a means to gather and collate information in such a way as to enable a better-informed decision. Certainly the value of the tool is as much to do with the quantity of effort that goes into using it and the interpretation of the results, as it is with how well each part is performed.

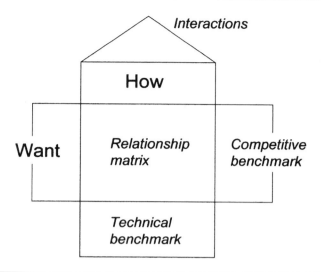

Figure 5.4 House of quality in outline

The use of QFD in the first stage is to identify the metrics that can be used to measure customer quality. The starting point will be a list of customer needs, and Figure 5.5 shows part of a customer needs tree. Identifying customer needs can be a very challenging task, often clouded by the business viewpoint and an unwillingness to see things from the customer point of view. It can also be very difficult to see the customer need as just that, and not simply a business solution to the need or issue. Customer needs fall out from primary high-level requirements and manifest themselves in sharp-ended necessities for particular characteristics from products and services, which if not met usually result in an issue with some product or service. Getting to customer needs in Six Sigma can often be best achieved by finding out what the current issues are; however, with new products and services this is often difficult in the extreme. Unlike Six Sigma improvement projects, where the problem is often clear, DFSS must begin with the assumption that plausible customer needs are likely to be based on similar needs found elsewhere. People, generally, work automatically in any situation to assess, pattern-match to a past experience, and then move forward with assumptions of what to expect based on past experiences. This is a two-edged sword, as it allows the new to shock and exceed expectation (for a while) but it sets deep-seated and almost unconscious perceptions of what is routinely expected. For someone launching a new web-based information facility, where nothing existed before, the best way to identify key customer needs is to map out similar situations, such as newspapers. A primary need may be for information, with second-level needs for added value, timeliness, cost and ease of use. There is no right or wrong way of continuing this process and many sub-level needs can be attached to the tree in various ways. The important point is not to correctly associate each part of the tree, but to identify every need and not miss any. In the design of a new Internet service, primary customer needs will come from existing requirements of information services, but also new needs and expectations for speed, efficiency, convenience and even entertainment. Clearly, too, where computers are involved, there is often the expectation that it won't actually work or be of benefit, and a very real customer need will exist for appeasement and being wooed, and then in not being let down!

Once needs have been fully identified and clarified, the team must rank them in order of

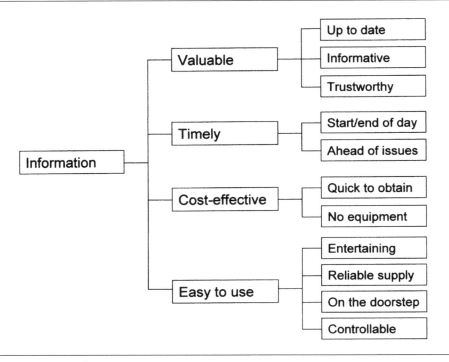

Figure 5.5   Customer needs tree

importance. The use of Kano analysis can help sort out basic needs or wants into the three primary classes of 'must haves', 'one-dimensional' and 'delighters'. The traditional concept of customer needs analysis was a simplistic 'one-dimensional' or linear model where more is better and less is worse. This is certainly true for a great many customer needs, such as speed, where there is an expectation of a given delivery or performance. Achieve this expectation and the customer will be nothing more or less than neutrally satisfied. Go faster and the customer will be pleased, faster still and the customer delighted; conversely go slower and the customer will be disappointed, slower still and the customer annoyed. This model is in reality far too simplistic, and Noriaki Kano is credited with introducing the idea of 'must-have' requirements, which are absolutes that cannot be left out. The 'must-have' needs, such as accuracy, reliability, consistency and safety (which can include all of physical, financial and psychological), are those which have to be fully delivered to achieve neutral satisfaction; failure to meet this class of requirements any less than completely will always result in dissatisfaction. The Kano model has been further extended to include the idea of unexpected needs or 'delighters'. Where customers are not expressing a need, or have little expectation of such a need being fulfilled, then actively meeting such a need leads to customer delight, which is very important for the commercial success of new products and services. In the design of the new, Kano analysis is a powerful tool to help identify and separate the primary groups of needs, since it is not easy to trade off between radically different customer requirements. Any new design must continue to *totally* satisfy the essential 'must-have' requirements and such needs are often overlooked. It is in the area of linear needs that the team must work hard to radically move forward delivery performance beyond the currently expected, often by using new technology or a fresh approach towards the problem. The third category of need, the unexpected delighter, is a real benefit in new design, since failure to deliver will not engender a negative response; however, a positive delivery will easily excite the customer. The very nature of 'new' suggests that something must be better or improved, and with Internet services speed, convenience and other novel approaches to traditional aspects of invoice payment come to mind. For example, the number on an invoice is not traditionally something that the customer can change; however, with a customer-driven web-based system there is no reason why customers cannot choose (within reason) their own number. The danger with such an approach is that the novel feature, so eagerly championed by marketing or technology, can just as easily turn out to be a damp squib as a market winner. The problem is that such 'customer needs' are in fact solutions or features and not needs at all. Customers don't *need* to choose their own invoice number, but rather they have a need for *convenience* and *ease of use*, which may reduce to 'getting each invoice through our system', the issue being that currently *your* invoices have to be related back to *our* purchase numbers. A 'feature' to meet this need may indeed be to allow invoice numbers to match purchase order numbers more easily, but this is part of the next stage of the design process.

What goes across the top of the first HOQ are plausible measurements that can or could possibly be taken from the existing or new product or service. If the customer needs include speed, accuracy and timeliness of invoices, then potential metrics are time taken to produce one invoice, number of errors per invoice, days late or early against expected target, number of invoices produced, value of income generated and so on. Much like any part of design, generating possible metrics is a balancing act between what is a dream and what is a reality, and there is no reason why the dreams should not be used. Certainly a few dreams may generate better metrics than simply relying on the old and tired existing counters. QFD is used, in the relationship matrix in the middle, to see and then numerically rank how well each measure relates to (can gauge) customer satisfaction for a need being met. The time taken to print and post an invoice does not relate in any way to how accurate the invoice is, but does relate partially to how timely is its arrival. If this tool is used effectively and with an open mind (focused on the customer rather than closed in on the company viewpoint), then the team often sees that traditional measurements relate very poorly to gauging success in meeting customer needs. This is a large part of what the longer-term Six Sigma culture is all about, as many organizations are slowly but surely turning corporate and fiscal metrics over to ones that better measure (better relate to) customer satisfaction. Often new metrics have to be introduced to fill in gaps missed by more traditional measures; also each measure has to be fine-tuned so that it can relate better to more needs.

Combining the ranked order of customer needs and the suggested list of metrics into the QFD diagram will ultimately allow a selection of the minimal set of metrics which most adequately gauge the ability of the newly designed product/service to achieve customer satisfaction. This should be a good set of CTQs, the smallest possible group of measures that are critical to customer quality, easily measurable, as well as actionable in the new design. Benchmarking again can play an important part in QFD, although for simplicity in smaller projects this work can be much reduced. The right-hand benchmarking area is an attempt to compare the offerings of the competitor market in terms of its ability to satisfy the identified customer needs. This should include three or so direct competitors in the new field, as well as the home organization. Technical benchmarking across the bottom provides an indication of the strength of the organization in achieving competence in the area of the metric. Although the aim is to give the customer exactly what they want, a good project team will adjust the final CTQ selection to match customer needs with corporate ability to deliver.

CONCEPTUAL DESIGN

Once a good set of CTQs has been selected and approved by the business, the team will move on to working in more depth on the solution concept and to determining a working set of CTPs to conclude the design brief. Again this is a critical area in DFSS and will be further expanded in Chapter Seven. This conceptual design stage will frequently take the form of a two-part undertaking, one part of which will be to construct a second QFD diagram to help rationalize appropriate design features, and the other part will be to further refine the concept and to develop suitable critical to process (CTP) characteristics. The concept will then often be refined yet further, when the designers will attempt to remove potential failure and error modes, and the capability of the concept to perform is modelled and measured. Overall this is often a difficult task, with a subtle transitioning of the design from a business concept solution (emphasis on the *concept*) to a solution concept (emphasis on the *solution*) and then to a more substantial design concept (emphasis on the *design*) building on all the work from the customer needs analysis. The conversion of CTQs to CTPs is likewise challenging, as it requires consideration of both the potential design features as well as the CTQs themselves. Good results are achieved by looking at both aspects simultaneously rather than in sequence, which is difficult in practice. Ultimately success is seen in both a workable design concept as well as a set of actionable CTPs. A good CTP is backwards related to the customer and the relevant CTQ, and forwards related to the actual product/service and feature to be provided, so as to ensure a sound constraint of the proposed design.

FROM METRICS TO FEATURES

The first house of quality has provided a set of metrics to measure customer satisfaction and quality, and these subsequently form the second round of 'wants', moving from the top of the first HOQ to the side of the second HOQ, as shown in Figure 5.6. The 'hows' are now the first-level set of potential features to be offered in the new design, and the use of QFD will here clarify which features best deliver to the customer CTQs. This requires a degree of development of the solution concept with a range of several bold new features, and preferably with a number of alternatives from which to choose. For example, in the first stage it might have been seen that customers need *timely delivery*, that is they require the invoice to arrive on or close to a given day of the month. A simple but effective metric to use is a count of the number of days either early or late for the arrival of each invoice, better still if measured against the exact date the customer wants the invoice. There may well be many alternative features in the new offering that could deliver the outcome required, and the use of QFD will help in sorting out which feature to select. Current practice might be for all invoices to be printed on the last day of the month. One new feature might be for each customer to select the day they want, from a choice of four (day 4, day 11, day 18 or day 25). A second alternative feature might be to issue invoices each and every day of the month, as required. Yet another feature might be to allow the customers to write their invoices themselves, when they want. Naturally some potential solutions like this come with a price tag attached, and often cultural, corporate, government or tax issues may hint at the impracticability of many such solutions. Value added tax (VAT) in the UK requires invoices to have an official tax-point date and in many cases the invoice date must be the date of supply. To provide a 'named-date' invoice arrangement might require a corresponding 'named date of supply', which will certainly generate many conflicts of interest, if not real conflict and practical difficulty. Part of the use of QFD is to help deal with this area of conflict resolution and both the relationship matrix and the interaction 'roof' are there to show where one 'how' or 'want' conflicts with another 'how' or 'want'. Referring to the example on invoices, the first-stage work in arriving at a group of CTQs (only

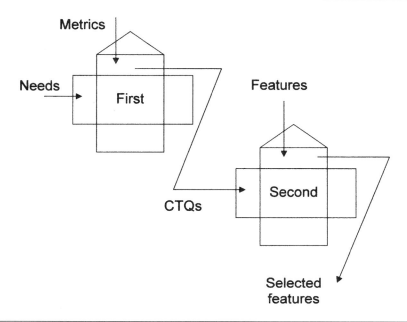

Figure 5.6   Sequential houses of quality

one of which is shown) can now be extended by adding the new design features. The example shows the CTQ with numerical limits set, which in itself may encourage a few new ideas, as presumably part of the reason for conducting this DFSS project is to devise a new design that overcomes existing limitations in this area.

- Issue – invoices do not arrive when I want them to
- Requirement – invoice arrives on the (whatever) day of the month
- Need – timely arrival of invoice (possibly and/or choice of invoice date)
- Metric – days late or early from the (whatever) day of the month
- CTQ – invoice arrives within plus or minus two days from expected.

Feature 1 – invoices printed once a month
Feature 2 – invoices printed each week
Feature 3 – invoices printed daily
Feature 4 – customer prints own invoice.

Clearly from the above it can be seen that feature 3 is better than either feature 1 or feature 2 at (potentially) meeting the CTQ, although quite what feature 4 entails cannot be seen without looking at the rest of the QFD diagram and the whole of the new design concept. Feature 4 may well better satisfy a whole range of customer CTQ requirements and hence customer needs for speed, accuracy, ease of use and so on.

In many situations where speed is a customer requirement it will often directly conflict with, for example, accuracy, reliability and cost. Typically, too, the actual price charged for the product/service is part of the set of customer needs and again in conflict with both time and 'quality'. Businesses generally balance such conflicting needs against each other – first-class post (faster) costs more than second-class post (slower), and if you want to ensure that your item actually arrives (reliability *and* speed), then send it by special delivery! From the customer point of view, value and fair equivalence are the important factors; the customer chooses the level of added value that they are prepared to pay for. Once an appropriate level of value has been selected, the customer is looking for quality in the repeated delivery of product/service to the expected targets and limits without failure, at this level of added value. Helping to sort out such issues as speed, price charged and the need to meet regulatory and statutory requirements can be achieved by ensuring that business and environment are treated as customers with their own CTQs added to the frame. What is required at this stage is the (often) smallest and (certainly) most plausible group of (new) features possible for the new design that best satisfy each and every customer CTQ, and hence each and every customer's each and every need.

It is to be hoped that the team can both generate a wide range of potential features and then reduce this to a chosen few. In simple terms the alternatives range from the (perhaps modified) use of what already exists, use of an approach used elsewhere (often gleaned from benchmarking) or use of a more radical approach (often based on new technology). For the example of printing invoices, using the standard process of print and post but with new features for printing and more reliable posting may well challenge 'best practice' of outsourced 'print-n-post', and ultra-new web-based 'print it yourself'. Of course, it may well be that the current customer-defined target for invoice delivery of two days either side of the expected invoice date is fine today but will soon become outmoded. Any moment now someone somewhere will start sending invoices by e-mail so that they arrive on the exact hour the customer requires. Naturally the objective is to best meet the CTQs *within* the boundaries of a holistic corporate strategy plan, and not to use the most advanced technology possible just for the sake of it!

CRITICAL TO PROCESS

Given any one chosen feature, the question now becomes, what will the newly designed feature have to achieve in order that the product, service or process performs as required? Typically such features can be related to processes and functions within processes, where each function has a requirement of inputs to the process if it is to be capable of performing as expected.

Feature A – invoices printed daily, on date selected by customer
CTP 1 – customer must/can select invoice target date in advance of printing
CTP 2 – invoices printed and posted two days ahead of target date
CTP 3 – posted invoice takes two days to arrive

Feature B – customer own-prints invoices as required
CTP 1 – customer has ready access to the system
CTP 2 – invoice details are available ahead of when customer will want to print
CTP 3 – the customer is reminded to print on time.

In the first example, feature A, it has been decided that for invoices to arrive at the customer when the customer expects, they will be printed daily. This requires (among other things) that the chosen invoice date must be ascertained from the customer and entered into the system, the invoices must be printed and posted in sufficient time, and that time taken in posting must be well understood and repeatable. Feature B has a very different set of CTPs, and it may well be that part of the work involved in selecting alternative features is a precursory review of likely CTPs. Good CTPs will also include high-level system requirements, such as volume of business and costs involved. There is little point in specifying a feature with delivery to just one customer in mind. Often such features will be used in the hundreds and the CTP characteristics will of necessity also imply:

● ability to handle a volume of transactions;
● provision of the necessary roll-out, training and technical support;
● reliability and repeatability in use; and
● business targets for costs and ongoing support.

Figure 5.7 demonstrates the theory behind the importance of identifying effective CTPs. For any given process the output from the process of interest, a Y, will be just one of many CTQs that matter to the customer. For the process this Y is seen as a function of many inputs or Xs as described by the equation:

$$Y = f(x_1, x_2, x_3, \ldots x_n)$$

In order to control the output Y (and thus give the customer what they want and expect), it is much better to control the input Xs, and in design this goes further to also include designing the behaviour of the process, or defining and designing the function f(. . .). At the conceptual stage the aim is to relate the process (and the behaviour of its function) to solution-independent key features, and to constrain the critical Xs and thus ensure the capability of the output.

EVALUATION AND REFINEMENT

Part of the process involved in generating and selecting alternatives for the conceptual design features must include the analysis of risk, evaluation of capability and elimination of failure. The substantial use of already-existing approaches will be safe from the unknown, but carry a risk of failing to excite and radically alter inherent capability. Using radically new approaches involves considerable risk, with a step into the dark, and often an adjustment of something already in use somewhere else is a good compromise. Inevitably and often regrettably, design by incremental improvement is both easier and safer than design through exponential change!

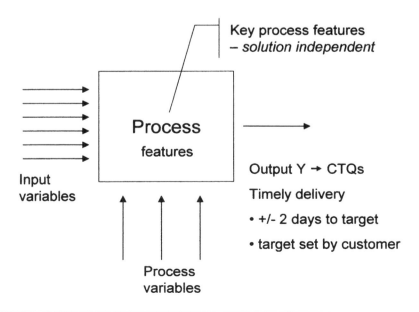

Figure 5.7 Importance of an effective CTP

Capability analysis for the new process will involve some form of simulation and modelling or piloting on paper, with a long hard look to see if the design could actually work in practice. Figure 5.8 shows a simple approach to the evaluation of one potential new design for invoice generation. This process is in fact rather more complex than it might at first seem. With perhaps timeliness as the key customer requirement, the elapsed time for each process stage impinges backwards on a clock counting down to day zero. The average total elapsed time for the process is simply the sum of the average time for each constituent part. What really matters is the variation in the whole – the question being whether the process can work each and every time without failure; excessive variation might take one 'average' instance over the customer limit into failure. It is not possible to add standard deviations together; however, variance, which is the square of the standard deviation, can be summed. Total variance is the sum of all the component variations, and final standard deviation is the square root of this.

As an example, if the process consists of just three parts – print, stuff envelopes and then bag for posting – then Table 5.1 shows the results of simple capability analysis (all figures are in minutes). This is a real benefit of the DFSS approach, as this simple table may show clearly that the new process will not perform as required. The total time might well be far too long, and more importantly the variation may be wholly unacceptable. If the process time is normally distributed (which is rather unlikely in a time-related service situation) then 99.7 per cent of all outcomes will fall within three standard deviations either side of the average, and clearly if this is unacceptable then, as the cliché states, it is back to the drawing board! Taken to the extreme of six standard deviations (or six sigma) then the accounted variation in the process is well over one whole day and may indicate that 'Six Sigma' performance is just not possible. Evaluation is indeed a complex area, and the regular use of statistical modelling and simulation software is only just beginning to make inroads here. Particularly in the design of new services, where resource allocation and queuing theory are critical to ensure time-related requirements are met, the use of appropriate soft models can add tremendous value to the project. Design with numbers, particularly well before hard design has taken place, is of vital importance and it is only for want of effort that so many service processes are implemented without an iota of evaluation to prove how well (or badly) they will perform *before* the launch.

The use of the failure mode effect analysis (FMEA) tool on the conceptual design process can, at this stage, begin to look for areas of potential failure that need to be designed out of the concept. Again this is a large subject in its own right, and will be further covered in Chapter Eight.

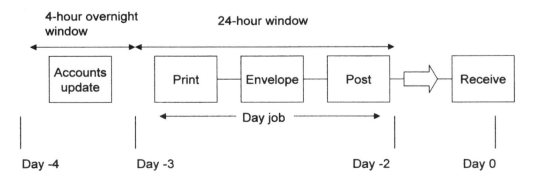

Figure 5.8 Process capability evaluation

Table 5.1 Process capability calculation

Process step	Print	Stuff	Bag	Total
Average time	240	360	100	**700**
Standard deviation	20	40	10	
Variance	400	1600	100	2100
Total standard deviation				**46**
WIthin one standard deviation		68%	654–746	
two		97%	608–792	
three		99.7%	562–838	

The design brief can now be completed and assembled from all the work undertaken to date. There is often little point in viewing just part of the picture; the use of QFD within DFSS is about looking at *all* CTQs together, but for simplicity in the invoice example above, the project team has shown well before any real hard design has been undertaken that:

- invoices matter to both customer and business;
- the customer has a need for the *timely* arrival of invoices;
- a good measure of the ability to meet this need is the number of days early/late;
- the target for customer satisfaction is zero days either side of target;
- a new design is required, which radically alters both speed and timeliness;
- a feature for the new design is 'customer prints own invoices'; and
- this feature requires customer access to the pre-generated invoices and a timely reminder to print.

Quite simply, if each new feature *can* be so designed and if all the process requirements *can* be met, then the CTQs *will* be met, and the customer *will* experience what they deem to be excellent quality. The challenge up to this point is to ensure that plausible yet exciting new features are generated, but within a framework that relates directly to what the customer needs for excellent quality. The tollgate at this point must be a major review by business, project team and technical design team (and the customer), with a formal acceptance and handover before moving on. The challenge going forward is to take the conceptual design and the CTP requirements and produce a working technical design that can be demonstrated as meeting all these design constraints.

DESIGN

A real difficulty with design is that it never really ends! The difference between *conceptual* design and *technical* or practical design depends on the subject matter and the size of the project; the dividing line may be almost invisible in practice. There has to be a point, however, at which the talking and thinking about design stops and real practical designing and development begins. The work prior to technical design encapsulates the strengths of DFSS in seeking a customer focus for a better way forward, together with the metrics that will measure success and the appropriateness of the new design. In moving away from the conceptual to the real design, three things are important:

1 The design as a concept and brief must be formally frozen to prevent scope-creep.
2 The concept, although well defined, must be solution independent.
3 The practical design must continue to be verified against the CTPs and original concept.

Clearly, the more that can be achieved in the conceptualize stage the better, as paper design will always cost less, contain less commitment and be faster than hard design. The defining balance is between over-designing the first stage, thus leaving nothing for the design team to work with, and under-designing the first stage, leaving too much room for manoeuvre or question. There must be finite room to solve the problem, and yet scope-creep is a serious business issue that must be firmly dealt with. If the concept has been well specified and scoped, yet without the taint of implied solutions, then the designer has no need to deal with business and customer issues and can concentrate on the serious activity of problem solving to find and select the ideal practical solution.

As in making a cake, there is always the danger of over- or under-cooking the design. Cakes, like designs, come in many forms, some light and fluffy, and others heavy with lots of fruit and nuts. It is folly therefore to even attempt to write out a sure recipe for designing anything from a moon rocket to a self-service café. Almost all that can sensibly be said is: ensure that you have all the ingredients required, mix appropriately (for the technically minded, avoid curdling the eggs and fat, and keep as much air in the mixture as possible to help it rise) and then cook for the right amount of time. Two serious points can be made. First, designers of products generally get the practical design completed well, but perhaps not to customer- or even business-focused targets, and the application of DFSS in the first stages will certainly improve the design process and also, it is hoped, the design. Second, service processes are often never designed at all and the application of DFSS will certainly facilitate the introduction of much-needed formal design into this area. Any good chef will try out a new recipe first – perhaps there is a need to use DFSS in simple Six Sigma projects, then move on to more complex situations and gradually build an understanding of the theory and practice of excellent design. To top off the analogy, the proof of the pudding is always in the eating!

What goes on at this stage will often mimic some of what has been completed before, and many technical designs may well use QFD at a functional level almost *ad nauseam* in stepping down from high-level concepts to low-level detail. The proactive use of statistical modelling and design of experiment (DOE) can bring both a real insight and a more formal approach to seeking the very best option from the multitude of choices to any one problem. The nitty-gritty of design has much to do with problem solving and a data-driven methodical approach will always be better than random or intuitive guesswork. There is no issue or guideline in pure DFSS as to *how* design is carried out, and reverting to a plan–do–check–act cycle or a similar process based on iterative improvement will certainly work well. The use of benchmarking, again, on a more technical basis will often lead to fresh insights for proactive solutions, prototyping and simulation can be used to evaluate and refine, and FMEA at all levels will further aid the elimination of sources of error and failure.

For a number of reasons the design activity in service processes often has to play a slightly different role to that in manufacturing. Typically services and the processes that drive them are fuzzier and less stable compared to neat and tidy manufacturing processes, and are also fundamentally different in that the customer directly experiences the service/process and often supplies the inputs to the process. Figure 5.9 shows some of the peculiar factors that need to be considered in service design, where the process is optimized for ease of use, the outputs optimized for maximum benefit, and the inputs optimized for minimal inconvenience. Here, too, the process interaction with the customer is very important, and points of contact, often called moments of truth (MOT), need to be designed for number, extent and functionality of customer intercourse. This is not to say that product manufacture can safely ignore service design. The world's best-designed washing machines, coffee makers, computers and mobile phones are only 'products' until the customer interacts with them, and then they often become facilitators of service process.

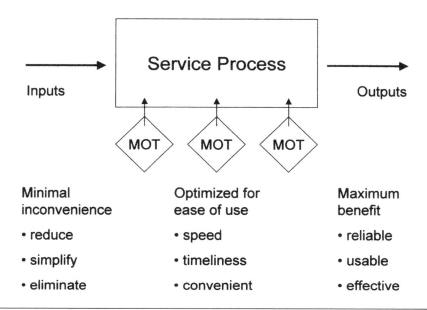

Figure 5.9 Typical service design issues

Whether the design is purely product, solely service, or a mixture of the two, the typical list of elements to be considered in practical terms will include:

- equipment and machinery
- materials and resources
- facilities and environment
- production and delivery
- information and IT
- human resources.

Also, the seven key elements to successful design, covered in Chapter Two, should be ingrained into any design process, although the practical consideration of many of these points will have started well back in the earlier conceptual design! If there is any real change to indigenous design in many companies, then it will be seen in the practice of design to imposed rather than self-generated constraints. The beforehand and perhaps new work in DFSS has, it is hoped, promoted not only a neat business- and customer-focused design concept but also a set of metrics and targets to design against. If the design brief requires invoice printing to take 240 minutes (with a standard deviation of 10 minutes) to complete 7000 invoices of A4 paper at 90 grams single-sided print, stacked in post-code order with no blank sheets, no missed pages, 0.05 per cent registration misalignment, and no running out of toner mid-print, then that is what must be delivered. It is always important to use hard figures to gauge performance; however, the end goal must be to answer a resounding 'yes' to all of the following questions. Does this solution deliver:

- Foundation – solve the need, and only the need asked of it?
- Form – look good, both aesthetically and internally?
- Function – work in use and application, each and every time?

- Formation – lend itself to ease of manufacture or delivery?
- Facilitation – enable low cost and effort in maintenance?
- Flexibility – facilitate future change, upgrade or disposal?
- Favour – engender a positive attitude of acceptance from the 'general public'?

Certain fields of design hint at some of the issues to be met with in pursuit of best practice. Kitchen design in the era of the fitted unit is little more than choice of alternatives in a layout that appeals. In a room two metres wide by three metres long, and given basic units that come in 300, 400, 500, 600, 1000 and 1200 millimetre widths, automatic permutation of all the alternatives by computer is a reality. Rule out the inappropriate alternatives and perhaps just six offerings can be made to the end customer to muse over and select from. Information technology is a much tougher area, as software development is perhaps one of the few fields of almost theoretical design. With computer instruction code there is nothing physical to see and touch; what importance has visible form in something few rarely see? Yet neatness of form in computer programs is in practice clearly an enabler for future maintenance and flexibility, and the generations to come may want to adapt or reuse old code. With nothing to wear out, computer code can remain in use literally for an eternity, so long as something exists to run the code. This fact, above all others, is the greatest difficulty with computer programming: given long enough, every design fault or failing (bug or 'feature') will rise to the surface. Computer programming also frequently demonstrates that in any design project 90 or 95 per cent of the work is often done well and to time, and the last 5 or 10 per cent takes for ever to finish. This has led to a very neat solution – do the first 90 per cent of the work, and then stop. Or, from the business point of view in running the project, set the target for 110 per cent, and then stop the design at 100 per cent completion. This may seem a strange approach, but it does work – this book was originally 11 chapters long.

IMPLEMENTATION

For many of the smaller DFSS projects the implementation stage can be successfully carried out by the business team that has led the project through the earlier stages, including design. For larger projects it may be necessary to enhance the skill set of the team by bringing in specialists such as designers, engineers and systems developers. Throughout implementation the principal aim is to test the full design for real and then to transition towards full commercial deployment and full-scale production. Full implementation will always lead to a real and viable product or service, and this may well need to pass through one or a series of advanced verification stages or 'pilot studies'. For very large projects, piloting is a must rather than an option, and should be a full simulation, including mock-up plant, offices or retail situations with full test loading and using real people. It is important to continue to use the full range of project management tools from earlier stages and for the team to work in tandem with the business and the customers. The results of implementation will often show weaknesses in the scale-up or launch programme, which will need to be addressed and rectified. Often what works well on the workbench or on paper does not transfer perfectly to factory floor, office or retail environment. Reasons for difficulty will be both inherent in the fundamental design as well as symptomatic of the shift to the larger scale. Inherent problems should be traced back to the earlier work in the DFSS project, as failure at this stage is more an indication of issues with the project approach and execution rather than with what has been designed. Feedback on the performance of the design methodology is very important for future projects and every opportunity should be taken to learn from such discrepancies and improve the design process itself.

In contrast, symptomatic failures in larger-scale pilot studies will often reflect aspects of support and environment that were either not expected, or were deliberately left out of the design scope and clearly come under a different heading. The availability of raw materials that simply cannot be supplied, bottlenecks in shipping in or out, and the inevitable technical issues often plague early implementation programmes. When first opened, the NatWest building in London demonstrated early difficulties during the lunch hour. With such a very large building and so many employees, the time taken to leave the higher floors and then get back to the office was longer than one hour, meaning that the traditional one-hour lunch was impractical. It could be argued that this is an issue with the original building design, or it could be argued that the design was fine but the implementation of a larger-scale office did not succeed. The difficulty was solved not by redesign but by positioning food outlets within the building, removing the need for everyone to attempt to leave and return all at the same time. Good design should take everything into account; however, as has already been noted, this is almost impossible, and excellence in design often comes by limiting scope, which in itself will often naturally exclude the more typically implementation-oriented issues. Often such matters will have to be dealt with 'on the run', and may benefit from a more aggressive and trouble-shooting-type 'can-do' attitude and support.

As well as the transition from prototype to production, the team will have to finalize a full control plan and business handover. The control plan should include all of the work completed during the project as part of a package to facilitate the proper monitoring of key metrics and process performance going forwards. Just as for Six Sigma process improvement, the entire product/service and process must be given to someone who will formally own and look after it. Such ownership will include not only the day-to-day running of the processes to given CTQs, but also a longer-term vision of gradual improvement using a customer-focused Six Sigma approach. Also, the project must be placed back in business ownership, so that the business can then review strategically the progress made and evaluate the next commercial step.

COMMERCIALIZATION

Often this stage can be the first outwardly visible sign of the results of months or years of work, and it is vital that the almost inevitable glitch that occurs with the launch of the new is retained within a sympathetic environment and not the full glare of heightened publicity. Brunel had his fair share of sceptics, including many who were sure that his bridges would fall down. Because he pushed his designs and engineering practice to the limit, the brick arches of the GWR over the river Thames at Windsor were the flattest then known (perhaps the flattest ever built in brick) and many critics eagerly awaited an outcome of total collapse. To build such a bridge required a wooden framework to support the growing spans of the brick arches until fully completed. Brunel ordered that the timber frames remain in place for longer than usual, even after they had been eased free and were actually performing no useful task. Brunel was never fond of either publicity or criticism, and this was probably for his amusement rather than for any practical purpose; eventually the timbers all fell down of their own accord in an autumn storm, and the bridge still stands. In contrast, today maximum publicity is often sought for the fledgling's flight from the nest and any failure is thus far too prominent. If the performing arts well understand the need to rehearse in part, then in full, then in dress rehearsal, and then hold preview nights, why not everyone else? The idea of charging less for the first offering reduces not only customer expectation but also the value of the damage done if and when failure does occur! The performing arts also enjoy the sensible practice of the understudy. Early railway companies frequently took the precaution of having an extra locomotive engine, under steam and waiting in sidings with almost one engine per station, just in case. Failure at opening night is not only a real possibility, it almost seems a certainty, and the first publicly visible engine failure for the Eurostar Channel Tunnel services was the inaugural run from London to Paris. With members of the press invited, any failure was going to be well announced; a spare engine was not standing by but in sidings miles away, and following failure of the locomotive, the necessitated changeover created a long delay. Thespians often cry 'break a leg!' at opening night, but this is definitely not meant in the literal sense!

The successful DFSS project can cap earlier success by ensuring a well-planned and successfully executed product or service roll-out in a phased and supported manner. Commercialization should start with the most stable, easiest and best-understood market segment, and this may well be the largest or the smallest customer. Whatever the chosen launch segment, the commercial acceptance of a new product or service is vital and requires the ability to deliver, in volume and without failure, factors often in addition to the inherent capability of the new design. Good design should have anticipated such requirements; however, the project must extend to dealing successfully with the practical launch to an eager commercial market.

SUMMARY

- DFSS projects are typically selected where several of the following criteria are met:

  - the undertaking covers a large scope, budget or impact;
  - exponential and not incremental change is required;
  - active or major design will be undertaken;
  - the introduction of (substantially) new products, services or processes;
  - new or radical technology is to be used for the first time; and
  - the meeting of customer expectations is vital for success.

- Projects begin with the identification of corporate leadership to ensure sponsorship, championing and ownership. A business case study is required, as well as a project team charter which will include:

  - scope of the project, problem and goal statements;
  - a project plan, team roles and responsibilities; and
  - a foundation product/service concept solution, and a sound business case.

- The creation of a concept solution is vital to begin the project and can be added to through best-practice benchmarking across competitors as well as investigative benchmarking in diverse industries. Focus groups and corporate dreaming sessions also add valuable input. Risk management and scope management are important, and MGP (multi-generation planning) can assist with defining the steps to market leadership and constraining the project scope.
- Customer focus is a critical aspect of the success of early stages of DFSS. The first step is to identify the customer needs around the proposed solution and to develop a number of potential measures that can be applied to the product, service or process. Using quality function deployment (QFD) a first house of quality (HOQ) is developed to identify the most appropriate and minimal set of metrics or critical to quality (CTQ) characteristics that will most adequately gauge the ability of the newly designed product/service to achieve customer satisfaction.
- Conceptual design stage takes the raw solution concept and refines it with a growing set of potential design features. The CTQs from the prior stage are then used in a second HOQ to evaluate

and select from this the best set of plausible design features. At the same time each feature has a number of CTP metrics and conditions defined which, if satisfied, will imply that the feature will meet the required CTQs.

● Each CTP metric is a complete statement of an input X critical to the process, which affects the behaviour and output of the process or product/service and thus the ability to deliver to the CTQs. Such metrics will often be accompanied by more precise numerical targets, limits and performance criteria such as throughput volume and restrictions on failure rates.

● The final design brief that passes from the business and customer focus to a more technical development will often consist of the refined design concept with outlined features and associated CTPs for each feature. It is important to freeze both concept and scope yet without imposing solutions to allow room for creative problem solving. Technical design continues by generating all the necessary practicalities and requirements for:

– equipment
– materials
– facilities
– production
– information
– human resources.

● Good design will proceed by locating and then evolving the ideal solution through benchmarking, capability assessment, simulation and pilot/trial, as well as risk and error elimination. Wherever possible the proactive use of data-driven simulation and modelling as well as the use of FMEA will clearly deliver a better result than intuition or guesswork, and the design must be repeatedly assessed for compliance with the CTPs and CTQs. As well as conforming to such specific customer and business metrics, the design must also deliver well on each of the seven key elements for good design, namely:

– solve exactly and only the need required
– be aesthetically and practically appealing
– deliver the potential to function at all times and without failure
– demonstrate ease of manufacture/delivery
– enable low effort and cost maintenance
– exhibit future-proofing for change, upgrade or disposal
– engender acceptance from the 'general public'.

● Practical design must adapt to the particular requirements of the project and product/service. Products often require extensive practical design and modelling, whereas computer programming is often a task involving the intangible and conceptual, with the design of services being somewhere in between. Closing a design project is often difficult, with the final 10 or 5 per cent of the work taking too long to complete. A simple answer is to 'finish early', perhaps completing some 90 per cent of a larger-stretch target.

● Implementation should move design from early prototype to full-scale production or delivery, often through structured piloting, where design issues and symptomatic problems with the larger-scale and commercial offering need to be addressed. This stage will also begin the formal handover of the project material, control plan and process ownership back to the business.

● Early commercialization must be undertaken in a structured and well-supported manner in a sympathetic environment away from the glare of damaging publicity. In large projects a phased roll-out of all aspects of the product/service supply should be undertaken over time to ensure complete success of the launch of the new without failure.

EXERCISES

Your organization is to invest substantially in an entirely new Internet facility to encourage your customers to open and manage their own purchasing accounts. These accounts will allow customers to buy from you on-line, track shipping and delivery and to make payments against their account without the need for paper invoices, remittance advice or aggressive credit control. Customers may be allowed to run their accounts in debit to an agreed spending and time limit, or may run in credit with a nominal monthly interest payment. The account will also allow the generation of reports of spending patterns as well as indicators of your own performance in shipping orders. The business aim is to eventually halve the amount of time spent on invoice production and credit control.

1 Write a brief business case saying why this project should go ahead. Include a projected usage forecast, as well as suggested cost–benefit predictions.
2 Develop an outline team charter, which includes a 'problem statement', description of the concept solution you envisage, and a project goal statement.
3 Identify the typical skills and cross-functional input you will require on the team to ensure that this project will succeed. Suggest a timetable for the project.
4 Develop an MGP as part of the first stage of the project, and clearly identify the scope and requirements for a first-generation delivery.
5 Undertake simple customer research and develop an outline customer needs tree.

CHAPTER SIX

Advanced customer analysis

Although this book paints a fairly bleak but perhaps nevertheless realistic picture of often poor and insipid design, many highly capable designers frequently do achieve outstanding excellence of delivery in their field. The failure of design is due rather to indifference and incompleteness in the overall execution on the part of the business ownership. Design For Six Sigma can bring very little to the design process itself that is outstandingly new or shockingly unknown, although as in every field of endeavour there is always room for improvement! Chapters Six, Seven and Eight focus rather on the three areas in which the greatest improvement in the effectiveness of commercial design is possible – understanding the customer, creative design with verification against the sigma metric, and design for reliability, and defect and failure-free operation. If DFSS is to bring any real benefit to commercial design, then these are the three broad areas where it is most likely to have both a major impact and a visible influence for the better.

The key driver for success of the outcome from a DFSS approach is to accurately identify, quantify and design to customer needs, wants and expectations. Within Six Sigma improvement there is a key element of customer research and analysis to determine each CTQ for the business; however, this area becomes of significantly greater importance within DFSS. A simplistic view of customer needs, requirements and focused metrics will generally suffice for any Six Sigma improvement project. In moving to the development of new products and services, two areas of difficulty arise – the fact that the design often deals with entirely new entities, and the fact that every single aspect of customer want must be fully considered. This multiplies the effort required as well as compounding the potential return available; however, the business viewpoint often only sees the extra overhead required for the up-front customer research. It has already been said but must be stated clearly again that DFSS is as much to do with hard and costly initial effort to identify the design requirements correctly and fully, as about designing *per se*. Clearly there remains a level of investment in customer needs analysis that will deliver nothing new, and this area often requires almost revolutionary and inspirational breakthrough to reach better understanding. Just saying 'these people are our customers and this is what they want' will simply regenerate the existing mêlée of mismatched needs and poor design.

There is the story of a dog food manufacturer that spent a fortune on the development of a new wonder mix, which dogs did not want to eat. Conversely there is the joke about dog food manufacturers who spend a fortune on customer research, only to find that the average customer is aged five, eats once a day and goes 'woof'. Almost everyone has seen a variation on the diagram showing the child's swing in a tree – what the business suggested, what marketing proposed, what development envisaged, what design delivered, what manufacturing installed, and yet what the customer really wanted was just one old tyre on a single rope.

To give the customer what they really want, and need, from good design requires:

- identification of precisely who the customer is;
- clarification of customer needs and requirements;
- generation of appropriate metrics to gauge delivery; and

- transition of quantified needs and metrics to design and features.

Ultimately a revealing and yet cost-effective insight comes from a fine balance somewhere between ignoring customers completely and overdoing the research. Early deployment of Six Sigma generally should have promoted a better customer focus and improved skills in voice of the customer (VOC) analysis. DFSS will often need to push this further, generally towards actually hearing what the customer is saying and often dealing with the messy conflicts of interest unearthed as a result. If the DFSS team has absolutely no experience in customer needs analysis, then the project will suffer and/or the team (and even the business) could suffer from overload and cultural shock. Even with experience and capability in this field, teams may well find that the business actually does not want to hear or act upon what the customer is saying, and much work and effort may simply add to an existing sense of frustration. All that may happen is for the typical end result of a bad policy decision, usually only discovered at the commercial launch stage, to now become an earlier battleground between business and project team. To know the customer well and to have a quantified understanding of needs and product or service delivery is the result of a journey that often takes much time and effort. The hardest part of the work may well be in convincing the business of the need for, and value of, early and rewarding in-depth customer research.

COLLECTING DATA – VISITING THE *GEMBA*

Many words in the Japanese language like *kaizen* are becoming almost second nature to quality, and *gemba* is one such word, meaning the 'real place'. In Japanese companies with active quality programmes people don't talk in the boardroom about what is happening on the shop floor; they visit the *gemba* to find out for themselves. The UK television programme series *Back to the Floor* revealed in documentary form a week in the life of one managing director of a large organization (one per programme) going back to the 'shop floor'. The difference was often profound: there in the boardroom were seen directors talking about restricting the number of small shopping trolleys to make shoppers use bigger ones and therefore buy more, and there at the sharp end of the business was someone handing out even smaller shopping baskets because the small trolleys had run out. The reality lies at the *gemba*: shoppers don't want to use large trolleys, so they use small baskets and actually buy less. The only people who know what they want (or at least have the closest idea) are the customers, and they are not often to be found in company boardrooms. The M25, the orbital motorway around London, is a classic example of research not at the *gemba*. Almost every road near to London radiates from the centre; before the M25 was built such an orbital route was almost non-existent, yet forecasted traffic figures were substantially based on the then current circumventing routes. When the new road was completed it became easier to travel out to the M25, go round a bit of the circle, and then back into London as required; traffic levels rapidly exceeded initial estimates, and this road is now commonly regarded as Europe's longest traffic jam! Of course the *gemba* for the M25 did not really exist at the time the initial research was undertaken. However, if there is any intent to introduce the radically or even conservatively new, then it is vital that the entire entourage of business, project team and vested interests locate and proactively visit the most appropriate *gemba* possible.

Just as Einstein talked about the space–time continuum, so quality project teams will in years to come talk about the customer *gemba*. If you want to sell burgers to little green men from Mars, then you must visit Mars to understand the Martian customer *gemba*. As gravity is different on Mars, the burgers will turn out differently and also the Martians might not like mayonnaise – there is simply no point in conducting the customer research on Earth. The customer *gemba* is the real here-and-now place where the customers live and work, doing customer things and thinking customer thoughts. The only way true customer-focused data collection and analysis can take place is when it is undertaken from within the customer *gemba*, with both eyes and ears fully open, and this is even more important for the development of entirely new services and products. If there is a need to design a new type of dog food, then the *gemba* will include real dogs and real owners, both of whom are quite capable of expressing an opinion. Existing processes, services and products naturally already co-exist partially within the customer *gemba*, since existing customers buy, consume and provide feedback. Mobile telephones have a real and (partially) understood customer *gemba* in which customers decide to purchase and use the latest models. The very latest idea (at the time of writing) is the disposable mobile phone, use once or twice and then throw away. This is an interesting concept, born out of frustration with existing phones rather than perhaps a real need for such a limited-use device. The danger is that, when introduced into the marketplace, this concept will simply not succeed commercially; the good DFSS project team should work very hard to create a working or simulated customer *gemba* to take the idea to for testing and evaluation. Simply asking people in focus groups about a disposable phone will often elicit the 'that's a good idea' response (simply due to the novelty factor), perhaps even followed by 'Yes, I would use that if it were available.' The hard light of day may well reveal quite the opposite, and there is only one way to tell – artificially create a customer *gemba* within which to test the new concept. For example, find a wide-ranging group of potential customers who already willingly use a phone (mobile or fixed) in a place where they would like to phone but cannot, such as a railway station or airport. Perhaps they have no change for the pay phones or have left their mobiles at home, or the battery is flat. Make a number of standard mobile phones easily available (for free or for a small fee) and see who uses them, and who does not. Then find out as much as possible, such as who these customers are, what has happened to the potential customers who are not consuming, and why they do or don't want/need to use a 'disposable' phone.

People use telephones because of a deep-seated need to communicate and keep in touch, and people use mobile phones because they meet a wider range of needs or perhaps meet one or two needs better. Mobile phones are always there when you want them, they can be used on the move (are not tied down by a piece of wire) and above all they offer freedom and don't require loose change to operate. The battleground for commercial success in the disposable stakes is likely to be fought over just one or two customer needs such as freedom and personality.

CUSTOMER NEEDS ANALYSIS

Only if consumers really need something will they want to use it, and it is the shifting pull from conflicting needs that ultimately drives the shape and form of the ideal end solution to a need. Everyone has a basic need for shelter, and the typical 'house' has evolved to provide exclusion of inappropriate climate and animals, and inclusion of people and possessions. From this perspective the ideal solution is a tin box with a roof and door; however, lower and additional needs often radically alter the practical expression of the conceptual solution. If there is a need to move freely to follow food, then tents and tepees are seen. If there is a need to use the only material available in a sparse landscape, then igloos are seen. If there is a need to conserve space, then the narrow merchant houses typical of Amsterdam are seen.

Move an appropriate solution for a set of needs to a different environment where the needs have changed and the solution rapidly becomes inappropriate. Igloos in Amsterdam don't work, not simply because they are impractical but since they do not better satisfy the full range of customer needs. An igloo is easier to build than a brick house, but most of the year they melt and break the (often only implied) need for consistency and stability, which has its foundation in the need not to have to rebuild the house each day. In the UK the vast majority of houses are built of brick or similar, which often makes picture-hanging a chore, requiring as it does a fixture set into the masonry of the house wall. When the DIY expert steps out to the local store for a masonry drill, the prime need is not for a drill, but rather for a decoration on the wall to satisfy the need for self-expression. No one needs a drill, but rather a hole, and no one needs a hole, but rather a fixture to go in the hole, and no one really needs the fixture, but rather a hook on the wall. And yes, no one really wants the fixture either, just a picture hung. At each level the basic need is subjugated to a best-fix solution, which then often becomes a lower-level symptom of the prime need. The very real danger is that organizations say 'Look, there is a person who needs a disposable mobile phone', when in reality what that person needs is convenient and cost-effective personal communication, and the two are certainly not the same and may not even be well related.

People need to survive at a physiological level, gain shelter and food, express deeper needs of self-expression and so on. No one *needs* a mobile phone; they *use* one to facilitate the meeting of deeper needs. If the basic need satisfied by a mobile phone in use is freedom from physical constraint and worry, then having to keep topping up the phone with credits may be counter to this need. A disposable phone with a limited credit allowance and no easy way if at all to top up credit may indeed have a large potential market from business users, who might have left their phone at home and 'need' an alternative. Such users, however, may not want to be tied to a fixed limit when making expensive business calls and would simply revert to a fixed telephone using a credit card or similar – there is perhaps a greater need not to get cut off in mid-conversation. The solution must ultimately satisfy as *many* and as *basic* needs as possible, and not just simply address either the symptom or more disparate needs. Successful customer needs analysis is an art in itself, and the greatest trap for the unwary is to confuse a design solution or feature with a real need. Get the need wrong and the entire solution becomes hypothetical and inappropriate, as can easily be seen where alternative solutions go more directly to the need requirement rather than tackling symptoms. When picture manufacturers include a self-hanging hook on the frame, suppliers of masonry drills lose business. If disposable mobile phones do not satisfy a greater set of basic needs than a fixed phone when the mobile is missing, then demand will never grow beyond that of a curious novelty.

NEEDS ANALYSIS APPROACH

In theory customer needs analysis is a powerful way to begin mapping from basic 'needs' or 'wants' to 'hows' or 'design features', retaining a strong relationship between the two. However, in practice it can be very difficult to achieve for the above reasons. To be successful, analysis necessitates, first, identifying and segmenting the customer and the customer *gemba*, second, facilitating the voice of the customer to express the real need, and third, analysing, quantifying and drawing sensible conclusions from the work. Often the best approach will be to move forwards jointly on customer/*gemba* identification, segmentation and needs analysis all at the same time, since all three areas are highly interrelated. In designing a radically new hotel and checking-in facility, the business traveller is a distinct segment of all users, has many needs that are different to those of the non-business traveller, and has a unique customer *gemba* in which booking, travel and consumption operate. The most effective customer needs analysis will come from setting up a new and perhaps pseudo *gemba* based on the future Internet-aware business traveller in action. Clearly setting up such a *gemba* will itself require some prior understanding of this segment and its particular behaviour and needs.

As it can be so very difficult to conceptualize needs rather than features or solutions, Table 6.1 provides a suggested list of high-level needs from which to work downwards. The service list encapsulates all the primary needs specifically expected from the typical service process exhibiting a great deal of employee–customer interaction. The service process must demonstrate knowledgeable staff, be accessible as required, be responsive (fast) and easy to use. Finally, safety is the prime need often forgotten until it is missing. For the typical product and supporting process, performance and fitness for use or requirement together with reliability co-exist again with ease of use and safety.

In using such a table, the aim is not to fit any product or service exactly to the list, but rather to provide a basic framework around which the detail can be more easily worked out. A good starting point is to realize the duality of product and service for almost any commercial offering and to consider and define each and every constituent part. As an example, consider the provision of one hotel room, which has clearly an element of both product and service. The product is the room, which has a size, location, facilities and other features. The services associated with this room are procurement (reservations), checking in, checking out and billing, maid service and room service. There are also processes involving the room which perhaps defy the exact label of product or service, such as getting to or leaving the room, using the door key, using the telephone and so on.

From the point of view of a typical (business) traveller, the room product has to meet needs for performance: size, cleanliness, quietness, warmth and light and so on; needs for fitness to requirement: size and comfort of bed, en-suite facilities, TV with satellite or cable, desk with computer points and others. There is also a need for reliability: the room is always there and does not change or become unusable. Additionally the need for 'ease of use' is extensive and covers such things as access, fiddle-free key and door lock, easy-to-use lights and shower controls. Safety is of course always in the background, covering such things as physical security, protection from fire, theft and inappropriate use of the telephone or mini-bar by cleaning staff. From the service point of view the list is similarly long and all-encompassing. Reservations need to be carried out with understanding and knowledge as well as speed and accuracy, and check-in should be a slick and well-performed process. Hotel staff must be accessible, responsive (speedy) and knowledgeable. The process needs to be easy to complete, as well as safe and reliable. If this is not already a long enough list, it should be noted that the room itself does not sit in isolation but rather co-exists with many extra support services and products, ranging from travel, concierge, public areas and the like. Also, service offerings are often less tangible than products and the service list may strike less of a chord than that for the product. Considered examples of typical failures in meeting customer needs will, however, soon show that service needs are just as important as product needs, if not more so.

The example used, that of 'hotel check-in', has many benefits since almost every reader will have direct experience of and can easily relate to the process, but it also has drawbacks. The 'hotel concept' is not new, and a reasonably clear customer *gemba* already exists in which to work. Of course, radical

Table 6.1   Service and product high-level needs

Service	Product
Knowledgeable staff	Performance in use
Accessibility	Fitness to requirement
Responsiveness	Reliability
Ease of use	Ease of use
Safety	Safety

new design for Internet-based concepts can be applied in such situations to sweep away the existing horrors of check-in. Why queue, struggle with luggage, answer the same questions each and every time and wait for a key that may or may not work? Why not book by telephone or on the Internet, guarantee the reservation by credit card, and then use the card number to obtain a key from an auto-dispenser or even unlock the door directly? The aim of a DFSS project is to introduce the 'new' more effectively by better identifying and meeting customer needs. Part of this work must begin with current failures. In beginning with existing performance, the secret is to identify clearly the fundamental need, bypassing solutions such as have just been described. The need from the check-in service is not for 'Internet booking' but rather that the service process is:

- accessible – check-in always available
- responsive – no queue and prompt attention
- knowledgeable – the required room is offered first time
- accurate – right room, right key
- easy to use – low effort (no luggage handling, on direct path to the lifts)
- safe – correct billing.

As well as flushing out all the primitive needs and then working down to more specific needs, the team must prioritize the list against some form of customer-based score. The use of Kano analysis at this stage is a powerful tool to divide each need into essential needs, linear needs, and unexpected needs. The cardinal ingredient here is the voice of the customer, and there is little point in allowing the team simply to brainstorm needs and rank them on their own! A good way to clarify need type is to ask the double question 'How do you feel if feature "X" is available/is not available?' For example, 'How do you feel about having the door locked?' and 'How do you feel about not having the door locked?' will clearly result in the conclusion that 'door locked' is an essential need. The question 'How do you feel about checking in within 1, 2, 5, 10 minutes?' is likely to show that the quicker the better; in other words, this is a linear need. The question 'How do you feel about not having to check in at all?' is perhaps a hint at Internet checking in, and will certainly be more problematic. Unexpected needs or extras are those things the customer does not expect and, if provided, will generate delight and much goodwill. In one respect DFSS is about such needs, moving as it does well into the realm of the bold and new. The danger is this: to ask any question it is often better to work with features rather than needs – both customers and the team will understand the tangible feature of a 'key' better than the conceptual need for 'security'. Customers often cannot define/specify what they need for products and services, even when asked, and may even guess their responses to such questioning.

Solutions and features should be filtered out from the final analysis, since what is ultimately required is something like:

- fast – short time taken (linear, 3.5)
- accurate – correct room allocation (essential, 4)
- easy – not physically diverted (unexpected, 2.5)
- responsive – no waiting (linear, 3.5)
- safe – no errors in billing (essential, 4.5).

The list of solution-free customer-need expectations shown above has been completed by classifying each need into one of the three basic Kano groups – linear or 'one-dimensional', essential or 'must-have' requirements, and unexpected or 'delighter' needs. Further, a numerical customer score has been calculated using an average of several respondents rating the intrinsic importance of each need from 1 to 5, 1 being not very important and 5 being of utmost importance. This shows that 'fast' (speed of the process) is a linear need in that faster than target will engender satisfaction and slower will engender dissatisfaction, and also that the customer rates this as 3.5 out of 5 in overall importance. 'Accuracy' is an essential need that must be fully provided to engender neutrality or else dissatisfaction results, and this is 4 out of 5 in importance to the customer; in other words, accuracy is slightly more important than speed. 'Easy to use process' is unexpected – the customer is not really expecting this, so achieve it and the customer will be delighted. In the majority of cases the customer will score such unexpected needs lower in importance, as shown in this example.

Naturally there may well be far more than just the one need under 'fast', and each score should range between 1 and 5. If the customer rates each need as 5, then that means everything is 'top priority' and of 'equal priority'. Since essential needs should be somewhere at the top end, linear needs perhaps across the range, and unexpected needs may well be rated incorrectly at the lower end, separating the needs into three distinct groups may be a good idea. In general, the objectives for practical customer needs analysis can be met as follows:

- start by identifying the various and distinct products and services;
- list the needs from the high level, going down two or three levels;
- the exact placement order in the tree is not essential – use appropriate affinity to group;
- use Kano analysis to identify different classes of needs – essential, linear, unexpected;
- get the customer involved, or at the very least confirm with the customer; and
- rigorously avoid any implied solutions or design features at this stage.

The last point can be very difficult to achieve, and the realization and acceptance of this necessity for sound customer analysis is often a stumbling block to successful DFSS projects. The traveller does not need a door key – they need security counterpoised against ease of use and 'key' is just one solution. Someone standing guard outside the door is an alternative solution!

CUSTOMER COMPLAINTS

A powerful way to bridge the gap between the existing and the potentially new customer *gemba* is to listen to current complaints, and this is a good tool for flushing out needs that might otherwise be missed. When a customer complains about a product or service, they are in effect protesting about a CTQ failing to deliver to their needs or to deliver as expected. Although frequently a failed CTQ will neither generate a complaint by the customer nor a follow-up action by the company, this can be a very powerful way to identify what customers require. Further, careful research has shown that the customer who complains is actually far more interested in continuing business than those who do not. Often the voiced protestation is a plea to the organization to improve service or product so that life can continue smoothly. Customers generally do not like changing supplier; there is a real need for consistency and conformity as well as a need for the lowest overall expended effort.

The complaint process itself has its own CTQs and each complainant expects the company to action a sequence of steps to redress the issue:

1 Co-identification of the failed CTQ
2 Presentation of sound advice which is accepted and agreed
3 Instantiation of an action to deal with the issue and root cause
4 Success of the action to achieve the agreed aim.

Failure of any one of the above stages is in itself a failed CTQ, which leads to multi-layered and compounded issues! Failure to see the problem from the customer viewpoint, failure to agree or advise, failure to take action or failure in action to achieve as expected and close the issue will all lead to further discontent. Often in such cases disgruntled customers present a tediously long list of issues, each point after the first prefaced by 'and then they . . . ' Aggressively listing all the issues with past experiences in checking into a hotel will typically reveal a wide range of problems due to needs not being met. Hotels that cannot be found easily, check-in staff missing when you need them, having to write out personal details at every single check-in, bookings lost or rooms not ready, being booked into the wrong room or type of room and door key not working are just a few that easily come to mind. Not only can this be a rich source of information and insight, but it also shows the importance of creating a pseudo customer *gemba* to work in. When someone invented the electronic door lock and key, little did they realize that a basic customer need was for consistency! I have seen intelligent and highly capable business travellers struggle to get into their room, simply because the door key was radically different to the last key they used and they did not instinctively know how to use it. Overcoming this difficulty for the introduction of the 'new feature' will certainly require a clear presentation of new ideas so that customers can easily and aggressively 'complain' in advance. Getting past the distrust and hesitancy of the new is a challenge, but how much better if the customer complained honestly long before getting to the stage of commercial production! As much as anything, the lack of a successful and working complaint procedure, perhaps even complaint *environment*, is an indication of the inability of the organization to listen to and hear the customer.

CUSTOMER SEGMENTATION

Chapter Three has already introduced the idea that customers of a product or service often come from many disparate groups. The vast majority of organizations do not have just one customer, but rather a multitude, each with different outlooks and requirements for goods and services. Ideally the entire range of needs, wants and wishes can be subdivided by customer segment for easier understanding and a more cost-effective delivery. Organizations today leading in customer service and world-class delivery are realizing that the ultimate goal is a customer segment of one – each and every customer is treated differently and their exact needs are met. With modern technology this is more often an issue of corporate attitude rather than practicality; however, for the majority of purposes segmentation still does deliver practical purpose and efficiency at a higher level of granularity. Practical segmentation is perhaps more an art than a science, as division into parts will always be a compromise between efficiency gained and potential customization lost. The smaller the grouping, the more likely and better able will the company be to identify, quantify and deliver to exact customer requirements. In contrast, the larger each segment becomes, the fewer groups there will be, each with a slightly different set of requirements. As Six Sigma is, in theory at least, all about reducing and eliminating variation, a good place to start is with the allowed variation of and between customer segments. The starting point is to pool together every single potential customer possible without omitting anyone with a valid or vested interest. This must include those who are not (now or yet) customers. For dog food, the customer is clearly the dog, but also the purchaser. Often, too, there will be a third customer who actually feeds the dog – perhaps the parents buy the food and the child feeds the dog. Here we see three separate needs – dog requires something good to eat, parents require something easy to buy, and child requires something easy to feed to dog. Why not also include cat food customers, or those who don't have a dog simply because of the cost or inconvenience of feeding? In the hospitality trade, large hotels find that they have two basic groups of customer – those who actually use the room and those who interact with the process. Room users subdivide into business and leisure, and then further down vertically or in various forms of cross-subdivision, to smokers and non-smokers, single, double or family, conference, long-stay and so on. Division can be by any variable that forms a logical or practical divide into two or more groups with statistically significant variance of needs. Smokers want a room with an ashtray and non-smokers want a room not previously inhabited by a smoker. Business users don't want to check in but just go straight to their room, while families on vacation want a little more pampering and fuss.

There are no hard-and-fast rules or tools for this work, particularly customer segmentation – just what seems sensible and can be backed up by multivariate studies on categories of customer and key needs. If the segmentation is such that 'in-group' variation of a key factor is very small and 'group-to-group' variation is large, then the segmentation criteria and critical factors have probably been well chosen.

QUALITY FUNCTION DEPLOYMENT

The concepts and tools that go to make up this branch of quality were first developed in Japan during the late 1960s, and have only slowly become more widely adopted. This tool is principally a team-based activity, used perhaps to break down the barriers between various factions within the business and a typical design project. Certainly the primary aim is to take clearly defined customer requirements and transition them to design features, while maintaining a good relationship and understanding between the two. The term quality function deployment (QFD) is a translation from the Japanese and the term house of quality (HOQ) is in common use in America (and the West) because of the house-like shape of the typical variant adopted in that country. There is a school of thought that a better translation is 'quality function evolution', with the word 'evolution' perhaps better describing the purpose and flow of the tool in use.

There is no right or wrong way to use this tool and approach; however, certain factors are commonly regarded as essential. The heart of QFD is customer needs mapping – a matrix that steps from the 'what (is required)' to the 'how (can this be best provided)'. The full HOQ combines the central customer needs matrix with technical and functional benchmarking, as well as a roof of interaction assessment, all of which will be covered in some detail. The main use of QFD has been within volume and consumer manufacturing; however, the tool can be applied with great effect in almost any situation. The benefits come from a potentially reduced development cycle time, perhaps by as much as a half or a third, and a much better development of a design that ties well to customer requirements. The drawbacks to using this tool should not be underestimated, and although it is often portrayed as playing a major role in DFSS, the use of QFD is not to be undertaken lightly. Unless the work in the first part of this chapter has been taken on board with a degree of gusto and enthusiasm, what follows will almost certainly be a paper exercise to bestow approval on a hollow design without any regard to the customer. In use QFD can be seen as an organizing and prioritizing tool requiring much thought and care in execution and any attempt to use it simply as a handle-turning tool to churn out a result must be avoided at all costs.

Putting the tool into actual use is almost as much effort as using it for real. It is not a straightforward tool to use: it requires a team that works effectively and proactively, and it requires an attitude of mind that may be difficult to engender in some organizations. It is not a tool simply to force on any team: time, effort, training and experimentation are all required and anyone thinking of using QFD for the first time in a major DFSS project is certainly heading for a surprise. In Japan the full use of the tool builds one house of quality after another, often ending up with what looks like a small street, and extensions to the tool also add rooms, basements and conservatories almost *ad lib*. What is described here is a simple two-stage approach that is appropriate for beginners, small projects and certainly challenging service or transactional DFSS work.

THE FIRST HOUSE OF QUALITY

The first-stage 'house of quality' will use QFD to determine the critical to quality (CTQ) metrics that will be used to both develop and gauge the performance of the design to come. Figure 6.1 shows a completed example HOQ, which is neither necessarily accurate nor useful, but just an example from which to explain the features and working of the QFD tool.

The 'what do we want', the 'wants' in this case, are the customer needs and are listed on the left. It is useful to group needs using the tree format and, for small diagrams, to perhaps only go down to level two. On the right of these needs are shown the customer score for importance of each need. Typically these go from 1 to 5 or from 1 to 10; however, other ranges can be used and it may well be appropriate to normalize the scores – divide each score by the sum of all the scores. If Kano analysis has clearly shown that essential, linear and unexpected needs have been scored by the customers in a very unbalanced way (for example all essentials at 5 and all unexpected at 1), then split the entire house into three separate diagrams.

The 'how are we going to get this', or 'hows', will be the potential measures that can be used to gauge the performance of the new product/service against customer expectation. This should begin with a long and exhaustive list of all possible measures, from which a selected few can be entered into the diagram. The starting point is the high-level concept solution provided by the business, and the team should look for both new and existing measures focused on both the outputs and the process itself. Good measures are those that can be used within the design stage and are also solution- or

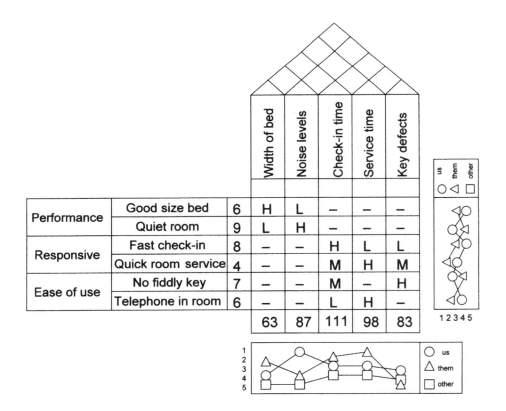

Figure 6.1   First house of quality

implementation-free. The most important criterion of a good measure is whether or not it can be used to determine if the customer is satisfied. Ideally each measurement can be easily taken, used independently of any actual design, and moves according to how well the feature being measured meets customer needs, requirements and approval.

Once the better measures have been selected and entered into the diagram (the order here is not important), the main purpose for using QFD can begin in earnest. The middle part of the diagram is a relationship matrix, and for each interaction between a need and a measure the team must agree the level of interaction on a four-point scale. Interactions are typically scored as high, medium, low or none, and the usual symbols used come from Japanese racing for first, second and third past the post! The criteria for scoring are somewhat subjective, but the objective is to rate the interaction as high only for metric and need, where a very significant shift in performance in delivering to a need, and hence the associated metric, corresponds to a significant shift in customer perception of satisfaction with meeting or failing to meet the need. High scores should go only to metrics where the (significant) majority of (important) customers agree that:

● the measure is an appropriate way to track this particular need; and
● a positive metric score would satisfy or even delight.

Medium and low scores go to a lower proportion and/or less important customers, agreeing that positive measures relate to positive satisfaction. From experience this part of the work is often the easiest to explain, and undoubtedly the hardest to complete. QFD is definitely a tool to use only in teams with a strong sense of teamwork and a good customer focus. This work simply cannot be completed by one person alone, and is almost worthless without good input from or on behalf of the customer. Teams will often aggressively question the point and benefit of QFD and so it is worth expending plenty of training, time, support and even play and experimentation before the work is carried out. The fact that this tool was introduced by the often-inscrutable Japanese should not be overlooked by the vastly different cultures of the West!

When the relationship matrix has been completed, the metric importance scores need to be calculated and entered at the bottom of the grid. Each high, medium or low is converted to an integer on a sliding scale, usually 9 for high, 3 for medium and 1 for low. Alternatives are 9, 5, 1 or similar; however, the over-importance given to 'high' often helps spread out the final results. For each metric, going down the column each high, medium and low is multiplied by the corresponding customer-need score on the left, and then each product is summed to a total. In this way, each metric is allocated a score which represents the ability of that metric to associate positively with many and important customer needs. This calculation is certainly an excellent candidate for the use of a spreadsheet!

The remainder of the work required to complete the first house can be regarded as optional within smaller projects; however, the full house will provide great insight and add much weight to the business case as well as the design and solution concepts later in the project. The right-hand 'room' is a summary of competitive benchmarking, perhaps taking two competitors and 'self', ranked on a simple scale against ability and performance to meet customer need. Such work should have been completed as part of the customer needs analysis, or even earlier as part of the business case for the project, and so completing this part of the diagram is not so much of a chore. The lower room is a technical evaluation or benchmark, again with two or three competitors and 'self' in terms of technical ability to achieve in each metric. This is more of a challenge and should be completed with the work to set metric targets and the determination of metric interactions (on the roof). This work is indeed more complex and will be discussed further in the next section.

Once the diagram is complete to the required level, the objective is to draw appropriate conclusions. The main outcome from the first house of quality is a determination of the most appropriate CTQs. This should be a minimal set of metrics which best gauge customer-perceived quality – experienced satisfaction of product, service or process in delivery. Certainly this list should be as small as possible, since metrics are expensive to put in place, to operate, and to use appropriately. Definitely 'the more the merrier' is *not* what is required! Certainly, too, the list needs to be complete and comprehensive in its ability to relate performance to customer-perceived quality. CTQs are *critical* to the customer, easily *measurable* and *actionable*, normally for improvement in Six Sigma projects but here for better design.

There are many questions that can be asked of the completed diagram. A strong score in the competitive benchmarking indicates an area of current market lead from existing products or services, and this can be a point of strength on which to build. Likewise a low score on the competitive but a high score on the technical benchmarking indicates an area of potential strength not yet exploited in the market. In the relationship matrix an empty row indicates a customer need that is not being addressed and one or more additional metrics may need to be added. Similarly an empty column indicates a metric of little use which can be safely removed. A fairly typical reaction when constructing the metric list is simply to go down the needs and add one metric for each need. This shows up as a strong diagonal line on the grid and often indicates a shallow approach to the work that has not fully investigated all the potential metrics. Clearly the metric that interacts well with several customer needs is much more valuable than the metric that interacts with only one. There is no guarantee that effort alone will reveal a large number of good potential metrics to use; however, a matrix with a good distribution pattern of scores across the whole is much better than a simple diagonal line. In Figure 6.1 it is clear that check-in time is a good metric – if the outcome is on target, then everything that matters to the customer must be performing well. Service time would probably need expanding into room service for cleaning, meals and so on. Notice that the performance block, which perhaps relates to the product of a hotel room, is very distinct from the service elements block. Clearly room noise is important, but may not be adjustable by changing service components once the hotel has been built and in such cases it may well be best to separate the product and service into two distinct QFD diagrams.

Strong negative interactions between metrics indicate the potential to benefit from adjusting the concept and/or removing one metric as a trade-off between the pain and gain involved. If going faster is better and higher quality is also better, but the two interact inappropriately, then a trade-off is required. Such necessary trade-offs are often seen between speed, cost and quality. Strong positive interactions between two metrics likewise indicate the potential to remove one or other metric. If going faster is better and not queuing is also better, and the two interact together (go fast and there is no queue), then only the one 'speed' metric is actually required. This part of the work can be both extremely revealing and a powerful incentive to the business ownership to make radical decisions early on in the design. Often the business wants both high speed and low costs, and where the two conflict the sensible approach is to adjust business expectations and the business concept solution to bring the project back into the realm of the sensible. As well as working on behalf of the customer, the project team is also working for the business, and this is often a challenge. Costs, market selling price and risk analysis should all be kept in mind during this stage of the work and benefit may come from completing the QFD two or three times over: once for the team (to get some practice in using the tool), again for the customer, and a third time to fully integrate and consider business needs. In more complex situations such interactions may be seen to act only one way, in that improved speed affects (either helps or hinders) quality but improved quality does not affect speed. The more able team will therefore need to distinguish between uni-directional and bi-directional interactions.

Naturally, after the conclusion stage the team may see the need to add and remove potential metrics and subsequently to revisit the diagram and re-evaluate their conclusions. In summary, here is a list of the stages to complete the first QFD diagram, although the precise order is not necessarily that important:

1 Gather customer needs
2 Prioritize and order needs
3 Gather potential metrics
4 Complete relationship matrix
5 Undertake competitive benchmarking
6 Complete technical benchmarking
7 Set metric targets and identify interactions
8 Evaluate and draw conclusions.

A degree of complexity arises from the need not to mix different data types within one single QFD diagram and to use the most appropriate phrases and terminology. Keeping to a defined class of customer needs and metrics or functions can often be very difficult, as formal definitions of what is a need, metric or function can be very dry and there is the ever-present temptation to drift back to solutions. The primary need of a hotel room may well be sleep, and a measure of this is number of hours of undisturbed sleep obtained (target of 7.5, with limits to suit). An alternative measure comes from the answer to the question 'How well did you sleep last night?' The function here (what a product does or what the service performs) is 'facilitate sleep' – facilitate is probably a better word than 'provide', which might better apply to a sleep-inducing drug! To get a good night's sleep might require a comfortable surface, covering and correct temperature, and exclusion of light and noise. The feature to provide covering is typically bedclothes such as duvet or sheets, which are themselves terms of solutions and should not be used. The practical requirement of the bed covering will be weight, extent, material composition and thermal properties and so on. The better QFD diagrams work well when the team talk about the function of 'sleep-promoting covering' with metrics to measure how well the 'sleep-area covering material' covers, stays on the sleep area, retains heat and has a low tendency to promote allergic reaction. Such a way of working does not come overnight and may well require much practice!

SETTING TARGETS AND LIMITS

The work involved in setting numerical targets and limits for each metric is complex and worth serious discussion in its own right. Each metric will have potentially both a target and two or perhaps just one limit, and the challenge is to set numerical expectations that can be used both as a goal to aspire to as well as a yardstick to measure against. Figure 6.2 demonstrates the complex principles involved in the example of time taken at a hotel check-in desk. First consider the ideal situation where check-in time taken is the only issue for quality, and just for the one 'typical' customer. Clearly if the check-in process takes far too long this customer will be dissatisfied, and conversely there is a point at which the time taken matches exactly what was expected and satisfaction is at 100 per cent. Between these two points the satisfaction experienced will shift from zero to maximum as the time taken decreases. Somewhere there has to be an acceptable upper limit, which divides the grey into two distinct areas of acceptable and unacceptable delivery. On the diagram a limit has been drawn at

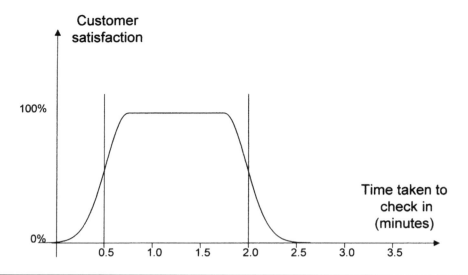

Figure 6.2   Basic customer satisfaction model

two minutes, which indicates a customer experience resulting in about 50 per cent satisfaction. The question is, what is an acceptable limit? For very many cases involving elapsed time in service processes there is often also an invisible lower cut-off to satisfaction, as many customers would be highly suspicious of or even affronted by a check-in process that took less than 20 seconds. In reality there exists a short plateau of 100 per cent satisfaction, centred on the customer's expectation, which is generally based on past experiences and may well shift from moment to moment. Customers do not go around with stopwatches, and dissatisfaction will often at first grow slowly once the time has perceptibly slipped beyond the expected and anticipated ideal. The target for this CTQ should therefore be set to this unspoken ideal, and if every delivery is achieved on target then every customer will be satisfied. Knowing that variation is part of both life and process, the Six Sigma approach is to set absolute limits for this key process metric at the two points where customer satisfaction suffers significantly. Whether the company sets limits when satisfaction has just begun to slip, or waits until it has begun to fade rapidly, depends on attitude and situation. What does it matter if a business traveller is unhappy with check-in? Naturally the customer who is happy to begin with, and who experiences no other issues, may well accept a two-minute check-in and recover with a smile. On the other hand, the disgruntled business traveller who has just been delayed at the airport, the taxi rank, and has gone round the block twice looking for the hotel might well and justifiably explode at any such affront. Or, quite simply, the next customer might be from an agency looking for a fast check-in since they want to site the next 200-delegate conference at the hotel with the snappiest service. Industry has in the past accepted the 50 per cent cut-off point for the limits; however, 80 or even 90 per cent is a much more reassuring figure for the service industry.

Of course the often-unanswered question is whether or not a plateau of 100 per cent satisfaction actually exists. If it does, then the limits can be safely positioned at the extremities of this plateau. If, as Taguchi holds, satisfaction is determined by a loss function, then the use of limits is rather impractical. Figure 6.3 demonstrates the difference between the two schools of thought. The basic Six Sigma approach is to set the target mid-plateau at 1.25 minutes, and to place decisive upper and

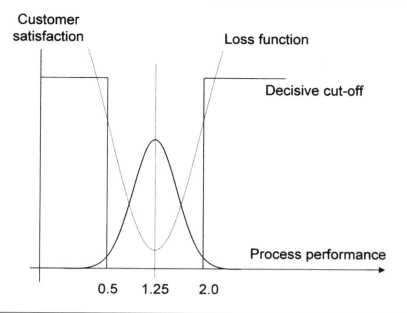

Figure 6.3   Advanced customer satisfaction model

lower customer limits at (for example) 0.5 minutes and 2.0 minutes. This says that, if check-in time has an average at 1.25 minutes, and a variation such that the vast majority (999 996 out of one million) of the instances of check-in occur between 0.5 and 2 minutes, every single customer will be sufficiently satisfied to rate us as a world-class quality company. The Taguchi loss function drawn on the same diagram shows that dissatisfaction changes as something close to a quadratic curve and the outcomes are almost identical, although the amount of check-in time distribution that falls outside the two variant cut-offs will be different according to the method used. Manufacturers may well deal with just one customer for a particular CTQ; if the company supplies a unique product to one customer, then both sides may be able to agree one set of targets and limits and this may then mean that the simple pass/fail approach is quite acceptable. For service processes there are very many customers and each comes to the service offering with typically differing expectations, even allowing for appropriate segmentation. Figure 6.4 goes some way to expressing the difficulty experienced and shows the satisfaction distribution from a large unique segment of customers, when the entire group experiences together a number of different outcomes.

Clearly Taguchi is more correct, as customers do not pass from happy contentment at 1 minute 59 seconds to apoplectic rage at 2 minutes and 1 second. However, to be serious, Six Sigma quality is all about real people (it is hoped, indeed, every single employee) in real companies continually improving and designing processes to make customers happy and satisfied. Setting limits, a difficult enough chore, should be easy and not require an understanding of quadratic approximations for a first-derivative Taylor-series expansion (and if you don't know, don't ask). The real work of setting the *target* is to find out what the (average, typical or important) customer wants and aim for that. The hard work of setting *limits* is to find a decisive cut-off point that works for customer, business and project team. If the customer need is essential, then tough limits will have to be set. If the need is linear, then consider the competitive market and aim for a stretch above and beyond the current

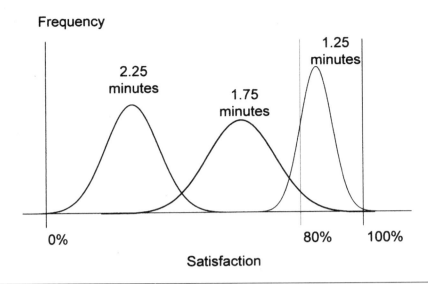

Figure 6.4   Customer satisfaction spread at various outcomes

competition. Of course design for the new is about radically pushing back the boundaries of the inherent capability to deliver. If speed of check-in is indeed important to the customer, and if today people expect about 1.5 minutes and over 3 minutes is a decisive black mark to the hotel, then the team should ideally consider a new process that can provide check-in in 30 seconds. The limit should not be set on the borderline of satisfied/not satisfied; it should be so far away as to rewrite the rules, and quite what the company does with this new capability is then up to the business! During World War I on the battlefields of Flanders and the Somme, hand-to-hand combat across acres of mud often shifted the front line by no more than feet or even inches a month. When the experimental armoured tank was first introduced to practical warfare, it punched a hole in the enemy lines and advanced by a dozen miles or more – almost all of which was utterly lost the very same day since no one in command expected such an outcome. As Groucho Marx said in *A Night in Casablanca* – 'If a guest orders a three-minute egg, we'll give it to him in two minutes.' Take the competition by surprise!

To finish off the HOQ, the targets need to go at the bottom of the diagram – limits are generally more useful later when refining and evaluating the design. The target goals at the top indicate if up or down is good (usually where there is only one limit) or if on target is required. The roof is a consideration of any interaction between the metrics, scoring between ++ for a strong positive correlation, to XX (which looks better than −−) for a strong negative correlation. Unless the team becomes really interested and involved in the use of QFD, the roof is not always completed.

SUBSEQUENT HOUSES OF QUALITY

The first house has, it is hoped, generated a very good understanding of the customer and has promoted the most appropriate selection of CTQ metrics, which will position the team well on the way to fully identified critical, actionable and measurable characteristics with associated numerical targets and limits. The second house will now use these metrics on the left-hand side as the 'wants' and position a number of alternative design features in the 'hows'. Here the aim is to select the best (minimal) set of features for the new design concept that best provide the inherent ability to deliver to the CTQs, and Figure 6.5 shows a simplified example. In Figure 6.1, the first house of quality, the

		Number of hotel staff	Separate staff lift	Key card (electronic)	Weekend special rate	'Ultra-plush' room service
Speed of check-in	9	H	L	L	L	–
Speed of room service	8	L	H	L	–	M
Count of key defects	7	–	–	H	–	L
Bed age (nights used)	5	–	–	–	L	–
Length of average stay	5	L	–	L	H	M
Eat-in to nights'-stay ratio	4	L	–	–	M	M
		98	81	85	71	68

Figure 6.5   Second house of quality

three main metrics for the service offering were seen as check-in time, service time and a count of room-key defects. Although Figure 6.5 is only an example, it is often seen that such metrics will be fine-tuned and perhaps also added to in the transition to the second HOQ. The age of the bed has been inserted, as have the length of stay and a ratio of the number of nights to the number of times the guest ate in the hotel; these are perhaps metrics with a strong business rather than customer focus. With a range of service features to choose from, the outcome shows that the more product-oriented metric of bed age is not really related to service features and should belong in the product HOQ. Also note that 'number of staff' scores top and 'ultra-plush', the new luxury offering, scores bottom. This is, at least numerically, due to the fact that for 'ultra-plush' the strong correlations are with the business metrics, which are naturally rated low by the customer. QFD is certainly not a tool to use to simply ratify a good idea, since the outcome may surprise or even offend and an inappropriate focus in the first HOQ will simply compound the problem further in the second HOQ!

The enthusiast can then progress with yet more houses, each one taking a refined set of features for the 'wants' and progressing down to functions and sub-functions. This is where the name QFD comes from – a gradual and logical process by which functions are evolved (deployed) to deliver the level of customer quality required:

● customer needs
● CTQ metrics
● functional requirements
● design requirements
● CTPs.

The objective in using a series of houses one after the other is to assist with the gradual shift in emphasis from the solution concept to firm design features. At the beginning of this process the focus will be on the product and/or service offering to the customer, centred on the critical characteristics of the offering that matter to customer-perceived quality. At the very end of the design process the focus should have successfully and fully transitioned to design features, functions and the actual process by which the product and service will be generated and proffered. The common thread in all of this work is to retain throughout the customer and business requirements for delivered and experienced quality, value cost and profit, and to arrive ultimately at a set of critical to process constraints, which will ensure successful design. In the hotel example, the product is a 'room' and the service is the 'check-in', both of which may have many customer CTQs. Considering just the check-in service and speed as the CTQ, clearly an appropriate metric is time taken to check in. Potential high-level features might be 'standard check-in', 'business check-in' and 'slip-stream check-in', the new electronic offering. If the 'want' is a 1.25-minute check-in time, then each alternative can be evaluated against this and all the other myriad of CTQs to identify the best potential set of design features. Going further still will enable the features to be expanded to functions, then sub-functions and so on. The preferred choice might be the existing manual check-in process, and a typical associated CTP might be that at least two members of staff are constantly available day and night. Naturally there will be other CTPs such as the availability of room and hotel data, speed of system update and printing and so on. The entire basket of CTPs will often be a complex mix of design features and sketched processes together with specific requirements that must all be satisfied if the process is to deliver world-class quality in performance.

As a brief example of the entire end-to-end work required, consider a telephone call centre providing a specific help-line service. The customer need is for speed (both in answering and the overall duration of the call), polite and well-informed staff, together with easy access, such as a memorable telephone number and a short but effective voice-activated menu system. The requirement of the 'product' – the help – is for appropriate and beneficial information, which will be a correct answer, and more specifically perhaps, the same answer each time. This last point is becoming more and more critical as the typical level and importance of information provided by such call centres increases. A specific CTQ is that, for 100 per cent of calls with the same question, the caller will get exactly the same (and correct) answer each time. One of the team's design concepts to solve this may well be a database of questions that are matched to each call and from the match the correct answer is provided. Very similar in many ways to modern telephone directory enquiries, although there the match is for a number to a name. What might evolve from such a concept will be something along the lines of a process for matching the calls where the unmatched calls are dealt with by a special routine, which then adds the newly generated question and answer to the database. This will then typically promote a requirement of the process (the CTP) that something like 99.5 per cent of all incoming calls are matched to the database in 20 seconds, with a second requirement for manually answering the remainder in three minutes and updating the system database within a further five minutes. To satisfy the customer needs, the designer now has both the conceptual solution as well as a few well-chosen constraints that both shape the direction of the final design and permit effective evaluation of capability and performance.

The work required to identify, clarify and quantify customer needs is an *absolute imperative* for the successful introduction of new services and consumer products, particularly where there is a very substantial level of contact with the end customer. For simple items governed mostly by business-to-business product specifications, such as the infamous 'widget' where there may be very little customer contact and few services offered, the imperative is clearly more that of obtaining the defining metrics for the design of the production and delivery *process*. The weakness seen is far too much concentration on the product alone without considering the new process required. Such work, however, always benefits from due consideration of the explicit needs of both internal customers and the process itself.

SUMMARY

- Advanced customer research in DFSS necessitates:
  - identifying all the customers;
  - clarifying customer needs and requirements;
  - generating metrics to measure delivery to need; and
  - transitioning needs and metrics to design features.

- The customer *gemba* is the real place of the customer, where the customer lives, works and experiences products and services. True customer needs analysis can only take place at the customer *gemba* and for new products and services it may be necessary to create a pseudo *gemba* environment containing both customers and the (artificial) new product/service.

- Customers buy products and services because of the added value and experienced quality in delivery. The added value comes from the meeting of needs that stem from fundamental requirements for existence and self-expression, propagated downwards towards more symptomatic realizations of such needs. The greatest value is transferred when best meeting the maximal set of the most fundamental needs.

- Needs analysis is often complex, and may best begin at a high level working downwards. One practical high-level set of needs for products is:
  - performance;
  - fitness to requirement;
  - reliability;
  - ease of use; and
  - safety.

  For services it is:
  - knowledge of staff;
  - accessibility;
  - responsiveness;
  - ease of use; and
  - safety.

- Customer needs can be subdivided using Kano analysis into three classes, each with often quite distinct requirements for delivery and performance. Essential needs must always be fully met for maximum satisfaction; linear needs provide increasing or decreasing satisfaction from increasing or decreasing performance; unexpected needs excite and delight when met but do not cause dissatisfaction when not met.

- Customer complaints are often a good source of information on essential or expected needs that are not being fully satisfied, although the complaint process is complex and largely under- or incorrectly utilized by both customer and company.

- Customer segmentation is used to divide the whole customer base into significant component parts, each with a common theme of needs and requirements. Although the ideal level of segmentation is achieved with a division of 'one', so as to provide the maximum potential to fully satisfy each and every customer, appropriate segmentation often simplifies study, design and process operation without severely affecting delivery of customer quality.

- Quality function deployment (or evolution) is a tool for supporting the work involved in clarifying and selecting the most appropriate 'hows' for a group of 'needs'. Also known as a house of quality, the use of this team-based tool often requires extended effort, an attitude of meticulous precision and the avoidance of solutions to customer needs.

- The first house of quality diagram is typically used to transition from customer needs to critical to quality metrics, which are used both to measure performance and to design against. The execution of the tool includes a number of distinct stages:

  - identifying customer needs;
  - prioritizing and ordering;
  - gathering potential metrics;
  - realizing the relationship matrix;
  - completing competitive benchmarking;
  - undertaking technical benchmarking;
  - identifying metric targets and interactions; and
  - evaluating and drawing conclusions.

- The setting of numerical targets and limits for critical metrics is often a trade-off between the wishes of the customer, business and team. The use of decisive limits is typical to Six Sigma, whereas Taguchi exponents will use a loss function to evaluate the impact from reduced satisfaction as performance moves away from the target. However the targets are set, it is important to adopt an approach that can be used with ease and yet ensures an aggressive stretch that pushes back the boundaries of the achievable, both to excite the customer and to present an extended capability of performance to the business.

- A second house of quality will use customer quality metrics in the 'wants' and conceptual features of the new design in the 'hows' to identify and select the most appropriate set of features for further development. Subsequent houses can then gradually transition such features through to detailed functions and process requirements while retaining a strong relationship to guarantee both appropriate process performance and the associated customer's experience of quality.

EXERCISES

QFD is a major part of the DFSS approach and certainly a challenge to the novice. The following work will require considerable time and effort and cannot be undertaken lightly! This book is not intended to detail this tool to exhaustion, and students will find it appropriate to review other texts and sources of information. QFD is such a major topic in its own right that at least two major symposia are held internationally each year.

Go to a large airport, railway, bus station or shipping terminal, and observe people using 'suitcases'. Relate your own experience and that of family and friends in using a suitcase or similar object for holidays, business trips, moving house, going to college and so on.

1 Note the different types of suitcase in use, and the classes or segments of customer using them. Note the uses to which suitcases are put, and observe the many processes through which they pass – selecting and buying, packing, moving, handling, identifying and so on.
2 Clearly identify the 'product' and the product features involved in the typical suitcase.
3 Identify the many processes and 'services' associated with the use of a suitcase.
4 Identify all the customers of the suitcase and suitcase-related processes.

5 Roughly segment the different suitcase types and also segment the customer base.

What are the *customer needs* associated with a suitcase? Brainstorm and numerically rank your own list. Construct a customer needs tree to a depth of three levels, for a *generic* suitcase.

1 Identify potential metrics to use in measuring the effectiveness of a suitcase to meet the customers' needs.
2 Reduce this to a workable set of about five or six, and attempt to quantify numerical limits.

Select one customer segment, and either four suitcase-type segments (such as large-hard, trolley-hard, soft-bag, soft-backpack) or four distinct manufacturers of one similar type of case.

Build a first house of quality QFD diagram, placing the customer needs for just two levels on the left side, and your selected set of potential metrics across the top. Complete the central matrix and undertake both technical and competitive benchmarking for the suitcase-type segments identified.

From this draw conclusions and prepare a report highlighting:

1 The competitive advantages of the 'better' suitcase type.
2 The technical difficulties associated with this suitcase type over the others.
3 A selected subset of the critical metrics, which could become suitable CTQs.

More advanced students should additionally undertake the following.

Supplement the customer-needs brainstorming with a focus group conducted to identify issues and needs. Construct a customer survey about suitcases and question about 50 people within a distinct segment to identify or confirm:

1 What the primary customer needs are.
2 Which suitcase features delight and which annoy.
3 A ranking of the importance of all customer needs.
4 A basic weakness with either the suitcase product or one of the associated service processes.

Brainstorm a new feature of the suitcase product that might overcome this weakness and add it to your house of quality. Update the HOQ and critique how well your idea works in potentially improving the product or service. Complete the interaction roof for all the metrics and discuss your findings.

Identify precise numerical limits for the CTQs identified earlier, setting both targets as well as upper and lower limits. This may require yet another customer focus group and/or survey.

Fully critique your work, and summarize the benefits and costs of the entire approach undertaken. Come to a firm conclusion in your own mind as to whether the effort is worth the potential commercial gain. If not, how would you modify the entire QFD approach to be more cost-effective and yet still be of value to a DFSS project?

CHAPTER SEVEN

Practical conceptual design

After the exacting customer and process requirements for the new design have been made evident, it becomes very important that the design concept be developed creatively and yet with staged and careful evaluation. The two fundamental aspects for success in the conceptual design stage of DFSS are:

- free creativity in the generation of a range of alternatives with novel, new and inspirational features;
- the ability actively to measure, evaluate and select the most appropriate set of alternatives.

At the very core of any excellent design activity is pure creativity and inspiration, leading to something 'new' as an alternative to what already exists. Although this stage in DFSS has a great deal of commonality with any formal design approach, there are still aspects which need due consideration, particularly if formal design methods are not to be allowed to subjugate the inventive spirit. The requirement during the latter stages of the customer analysis and the early stages of development of a conceptual design is for the generation of a wide range of alternatives from a highly creative but measurable foundation. This is almost an oxymoron, bringing the two words 'creative' and 'measured' together. Children of kindergarten age are actively encouraged in creative play, where the two words 'creative' and 'play' adjoin quite at ease with each other. However, with advancing years the encouragement is often to replace all too rapidly 'play' with 'thought', and perhaps also 'creative' with 'constructive', and more often than not associate also 'dull' and 'uninspired'.

As in many other areas, the commercial need is for a fine balance between many conflicting demands and a balance that is not static but rather moves dynamically as the organization grows, changes and continually adjusts. The balance could be between riotous invention and over-rigid measurement, between aggressive complexity in the search for the new and over-rigid simplicity for lean manufacturing, and between free and flowing development and due inspection to defined metrics for customer quality. In totality this is a commercial balance between costs involved and benefits gained. In typical process improvement projects, cost–benefit analysis is difficult but nevertheless achievable. For DFSS the scales used to judge benefit against cost must be exceedingly large in order to accommodate all the aspects of creativity, complexity and measured evaluation.

CREATIVITY AND INVENTION

Many commentators express the opinion that each individual has the same inherent capacity for inventiveness and creativity. Although it is clear that the vast majority of employees in an organization do not use their ability for creativity to the full, simple training and changed environmental issues do not typically unleash creative genius in every single person. The plain fact is that creativity and inventiveness are activities of the mind, not of the body, and require mental rather than physical energy and prowess. If the managing director of a large organization were to walk around the company, observation would most often show the vast majority (if not the totality) of staff actively doing something of a practical nature, with very few just sitting and thinking and being creative. This situation is clearly not conducive to higher thought and certainly does not provide an environment for the proactive development of creative ability. In observation pure creative capability certainly does vary a great deal from individual to individual and is not a simple function of basic intelligence. Sadly, intelligence is often measured, most inappropriately, with the singular IQ (Intelligence Quotient) figure that is now long overdue for upgrading. An individual's mental ability is far better divided into several and often highly distinct principle areas, such as:

- logical thought;
- verbal reasoning;
- spatial conceptualization;
- artistic expression;
- social intercourse; and
- self-knowledge and realization.

Although none of the above actually touches on any physical aspects or athletic prowess, even excellence in physical skills requires agility of mind. World-class athletes often comment that success is as much mental attitude as it is physical aptitude. Indeed, it could be argued that almost everything a person is capable of stems ultimately from the abilities and involvement of the mind.

The ability of the human mind is quite extraordinary in terms of memory retention, processing ability, and range of thought from logical, verbal, spatial to artistic and social interaction. The ultimate ability must be that of self-expression and development of concepts, which can often be totally abstract and distanced from anything real and physical. There are still tribes deep in jungles in which counting progresses as one, two, three and 'many'. In contrast, our concept of numbers is now well developed and includes the idea of the power of a number. Here, a single number is multiplied by itself a repeated number (the power) of times. The number 2 to the power of 3 is 8 (2 x 2 x 2). The human base of counting is 10 since we have 10 fingers, and 10 can be raised to the power of 100 – that is, multiply 10 by itself 100 times over, which equals 1 followed by one hundred zeros. This number has been specifically named and is referred to as a 'googol'. In a leap of conceptual ability, 10 can be raised to the power of a googol (multiply 10 by itself a googol number of times) and the result is a 'googolplex'. The mind-boggling thing (if the reader can stretch to this concept) is that even a googol is a larger number than the count of every single atom in the visible universe. The mind of man can therefore extend, when required, to dealing with concepts beyond the realms of practical experience – here is a number that simply cannot be physically represented by a pile of counters.

The human mind grows and develops continually from birth to grave. Some individuals are better (more capable and/or more able) than others, but each of us can aspire to greatness. True genius, beyond greatness, is seen rarely and, for example, both Leonardo da Vinci and Sir Isaac Newton were outstanding in both their abilities and achievements. What are the characteristics commonly exhibited by such great individuals that reveal greatness of mind, intellect and, above all, creativity? Perhaps the answer lies in avid curiosity, the testing by experiment, an equal balance of both art and science, and an approach that embodies an understanding of the interconnecting systems. Design is fundamentally a problem-solving activity, but enhanced by the creative mind, particularly where the game plan is to arrive at something new. Typically the practical design process is more evolutionary than revolutionary, yet even here creativity plays a key role in helping to seek out the very best solution rather than retaining existing ideas and approaches. James Dyson has revolutionized the vacuum cleaner market with the introduction of the bag-less device. Dust and dirt are removed from the airflow by a vortex that uses centrifugal forces to throw the rubbish away, rather than using a bag-type filter. In a radical change to the very static development in the domestic cleaner market, almost unchanged for decades, Dyson cleaners have introduced several new ideas into the machine to make it a world-class product. To arrive at such a commercial success requires far more than just the idea: over 5000 prototypes were made and tested, followed by almost two decades of marketing and growth. Interestingly, commercial creativity can work in many ways, including an involvement with the customer – it was the Japanese who first took to the new vortex cleaner during the latter half of the 1980s. This was in stark contrast with the more staid Western countries, where the multinationals were reluctant to invest in the new machine and thus terminate a lucrative market in bag replacement. Just like giants of creativity such as Edison before him, Dyson has expressed many of the fundamental traits of the creative mind at work:

- curiosity and exploration;
- experimentation and testing;
- balanced outlook – science, art and commerce; and
- a viewpoint which includes the holistic system.

Edison is often quoted in this respect as saying: 'genius is one percent inspiration and 99 percent perspiration'. The argument over exactly who invented the electric luminescent lamp, Swan or Edison, can reach huge proportions; however, it is clear that Edison took the stronger lead and developed not only the lamp but also a business to generate and distribute electricity to light such lamps. Here business commerce and creative innovation become proactive partners to achieve more than each one could on its own.

When encouraging the individual to aspire to creative thought, it is worth noting that the human brain operates as two quite distinct halves, the left and the right. As well as dividing the entire body in two, with the left brain controlling the right-hand side and vice versa, the two halves of the human mind exhibit quite distinct 'personalities'. The left brain is typically the dominant half, particularly so as the majority of the population are also right-handed. Logical thought and physical tasks are undertaken by the left brain, with the right brain doing the more fiddly and creative thinking. To be creative it is necessary to think with the right brain; however, the left brain is by far the ascendant and often excludes the other half from becoming actively involved in tasks and activities. To encourage the right-hand side to come to the fore, the following 'trick' can push the left brain into 'shutting down' for a while to give the other half the chance to think for itself! Taking a simple line drawing, and placing it wrong way up on a table, and then attempting to copy it using the left hand does two things. First, the right-hand brain has to undertake the work, since there is neither a logical nor easily remembered way to achieve this, and also the physical action is being carried out by the left hand, which requires the control of the right brain. Even if the drawing is something that the left brain could copy from memory, being upside down typically makes it all too difficult! Second, the left brain becomes quite bored with the fiddly work involved and, having not a lot else to do, it effectively goes to sleep. After a few minutes the natural ability for creative thought should noticeably improve. There are of course other ways to achieve much the same effect, and it has been noted that the left brain goes into sleep faster than the right, which is why some of the best ideas come just before sleep or while daydreaming! The ability for just one individual to express a creative mind is often of little use to the organization. What is required, particularly for the larger and more important DFSS project, is for everyone involved to be creative in every aspect of the project. Innovation is the planned application of creativity to a problem, and such problems begin with the initial business case and run right through to the final close of the formal project. Creativity itself takes time, needs inspiration to ignite, benefits from acute focus, and can be very easily blocked by the simplest of barriers. To flourish, creativity must exist within an 'ideas culture', and such a culture will always require strong leadership, a formal structure, and visible proactive implementation of the ideas so generated. In this respect, the Six Sigma culture that is a prerequisite for DFSS brings much-needed leadership, a formal structure and methodology and also the rigour needed to see employee-generated improvements through to implementation and control. To extend this concept DFSS must also bring a strategy for growth through the introduction of the 'new'.

CREATIVE ORGANIZATIONS

The barriers to creativity are seen within the general culture of an organization, in an acute lack of time and money for R&D, in poor focus that cannot stay with the real issue, and such attitudes as the 'not invented here' syndrome. It is very important for healthy organic growth that each individual in a corporate team has one new idea a day seen through to successful implementation. Yet it is very much easier for leaders and managers to snuff out the spark of creativity than it is to fan such a spark into life. Progressive organizations make every effort to obtain and realize the ideas and creative drive of every employee as a means to continually improve. How much more important is the creative drive in the development of new products and services! The real challenge is to develop both the individual ability to be creative as well as the corporate culture to recognize, foster and support creativity. There are many tools that can aid creative activity, such as brainstorming, but it often comes down to a question of attitude. One of my past managers commented once that I was always coming up with ideas, most of which were totally impractical. This was not said as a compliment, as it should have been, but almost as a reprimand. The difficulty is that, in direct contrast to most management practice and theory, when generating creative new ideas quantity is far more important than quality. It is much easier to pick out the good idea from one hundred indifferent ones than it is to generate just one brilliant idea on its own. Who is to judge which idea is a good one and which a bad one? The adage 'The person who never made a mistake never made anything' is relevant in this respect. In the commercial world mistakes are often expensive, but rarely is the cost of a few mistakes balanced against the benefit of a few good ideas. If a DFSS project of any size in any organization is to achieve success, it is simply imperative that a large quantity of fresh new ideas be rapidly generated. This is often even more critical within the smaller 'excursion into design' Six Sigma project, where time and the rapid change from improve to design and back again tend to constrain creativity even further. The following list is a guide to some of the practical points required for developing and promoting the creative organization:

● create an 'ideas culture' in the organization – encourage, support and implement;
● provide ongoing training to develop latent creativity in *all* employees;
● identify those naturally gifted with a creative mind and utilize their skills to the full;
● use a range of team-based creativity tools such as brainstorming;
● encourage curiosity and exploration that borders on play and even dreaming;
● allow employees to make mistakes by supporting controlled adventure;
● provide resources, time and money for practical testing and experimentation;
● develop the widest possible outlook – science, art and commerce together;
● view all things as interconnected systems and think outside of the box; and
● provide a suitable environment with the right type and degree of pressure.

An example of the importance of corporate attitude toward creativity is the very old story of the matchbox company. For years the company had manufactured matches and had improved the process to a fine art. One day a stranger wrote to say that he had a suggestion that would save the company a great deal of money; however, he wanted £50 for the idea, which was a considerable amount of money given that the matches only cost a penny a box (240 to the pound in old money). The management thought long and hard, wondering what possible improvement could be made, but in the end they paid and the idea arrived. The box had two sides coated in sand to strike the matches on – the suggestion was to coat only one side. The man got his £50, the company saved that in a matter of months, and the customers had an equally satisfactory product. Had no one thought of this before? Quite probably many people had; however, the management thought that there was nothing left to improve upon.

Archimedes was a great thinker and demonstrated creative thought in various ways. As for many before and after him, the highly creative ideas come when the mind is able, when the environment is right, and when there is the right level of pressure applied. Often this pressure comes from necessity – necessity being the mother of invention. However, pressure can be applied by self as well as externally, and for Archimedes the pressure of the moment was to work out how to tell if what was in the crown was pure gold. Time out for bathing and the result was a brilliant new idea: both 'Eureka!' and Archimedes' principle have entered the history books! The challenge of providing both the right environment and the right pressure is seen more acutely today than ever before. Too much pressure to deliver is just as damaging as too little pressure, and the constant ringing of a telephone cannot be supportive of creative thought! There are a growing number of tools to aid the basic creative approach to inventing new alternatives, including TRIZ, which translates from the Russian as the theory of inventive problem solving (TIPS). The work of Genrich Altshuller, a patent investigator for the Russian Navy, TRIZ covers an umbrella of evolutionary design theory as well as basic innovation principles. In simple terms, there are only so many ways by which something can be changed or improved, and TRIZ includes lists and charts by which inventors can look at analogous problems to find solutions. Of course this is design by evolution from the existing, which is always going to be easier than the introduction of the purely new and revolutionary. The further study and use of such tools will always add benefit to the struggle to develop a corporate creativeness. However, in DFSS the aim must be to tackle with vigour and success the very difficult issue of proving that the new product or service is not only achievable but also of value to the customer.

Although it carries less inherent commercial risk, it is not always of value simply to improve on what has gone before. Birmingham International Airport in the UK is an example of the entrepreneurial spirit, where the transport connection between the airport and the nearby mainline railway station has for many years operated using the MAGLEV system. Developed from the pioneering work of Professor Eric Laithwaite, this was the world's only public transport system to use magnetic levitation and floating trains. Closed in 1995 after some eleven years of operation, it is to be replaced during 2002 by an almost equally bold new cable-drawn shuttle, fully automatic and currently only in commercial operation in one other location.

There is always the considerable risk that bold enterprise such as the MAGLEV will fail, either mechanically or in gaining favour with the public. In contrast it is often only radical and creative advance that can fully open the potential of the situation to truly excite the customer. From a commercial point of view, perhaps the best way forward is to bring proven and reliable technology (cable-drawn trains are by no means new) together with a creative and bold approach to meeting customer needs. The aim must be to use predictably stable technology in creative and new ways to challenge the existing limits to customer requirements, and not to challenge the technology itself – be creative in the *use* of the technology to deliver to the customer!

COMPLEXITY AND SIMPLICITY

It is the high ideal of any Six Sigma initiative proactively to change the processes by which products and services are delivered, with the aim of enhancing the core process that adds value, making the enabling processes and supporting functions more efficient, and eliminating any other waste and non-value-adding steps. The fact is that any expended effort, time, resource or material by either business or customer that does not directly contribute to or facilitate the promotion of increased value is waste. This ideal can be executed in practice through process improvement methodologies and Six Sigma is only one of many approaches. Lean manufacturing has been a driver for success in many organizations, particularly in the Far East, and is a large component of modern incremental and continuous quality initiatives such as *kaizen*. Such approaches look for just in time (JIT) supply chains, the elimination of waste (*muda*), control of supply–consume cycles with signals (*kanban*) and a tidy house (the 5 Ss: clean-up, orderliness, clean and check, standardize and discipline). Simplicity reduces variation and likelihood of failure, and also reduces manufacturing costs as well as transport, stocking and storage and assembly time. In contrast, complexity is often a part of the bold and the new, and very little aggressive growth can be achieved by sustained reduction in product and process complexity alone. An appropriate balance between the two extremes is vital for success in DFSS.

This is a fundamental question – whether to gain market betterment by incremental improvement and simplification, or by the bold advancement of current performance limits through innovation and the often associated complexity that comes with it. Figure 7.1 attempts to divide the two contrasting aspects of modern quality initiatives and to compare the advantages of the complex over the simple.

The horizontal axis shows the performance of a process, measured in terms of a key metric that is

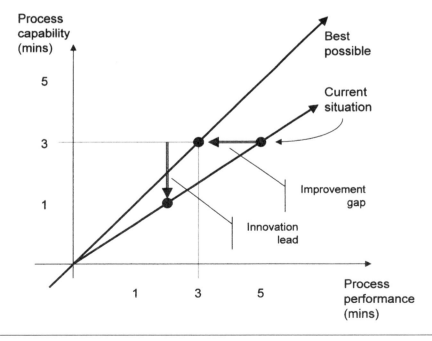

Figure 7.1 Improvement versus innovation

critical to customer-experienced quality. For example, this could be the time taken to check in at a hotel. Current *performance* is a typical five minutes, and this is plotted against the vertical axis, which is a measure of the inherent process *capability*. The very best performance or capability, under ideal conditions, is a limiting three minutes. The line drawn at 45 degrees is naturally the upper limit to perfection, where performance exactly matches capability. To reach this point current performance has to improve by two minutes, by eliminating the causes of waste and variation, and this is shown as a horizontal arrow marking the 'improvement gap'. In contrast, the vertical arrow shows the potential change as a result of innovation and enhanced capability by two minutes, perhaps through the introduction of new technology. If the process capability is (radically) improved to one minute, then the delivered performance could be almost any value, better or worse than before! However, the potential is that performance could be retained as a similar proportion of capability as before, and hence we see that performance has not only improved, it has in fact overtaken the best possible performance of the original process. Were the new process to perform just as the old process did at five minutes, then there would be a much greater potential for incremental improvement, but of course it is to be assumed that actual performance would be better than five minutes! In reality this is not an 'either–or' situation, as both one-off radical change and continuous incremental improvement should work together. Incremental improvement is often less expensive, has smaller payback and can deliver all of the time. Exponential change in contrast is more expensive, has a larger payback and potential, needs to work only in short bursts, and frequently must be associated at some point with incremental improvement to fully realize all of the gains. The benefits arise when both approaches are working in harmony. Often radical change will so alter existing processes that past incremental improvements are swept entirely away. Why squeeze the last penny of waste from a process when something new just around the corner will rewrite the benchmark? The wise answer is to review both performance and capability to form a reasoned judgement as to which approach to use – improve performance, or redesign capability. Improvement can only work successfully where there is room to improve, and as the gap between performance and limiting capability reduces, so do the returns from 'improve' Six Sigma. Electronic telephone exchanges are far more complicated than Strowger exchanges, which are also more complex than a simple manually operated plug board. Naturally the electronic exchanges can do far more than the older systems, but at a price; when first introduced, the Strowger system must have seemed very complicated compared to a plug and key system. However, once this level of complexity had become the baseline against which performance, capability and customer expectation were measured, the pursuit of simplicity was to ring the changes and achieve the simplest Strowger system possible. The question as to whether modern electronic systems are more or less complex than mechanical systems is a moot point. Although far more complex in construction and operation, many new systems have turned a corner and now offer a level of simplicity not seen in the older and mechanical devices. They are commonly smaller, easier to maintain, far less prone to failure and certainly less prone to variation in performance. The real benefit comes when advancement introduces a level of simplicity, even with apparently increased complexity underpinning the change. If mankind wanted to remain with the simplest product, service or process, we would still be living in caves. We accept increased complexity providing it also delivers increased benefit and return. From a commercial point of view, the breakthrough occurs when the increased benefit comes with reduced operating complexity, even though there may well be increased product or service complexity. The challenge in the hotel check-in example is to replace the existing manual arrangement – one person, a list of rooms and a set of keys – with something that is more complex, yet far simpler for the operating process and customer. Removal of the check-in process almost altogether, with an electronic key dispenser, is more complex, yet has the potential to be elegant and simple in operation. Such simplicity promotes reduced variation, error and waste, and also makes the task of later Six Sigma incremental improvement easier in realizing the inherent process capability as true delivered performance.

QUALIFICATION AND VERIFICATION

Typical design projects fail for a number of reasons, one of which is a failure to design satisfactorily before launching into implementation. The first part of this chapter deals with the value of developing creative yet simple solutions, and certainly the entire DFSS approach is one of designing first before implementing anything! Another typical failure is perhaps to design and implement first, and then to measure and evaluate later, if at all. Where evaluation is left to a post-production and commercialization activity, the results of such work clearly cannot be used as part of the design effort itself. It is vital for the success of any DFSS project – measured in terms of customer satisfaction and experienced quality – that new processes commence operation at between four or five sigma (or better). This is a departure from the normal approach in two ways: first in respect of the measurement to customer expectation; and second, since what is being measured is often the process and not simply the product. The normal Six Sigma approach is to improve processes, and thus the product/service delivery, by seeking out the most appropriate metric to gauge customer quality, and then to measure, identify weaknesses, improve and then remeasure and control using this vital metric. The only real difference between DFSS and Six Sigma as a process improvement methodology is that the measurements need to be taken *before* the process is in operation, which is certainly a challenge.

SELECTION OF ALTERNATIVES

Clearly the benefits from the DFSS approach are enormous, particularly if the proposed product, service and the associated process can be measured and thus evaluated while still at the design stage. The whole purpose of design is to achieve the most appropriate solution to the problem at hand, and this requires the ability to decide on a way to judge the best solution, then measure all of the alternatives, select the best, and implement with confidence. The process sigma metric, used as the core principle for the Six Sigma improvement approach, is an excellent candidate for a measurement tool. By converting customer needs, requirements and expectations to measurable targets and then associating these with a concept process, the team can use sound metrics to evaluate the potential of the design solution to achieve as required. For those well versed in setting product specifications and using them in the design stage this will not be such a shock as it will for the designers of services, who often specify nothing at all! The hotel room will certainly be specified and perhaps even measured after construction. In contrast, the check-in service and process will often not be specified and will rarely be measured. Even the manufacturer of new widgets may fail to measure and evaluate the production process, having carefully specified the new widget itself.

A powerful tool for selecting from alternatives is Pugh's selection matrix. By the time the DFSS team begin to work through alternative solutions, the issues of quality and price should have been raised and dealt with in the earlier work. This tool can then be used to make a decision based on pure ability to deliver to the chosen performance metrics. Stuart Pugh presented his work over twenty years ago and, again, this is only now becoming more widely used. Figure 7.2 demonstrates the basic use of the tool, using an example from mobile telephones. Here the customer requirements are listed on the left (in DFSS taken from the CTQs and the CTPs) and a number of alternatives are listed across

Alternative concepts for telephone solution	Coin box	Card phone	Mobile phone	Satellite phone
Criteria				
Speed of connection		-	+	S
Quality of sound		S	-	-
Stability of connection		S	-	-
Equipment needed		S	-	-
Lack of worry		-	+	-
Availability		S	+	-
No need for operator		-	S	-
Physical safety		S	+	S
Financial security		S	-	-
Use abroad		S	+	+
Not locked in		S	-	-
+		0	5	1
-		3	5	8

Figure 7.2 Pugh selection matrix

the top. Typically in detailed design these alternatives would be more elaborate functions; however, this tool works well even with high-level alternatives and concepts. One column is selected as the reference gauge, either the standard today or, more appropriately, the currently best in class, against which the others are scored as either better (+), worse (–) or the same (S). The conclusions are drawn from the balance between the totals for better and worse. In this case it is clear why mobile phones are gaining in popularity compared to using, for example, phone-cards! When the costs involved in implementing the various features are added to the picture the team will be able rapidly to select a design solution that also delivers to given cost targets. A real benefit in DFSS is to use this tool at the high level, with CTQs and customer requirements for products and services, and again at lower and lower levels for CTPs and process requirements. Inappropriate products, services and process features can be rapidly screened for and removed from the design, allowing greater effort to be expended elsewhere.

EVALUATION

The real power of the sigma metric within the DFSS methodology comes to bear on the design process when it is applied to the task of evaluation. If the customer has demonstrated a requirement for hotel check-in in less than three minutes, then clearly if the new process does not deliver, the customer will not experience world-class quality of service. Given two apparently equally good designs, the better one is that which not only has the capability to deliver in less than three minutes, but also is more likely to perform consistently as such on the opening night. Bringing effective evaluation into the design process at the earliest stage possible might be considered a handicap on the designer. In reality it should be seen as a liberator, since if the designer can exactly measure and evaluate how any one design will perform to customer expectation, then design can be bolder, more adventurous and often undertaken faster and without the worry of possible failure. In essence what is required is an 'experiment', conducted before the design is completed and with the aim of determining the behaviour of the new product or process. It is at this point that the practical undertakings of a DFSS project may well diverge, with a manufacturing team heading off towards statistical modelling and experimentation, and the service team left wondering just what to do next. The value of statistics and design of experiment (DOE) is certainly a subjective point and for many the heavy mathematics involved will be very off-putting. Just as the individual capability for creative thought varies from person to person, so does the ability to comprehend and use (advanced) statistics: what is simple to one may well be a complete nightmare to another! Historically statistical methods were first developed for use in agricultural research and rapidly moved into manufacturing industry from the 1930s onwards. Several changes have taken place over the intervening years and the aim today must be to promote the most appropriate degree of *statistical thinking* across each organization, whether manufacturing or service-transactional. The divide between pure statisticians and engineers can be considerable, not helped by the concepts and techniques involved. Today, with personal laptop computers and statistical software tools such as Minitab, almost obligatory for any Six Sigma team, the barriers between engineer and statistician can thankfully be removed. The work of Taguchi in this area has made a considerable impact, and, like Six Sigma, much debate! At a high level the efforts over the past twenty years have begun to focus engineering design towards excellent quality through three characteristics:

- a customer-focused drive for the highest level of product quality;
- the elimination of variation as the primary goal; and
- use of practical statistical methods for engineers and designers.

Design and engineering have never really had a big problem with being able to build a working prototype that meets customer and business requirements. The problem has always been with the variation from part to part once the item is in (mass) production. Whether using a more traditional sharp cut-off to customer requirements, or the Taguchi loss function, the validation stage during technical design has to show how well the product will meet requirements, even when the key metric varies because of changes in other factors. In manufacturing such work can progress down to a very detailed level, identifying the critical factors that affect the outcome or response variable and then determining ways to eliminate or control such variation. A great deal of this work can become part of a sound DFSS project methodology and indeed the axioms of both Six Sigma and the wider umbrella of 'Taguchi methods' make excellent working partners. The key components must be: keep a strong customer focus; identify critical metrics and requirements; work to eliminate variation; use the sigma metric to gauge performance; and make the best use of both statistics and business knowledge. Further discussion about Taguchi methods and the suchlike is outside the scope of this book and the interested reader is encouraged to turn to the growing number of works specifically on statistical and experimental design.

PROCESS MODELLING

What Six Sigma can bring to this work is the ability to better understand processes and to pre-calculate process performance. Indeed, this area may often be the only part that statistical methods can play in many service processes. A study and evaluation of the process performance is vital for the transactional DFSS project and may well provide revealing insight for any manufacturing organization too. The need here is to experiment on the process itself, to measure performance to the sigma metric, to identify, eliminate and control variation, and to do so with sound statistical thinking. The tool used is modelling, and, very similar to designing a new car where the prototype is modelled in clay to see what it will look like, the designed new process must be modelled to see how it will perform. Figure 7.3 shows a conceptual design for a new accident and emergency room at a hospital. Close study of such a process will show that there are basic similarities to many processes from dissimilar industries and with small alterations this could indeed become a hotel check-in process. What is required is the ability to model the new process and then run it as a simulation and pilot, all on paper or in a computer program. This is almost the reverse of Six Sigma projects, where real life is first process mapped and then measured. Here the team start with the metrics, construct a design solution and process, and then trial it to see how it will perform. There is a growing market for software to perform this quite intricate task, with various features and degrees of success. Modelling theory is a large and often complex subject in its own right, but the basic issue is this: a model will only yield answers to questions if it has first been constructed to do so.

Models are representations of something real, typically with reduced complexity, and are used to obtain information about the modelled item without the effort and expense involved in looking at the real thing. Physical models include such things as one-tenth-sized railway trains painted in new colours to see how they look, without actually painting the real thing. Paper models include maps and diagrams, to allow distances in the real world to be measured easily without having to measure for real. Statistical models include mathematical equations that represent the dynamic behaviour of critical variables, to allow experimentation and modification with greater ease. Process models are essentially process maps, with flow patterns and key information about entities that pass through the process and resources that are acquired and released by these entities during their journeys through the process. Very simple models are excellent in use, mainly because the simpler they are, the more

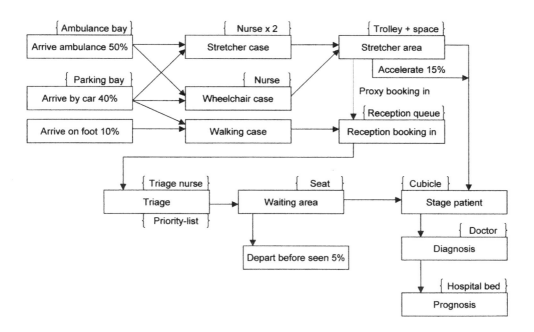

Figure 7.3   Simulation model example

likely they are to be correct. The converse of this is that the simpler model may not be able to answer the questions put to it. A model that says attendance presentation rate at the casualty department is ten each hour, and the doctor takes ten minutes to see each patient, will suggest that two doctors are needed. In practice the sort of questions DFSS needs to ask of such models is, if the customer has a CTQ of 'wait no more than one hour to see the doctor', how well can the process meet this requirement and how often does it fail? The more complex model can begin to simulate the process in a way that provides the potential to answer such questions. With a steady average arrival rate of ten patients each hour or one every six minutes, the interval between each patient arrival is best modelled with a Poisson distribution, where the random chance of none, one, two, three or more patients arriving in each six-minute time slot can be estimated. Adding numbers to the flow patterns, for example 40 per cent arrive by car, and of these 10 per cent need a wheelchair, will enable the likelihood for each potential process path to be further calculated. For time-based problems, each process step needs an accurate assessment of the elapsed time taken. This might be a fixed time for such things as booking in at reception, or more complex patterns such as the time taken by each doctor with each patient, clearly very dependent on the patient and case history. To be a highly realistic model the resources required must also be modelled according to real life – when nurses and doctors go for a meal break, then the processes that they interact with must be affected by the reduced resources. In experience, such modelling becomes very complicated and it is only the very best models that will give the very best answers. The typical single-patient arrival is truly random and follows a Poisson distribution – very rare in occurrence and totally independent of each other. Road traffic accidents, however, break the random pattern, although they are random events in themselves, as several patients will arrive almost at once and often require immediate and acute attention, bypassing the waiting queue. The patient with the dog bite, waiting for a tetanus jab, still has a CTQ of 'see the doctor in one hour', but might now be pushed further down the triage queue by an unexpected heart attack. Real life is a very complex mix of common cause and special cause variation, all of which must be present in the model if accurate measurements are to be taken!

For simple cases, spreadsheets with some form of Monte Carlo simulation are quite adequate. In more complex modelling, particularly for service and process models where the time and resource implications are often paramount, better software is available. The most sophisticated will not only allow for the process to be mapped and set up with parameters, but will then actually move icons such as ambulances, patients and nurses around the map, all the while gathering data for later analysis. By this means the team can clearly see how the process performs and can demonstrate where the problems are and hence make early improvements. The success of such efforts can lead to a determination of a predicted distribution of patient waiting time, or a count of the defects against opportunities, either of which can then be converted into a process-sigma value. The short-term implication is, if the customer wants to wait no more than one hour to see the doctor and only 60 per cent actually do so, then this will be a 1.8 sigma process. This can then lead to changes in the design or process operating parameters (remove a step, add a doctor, reduce the doctor–patient interaction time, or change the shiftwork patterns) that will improve the process. Long-term benefits are that the team can retain the model and keep it updated as part of the ongoing control plan. Modelling does not have to be just processes or products and often a mixture of various types of models may have to be used in any one project, each with its own associated difficulties. Modelling techniques are continually improving, and flow-dynamics theory can now provide real help with the modelling of such challenging situations as fires and the movement of large crowds of people within buildings. The critical steps involved in using process modelling are:

- decide on the process to be modelled, and for what reason;
- obtain accurate data – mapping, flow rates, resources and times;
- simulate appropriately for the process against real-life conditions; and
- measure key metrics and draw conclusions from the model.

It is always a good idea to test the model against real life and for this reason it is often good practice, although expensive, to incorporate more data in the model than are actually needed for the project. If the example model included doctor–patient interactions, then a count of patients seen in real life should relate to the count from the simulated model. It should be borne in mind that such work as this is both very important and valuable to the project, and also can be very demanding and expensive to conduct. The real benefit has to be seen in a clear validation of process performance, well before the final design is committed to anything near commercial launch. Modelling and simulation should begin at the earliest stages in the conceptual design and must continue right through to piloting. The best test for any new product, service or process is to try it out for real! The other point is that DFSS is about balancing the conflicting needs of a multitude of CTQs and often this can only happen when the team tests the process under duress. At the highest level of modelling every possible factor will be considered and the team will counterpoise all the factors and metrics to achieve the best possible solution – something that is in reality extraordinarily difficult and inevitably a compromise. Far better to have a measured and verified compromise than just pure guesswork!

COSTS AND BENEFITS

The majority of Six Sigma improvement projects will deliver benefit from the improved process well in excess of the costs involved in training, running a team and implementing the changes. Design For Six Sigma cost–benefit analysis is altogether more complicated – if such work in Six Sigma is difficult, in DFSS projects it often borders on the impossible. It may seem strange to discuss cost–benefit analysis at such a late stage in the project; however, the Six Sigma approach focuses on the ability to measure not only the customer experience of quality, but also the financial costs associated with poor quality. With a new product or (service) process, it is only at the final verification stages of the design that the team will have available the necessary projected performance measurements to be able to assess the financial impact. Potential financial benefit in the typical DFSS project can be almost unbelievable. For a new product with an entire life-cycle revenue of £10 million over ten years, simply getting the product to market six months early delivers at least £250 000 (or thereabouts) more revenue cash flow than might be expected in the first year. True, this might simply be moved from the back of the product life cycle to the front, but it is still cash in the bank this year! If the overall market share is further increased during the entire life, simply because of being early, then anything up to another 10 per cent or £1 million might be seen over the ten years. Added to this the benefits from earlier and stronger customer loyalty through better quality, and the profits from an entire repeat product which otherwise would not be launched, could be justifiably counted in the equation. All of this hinges on the 'if' and 'maybe'; however, the astute business will realize that being a late entry, losing market share, and being regarded as the 'second best' or 'also ran' in, for example, the mobile phone market does indeed lose money.

There are three principal areas in which the DFSS project can return real and hard financial savings. Running any new design as a DFSS project implies benefits from:

- reduced time and cost to design – and thus getting the product/service to market sooner;
- better added value of the final product and service – and thus stronger customer loyalty and sales;

- lower costs to manufacture, maintain and redevelop – and thus reduced operating expenditure.

Naturally turning potential savings into real money is very important and if the DFSS organization is to see improved figures on the bottom line, then hard savings must be made and, more importantly, increased revenue must be achieved. There is a contradiction in any large DFSS project in that the early stages of the project will add time through much 'up-front' work, and the only way that real cost and time savings can be captured from the process of the project itself will be to apply strong rigour and control. The aim is to ensure that the path from the start of the project to the final design is as short as possible, with no fancy frills or excursions into pointless invention, trials or testing. Improvements to a long-winded design process can include such things as concurrent rather than sequential design, and the DFSS methodology aims to remove the need or risk of having to revisit any major work at any stage. It is quite clear that, for the small project, the extra overhead of customer analysis and conceptual development will do nothing but add to the burden. It is only for the larger projects – both subject matter and teamwork – that savings can be made by compressing the stages from concept to implementation. This is achieved through a rigour and structure that bring the conflicting internal interests together with a clear focus for the project direction. When business, customer, engineer, designer, implementer and end user all work together in unison and agreement, the process of design will be much slicker and faster and, above all, less expensive and wasteful. Making sure that this is expenditure that is now saved is a matter for the business and one that clearly requires a form of measurement of the project itself. Getting better added value into the product and service, to increase sales, loyalty and customer base, is a matter for the project team working on behalf of the business. Again, where the measurement systems are in place to track such matters, over time it will be possible to show the difference between 'traditional' design and Six Sigma design. This metric must include objective analysis of the failure to deliver to customer requirements. Being honest that the latest product offering is losing sales is the flip side of the coin for better design gaining sales, or at least not driving the customer away quite so effectively! Similarly, it is an obligation of the business culture and effort to accept the cost of failure as part of the benefit gained from the DFSS project work, wherever failure has clearly been avoided. The real difficulty is in being able to place a figure on the savings gained from not falling down a hole in the pavement! Getting returns from lower manufacturing costs is a matter for both business and team. If the team designs a better way of checking in at the hotel with a saving of five pence each time, realization of such benefit will again require a measurement system, elapsed time and business activity and control to maintain the saving and realize the gains.

In contrast, the costs involved with undertaking a DFSS project are quite discrete and really amount to the extra effort and expenditure over and above what would normally be consumed by a 'traditional' project. There are other benefits from DFSS in terms of long-term strategy, customer awareness, teamwork and an extension of the culture of continuous customer-focused quality, but the conflict still remains that the costs of DFSS are likely to be much more evident than are the benefits. Generally it is up to the business to realize the savings, both in the short term by driving design and implementation projects with more rigour, structure and a better strategy, and in the long term by actively seeking, measuring and accrediting the returns. In an atmosphere where the short-term quick fix prevails over the long-term reward, companies will always plant short-term low-value crops such as potatoes, and not bother with long-term high-value crops such as asparagus. Why bother with DFSS? This is a real question that the project team can play a part in answering, using the tools of customer analysis, evaluation and modelling to predict performance, and a question that the business needs to answer through supporting a culture of broad-based, long-term and open measurement.

Much of the gains come from improving the design process, better understanding of the customer requirements, and reduction in risk and failure. This implies a need to measure the design process, the meeting of customer needs, and the costs associated with failure. Such metrics only operate if they are actively built into the project work, become part of the designed solution, and are suitably championed and managed by the business as an ongoing activity.

SUMMARY

- It is important that the conceptual through to practical design of a new product or service is creative, with new and inspired features, yet also fully measured and evaluated against customer requirements. Ultimately the contrast between creativity and measurement requires a fine balance by the business between cost and benefit.
- Creativity of the individual is vital if the project is to add innovation and inventiveness to the product or service. Both creative ability and expression vary from individual to individual. Creative people naturally demonstrate:

  - curiosity and active exploration;
  - experimentation and testing;
  - a balanced outlook – science, art and commerce; and
  - a holistic-system viewpoint.

- Proactive companies need to promote and develop a talent for creativity in their staff. To achieve this any organization must:

  - create an 'ideas culture' of encouragement and implementation;
  - provide all employees with training to develop latent creativity;
  - identify those naturally creative and utilize their skills to the full;
  - adopt a range of team-based creativity tools such as brainstorming;
  - support relaxed, even unconstrained, curiosity and exploration;
  - accept and accommodate employees' mistakes;
  - provide administration and real resources in terms of time and money;
  - develop a broad viewpoint that includes science, art and commerce;
  - view all things as interconnected systems, yet think outside of the box; and
  - provide both the right environment and the right pressure to foster creativity.

- Although methods and tools exist to aid with innovation, such as TIPS (theory of inventive problem solving), these typically automate the *iterative* model of design by incremental improvement. DFSS aims to take a single giant leap forward in process capability to meet customer needs, using creative and new approaches to an existing problem together with predictable and lowest-risk technology.
- Incremental improvement is often associated with simplification, while exponential change implies an increased complexity. Infrequent and short bursts of exponential change open greater potential for payback but at a high price, whereas continuous incremental improvement will generally provide less expensive but smaller returns. A good DFSS solution increases the complexity of the functionality provided to the customer, and yet simplifies the operational aspects of the process, leading to reduced variation, error and waste. Exponential change projects will often need to be followed by repeated incremental improvement to realize the new inherent capability to deliver the enhanced performance required.

- The difficult task of selecting between alternative solutions and features can be assisted by the use of the Pugh selection matrix. This tool can be used at many levels within the DFSS project to evaluate performance against a basket of customer or process requirements.
- The benefit of the DFSS approach is seen in the ability to evaluate potential solutions against customer requirements using the sigma metric early on in the design. Although the actual design process will vary considerably across differing industries and design projects using a range of tools and statistical approaches such as 'Taguchi methods', the common theme is to:

  - keep a strong customer focus;
  - identify the critical metrics to design against;
  - work always to eliminate variation;
  - measure objectively to customer requirements;
  - make the most appropriate use of statistical methods; and
  - embody the highest levels of engineering and business knowledge.

- Modelling is an important tool in the cost-effective development of design solutions. Process modelling is essential in service design and can add real benefit to manufacturing projects. This tool, either on paper or in software, allows project teams to fully test and evaluate critical performance metrics and process behaviour through simulation. Such models will only supply sound answers to questions where they are based on accurate data from the real world and are appropriately and sympathetically constructed.
- Cost–benefit analysis for DFSS projects is complex and often difficult. Additional costs come from the quite considerable effort and resource required at the beginning of each project, which may well be inappropriately large for small design projects. Benefits are both hard savings and soft returns; the hard savings come from:

  - improved design processes leading to reduced time and cost involved;
  - faster-to-market returns in cash flow and overall market share;
  - better added value in the product or service leading to better sales;
  - increased customer-experienced quality resulting in higher loyalty;
  - reduced operational and manufacturing costs; and
  - lower ongoing and second-generation costs.

- Whilst it is important for the project team to evaluate costs and benefits, it typically falls to the business ownership to fully identify and associate with the long-term costs returns from the large DFSS project. Only when an organization views the long term, ensures appropriate measurements are taken, and enthusiastically champions both the ideal and practice of DFSS, will it be seen to be really beneficial to the organization.

EXERCISES

The typical English breakfast includes a serving of toast – uniform slices of bread (typically 12 x 10 x 1 cm) that have been 'grilled' to a light brown colour and a crisp texture (traditionally served with butter and marmalade). The cooking process is fairly simple, requiring heat for a short period of time; however, the specific need for repeatable performance and ease of use has prompted the development of the domestic electric toaster.

One highly desirable characteristic of toast is crispness without any symptoms of sogginess, which can often be induced following cooking should the residual steam from the bread fail to fully disperse from the toast. Some hotels serve the toast after cooking wrapped in a cloth to conserve heat, which also conserves moisture and is thus liable to make the toast soggy.

1 Arrive at a new concept for a toaster, or new features of existing and typical toasters, which specifically eliminate any possibility of sogginess and so ensure the 'perfect piece of toast'.
2 Generate several alternatives for the key feature and use a Pugh matrix to select the best.

Look at a small building, such as a house or office that you know well, and consider the task of renewing all the plumbing and wiring, with the specific aim of bringing the wiring up to date with electricity supply and telephone/computer networks. You should also add a security system as well as video/audio and services monitoring. Construct a plan for the work – committing nothing to paper or computer. Ensure that you have considered every customer of the product/process, and attempt to refine your plan by eliminating potential issues beforehand.

1 Have you thought of everything?
2 What process did you follow to be creative and inventive in the solutions adopted?
3 Repeat this work as a team activity and note any difference in outcome and execution.

Design a very simple process for queuing at a service point, such as a ticket office. Using just one CTQ for queuing time, model the process using a spreadsheet or similar and evaluate the performance with random data. Take an arrival rate of one person every two minutes, using a Poisson distribution, and a time to serve using a normal distribution, average of one minute and standard deviation of one minute (a log-normal distribution might be a better model of real life).

1 If the customer CTQ is 'queue for less than one minute', what is the process-sigma capability of this design?
2 What changes could you make to the model to increase process performance to six sigma?

CHAPTER EIGHT

Robustness and reliability

One of the primary reasons for the lack of rapid and successful market penetration and capitalization with new products and services is the very high rate of failure at launch. Failure to deliver as expected, failure to perform as required, and failure to sustain satisfactory performance are three key areas for customer disappointment. Failure in regular use, specifically as a result of product design failure, can also be catastrophic, leading to total collapse of market confidence as well as large compensation and reinstatement costs. The cost of failure in existing products and services can be considerable; however, for new ventures such costs can completely dwarf the original design project outlay. Failure can be roughly categorized into three areas of impact:

1 Failure to meet specification target or limit
2 Failure to satisfy the customer
3 Catastrophic failure of product or (service) process.

For any product or service, delivery of any one instance of the offering may fail to hit the target or be outside of the specifications. From a purely sigma-metric point of view, this is a 'defect' and effectively reduces the process performance figure. Such failure may or may not affect customer satisfaction, depending on how well the targets actually relate to customer perception of quality. It is useful for the work required for failure analysis and prevention to step away from customer satisfaction *per se*. In simple terms, products and processes either fail or they do not, and it becomes very difficult to attach a measurement to 'degree of failure' rather than simply a 'count of failure'. It can be very useful therefore to retain the distinct cut-off limits of customer critical to quality (CTQ) metrics rather than use loss functions, and then relate failure directly to 'away from target' or 'out of specification'. In contrast to what has just been said, there is always an element of failure that does indeed relate back to customer requirement and, for the new offering, failure may well include inability to gain favour or excite the consumer. Such failure is more attributable to the strategy and conceptual development of the new product or service, rather than to the actual instantiation of the new offering. By the time the DFSS team is working on the design concept and actual solution, it is far too late to be considering failure such as *total* inability to deliver what the customer wants. Since so much was said in earlier chapters about the vital importance of customer analysis and corporate strategy in early stages of design, this chapter will concentrate on failures of product and service to deliver functionality and formation, rather than failure to deliver foundation and to gain favour.

Catastrophic failure is a total inability of the product or service to complete the delivery of any one CTQ. Such failures are almost certain to directly and negatively affect both customer loyalty and the fragile new market, and can often sound a death knell for the new commercial offering. The goal for the successful commercial launch of any new product and/or service must be to:

- reduce the risk of failure to deliver to basic customer needs – suitability;
- eliminate variation and deviation from customer-defined targets and limits – robustness;
- remove the causes of failure at instantiation to satisfy the customer – reliability; and
- prevent any form of catastrophic failure from occurring – stability.

In the example of the hotel check-in, the customer is looking for both a product (the room) and a service (check-in). Putting aside for the moment the issue of suitability of the new offering, this chapter will consider the issues involved in the design of new products and services specifically for robustness, reliability and stability. If the customer wants check-in in three minutes, doing so in four minutes may or may not lead to customer dissatisfaction, but it certainly does indicate a process that is not performing as robustly as required. Even if the process delivered at two and a half minutes, there may well still be far too much overall variation, leading to potential dissatisfaction and poor performance. A key element of excellent customer quality is total reliability measured in terms of small variation, and this often rates as the number one requirement from any product or service. Clearly the worst case is not being able to check in the customer at all, or perhaps in allocating the non-smoker to a smoking room. Whilst Six Sigma improvement projects perform extraordinarily well in reducing or eliminating variation and the root causes of failure, prevention of any form of catastrophic failure must be the number one priority of the DFSS design team, closely followed by the need for robust design generally. Indeed, the term 'robust' can be used to cover a multitude of issues from poor performance and excessive variation, to issues from poor reliability and high rates of failure. In considering the 'new' rather than the 'existing', excellence in design must be about designing out defect and designing in the highest degree of robustness to any form of failure and variation.

FAILURE AND ERROR

Failure and error are really two distinct areas: error is due to human misjudgement or operational mistakes; failure is due to component failure, design failure, as well as failure due to the unforeseen circumstance. Failure mode effect analysis (FMEA) as a tool is a powerful means to evaluate current products and services, as well as future processes during the design stage, so as to identify and deal with any type of error or failure. The case of the Tay Bridge disaster clearly indicates the need for due consideration of every aspect of the insidious nature of failure and omission – poor design, bad construction, and slapdash operation and ongoing maintenance were all contributory factors to the collapse of this particular bridge. It is important in DFSS to deal fully not only with the practical aspects of FMEA, but also the nature of failure and error and the importance of a correct attitude towards this complex area. Understandably, notorious bridge failure is typically of the catastrophic type, of which many examples can be found, particularly from the railway age. In fact, the early operation of the railways is a good area in which to study the nature of failure and error generally; however, it will be helpful first to review the current theoretical understanding of failure itself.

MURPHY'S LAW

History attributes the origins of Murphy's Law to Edward Murphy who in 1949, while working for the US Air Force, stated that 'If there are two or more ways to do something, and one of those ways can result in a catastrophe, then someone will do it.' Very quickly this became popularized and associated with the broader saying, 'Anything that can go wrong will', although this adaptation is more correctly a derivative of Finagle's Law of Dynamic Negatives. Many scientists seriously doubt the validity of what is arguably through experience one of the best-understood laws of nature. From careful observation the one principle that 'catastrophic and costly failure is inevitable' can be divided into three axiomatic parts as follows:

1 If something can go wrong, it will.
2 When something goes wrong it can cause the greatest amount of damage.
3 Failure relates ultimately to the simplest cause.

The first part is very similar to the 'Shakespearean monkey' theorem. Take one monkey sat in front of a typewriter, wait long enough, and the monkey will type the entire works of William Shakespeare. All potential errors and failures will always arise, given a sufficiently long period of time. As a corollary, the more often a product or service is used, the shorter the elapsed chronological time before a particular failure is seen; failures will happen, but clearly relate to the frequency of use. Scientists have refuted the second part; however, such research work is fundamentally flawed. As physicists know, Nature conserves energy and hides from inspection – as typified by Heisenberg's Uncertainty Principle. At the atomic level, if I know exactly where an electron is I am unable to tell precisely what it is doing, and vice versa. Bread, buttered on one side and accidentally dropped, will more often than not land on the buttered side, thus causing the most damage in that it is no longer edible. In testing this theory in a laboratory, Nature of course knows that the buttered bread is not actually going to be eaten, so there is no damage associated with it falling on any particular side and hence no difference is seen. In the real world, rather than the laboratory, Nature clearly understands that falling on the buttered side causes the greatest damage. A corollary to the second point is that Nature typically waits until the expense of potential failure has been maximized – often what goes on the carpeted floor is the very last piece of toast covered in jam, leaving nothing else left to eat. The third part is perhaps the most frightening of all, in that any failure is typically caused at root by the simplest and often least significant cause. In real terms this implies that the real causes of failure are frequently overlooked in favour of more prominent symptoms. Again a corollary to the third part is that failure often compounds and aggregates. The ultimate catastrophe is generally the result of a chain of events starting from something insignificant, with failure expanding to affect parts of the system that have not themselves failed. This is similar to the domino effect, where the failure of one component in a system will trigger the failure of a second. Where each failure triggers more than one cascading failure, then failure will multiply like a virus to swamp the system. Although this should only apply within the immediate system, there are unproven cases where it is believed that the failures have actually jumped to nearby but disconnected systems. Many computer users, for example, report that failure of the computer screen has caused a failure of the telephone or office light or even the coffee machine next door.

If any reader doubts in any way the validity of the above (albeit slightly humorous) discussion, then consider the sequence of events that led to a head-on collision at Hull Paragon station in 1927. Figure 8.1 is a schematic of part of the track layout at the approach, controlled by the (then) modern electro-pneumatic signal box – a power-assisted interlocking frame with short levers arranged in numerical order. Train B was running late, and one signalman was clearing the route behind the train, while a second was setting a second route for train A incoming to the station. The slip-point number 95 was protected not only by signal 171 but also by a set of bars along the rails at the point itself. Once the signal had been set to clear, as it was for train B, it was not possible to change the points, and when the points moved the protecting bars had to rise and fall, which was prevented if a train was actually over the points at the time. The first signalman, in haste, and against company regulations, returned signal 171 to danger before the end of the outgoing train had passed, leaving some 38 feet between the locomotive and the points – about 1.7 seconds of time at the then estimated speed of the locomotive. The second signalman needed to change levers 96 and 97 for his route, but changed lever 95 in error, which took about 1.3 seconds to effect. Clearly 1.3 seconds can fit into 1.7 seconds, and the slip-points changed, allowing train B to pass through point 83 although set against it, and the collision then occurred.

It is not really a surprise that something such as this would eventually occur, assuming that it was

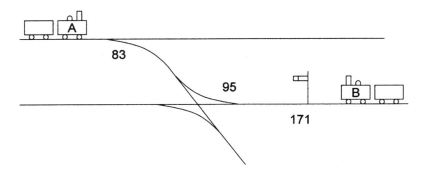

Figure 8.1   Train collision at Hull, 1927

even remotely possible for it to happen in the first place. What is astonishing is the commonplace reluctance to accept that if a failure mode is *possible*, then that failure mode is *inevitable*, and it is this simple fact of inevitability that must drive designers to eliminate failure and error by any and every means possible. To successfully defeat the almost uncanny ability for failure and error to occur and cause the greatest possible damage and hence commercial expense, it is necessary to reduce the likelihood and impact of failure by one or more means as follows:

● reduce the occurrence (frequency) of failure;
● reduce the impact (cost) of failure;
● eliminate failure (defect) at the root cause; and
● prevent failure from spreading.

Since failure typically begins with the simplest cause, a very successful approach is to snuff out failure at the source. Encapsulated in the Wilkins observation – 'it is necessary to stop a myriad of little things from failing' – success is achieved in practice by paying great attention to minute detail, and this attitude needs to become part of not only the DFSS project, but also the ongoing process and control plans.

ATTITUDE TO FAILURE

It has already been stated that both DFSS and many of the tools used relate more to attitude of mind rather than to a concern for their execution. Failure is often difficult to analyse when seen in hindsight and almost impossible to predict. The study of past errors and failures in well-defined systems is a good place for the novice to begin to realize the substance of the popular version of Murphy's Law in action. Unless the team members involved in a new product and service offering are actively prepared to accept that failure will occur, will be expensive, and can be prevented or reduced, then little benefit will arise from such failure analysis. Also, unless the business realizes the full cost and impact of failure, there is unlikely to be much emphasis on expenditure and effort to prevent the possible disaster, and even less interest in the possible hiccup.

It must be remembered at all times that almost all failure (of any magnitude) can be either prevented or the effects mitigated. The cost involved can be enormous; however, the majority of failures can be precluded through careful design of both product and operating process, likewise for services. This can clearly be seen in the history of railway accidents, still very poignant in the UK as at the time of writing there have been four major incidents in less than a four-year span. Railways are interesting case studies for failure, and the book by L.T.C. Rolt, *Red for Danger* (various publishers since 1955), is an excellent history of catastrophic accidents from the first railways up to 1957. In the early days failure was almost endemic and the main drive was to eliminate the basic cause of the accident. After the end of the railway age and into the early 1900s the emphasis shifted towards mitigation of the effect. Reading about the slow change in attitude towards such things as signalling, fire safety and robust operating procedures, one is inclined to wonder how companies could stare almost certain calamity in the face without pause for thought, until jolted into action by yet another disaster. Against what would seem almost common sense, such a soft attitude to failure still remains, as demonstrated by the Channel Tunnel fire in 1996. The open-type wagons used for conveying freight lorries through the tunnel had been the cause of many debates on safety and it was recognized that a vehicle fire within the tunnel would probably occur several times annually. The safe operation of heavy goods vehicle shuttles was assumed to be assured through early detection and control procedures, rather than overt attempts at fire prevention. The design of the trains ensured a 30-minute resistance to fire, assuming that the train would continue the journey and exit the tunnel in no more than 24 minutes, when the fire would be dealt with in the open. In the incident that caused the 1996 fire, it was seen that the detection was ineffective and the control procedures not fully adhered to. Finally, with so much reliance on the ability of the train to exit the tunnel, the fire caused an indicator alarm to operate falsely, which prompted the driver to halt the train mid-journey. The fire, now far bigger than had been anticipated, brought down the overhead power lines, cutting off both traction current and communication systems. The damage to the tunnel lining was significant as a result of the intense fire and the type of concrete used, which was not fire-resistant. Fortunately no one was seriously injured; however, services were severely restricted for some time and the negative publicity this event generated was clearly unwelcome. Here the attitude was to accept the inevitable cause of failure, and then to rely heavily on detection and control to help mitigate the effect. Clearly the better attitude is to prevent the primary causes of failure in the first place, then to mitigate the effect, and finally rely on detection and control as a last resort, and to do so with robust and automatic systems without requiring human intervention.

One of the prime objectives of railway safety is to prevent two trains from occupying the same section of track at the same time. Early control was by the use of fixed time slots, with locomotives dispatched at regular intervals, the folly of which became apparent very quickly. The signal and block system was then introduced, with defined blocks of track controlled by signals, which were initially raised to indicate danger and again disclosed an inherent weakness. It would seem that almost every single approach to the problem has been used over the years, starting with the most inappropriate and working upwards to the most appropriate, and also perhaps the most expensive. If this is merely a matter of financial concern, then the pressing need is to adopt the most overall cost-effective solution, which must be fully worked into the design concept from the very beginning. The most robust solution is not necessarily the most expensive, and a long-term view is required to balance any initial costs involved against potentially costly failure. Again, this is an issue of corporate strategy and yet another reason for the DFSS project to cover the wider aspects of the business objectives. It is far better to remove the fundamental possibility of the primary cause of failure than to try to fight it once it has appeared and taken hold. The signalling system used on the early lines of the London Underground remains almost unchanged since the early 1900s, and enjoys the best safety record of any comparative railway in the world. Continuous track circuits operate both the signals and a line-side stop-arm, which causes any train passing a signal at danger to apply the brakes and stop in a safe distance. Although the system is very reliable and operates on the 'fail-safe' principle, infrequent failure still does occur, caused by defective equipment, incorrect rewiring after maintenance and the failure of secondary manual procedures adopted when operational problems arise.

Of course, often the safest solution is also the simplest and may well be overlooked in the inevitable desire for the exotic and technologically advanced design. For many small railways, safety is still totally assured without the need for any complex signalling or control under the 'one engine in steam' rule.

FAILURE MODE EFFECT ANALYSIS

The failure mode effect analysis (FMEA) tool was first developed by the US military from about 1949 onwards, has been adopted more recently as a *de facto* quality tool by the automotive industry and is rapidly gaining in popularity almost everywhere. Use of FMEA is fairly widespread, and it can be applied equally to products, to processes, and to new designs. Like quality function deployment (QFD), it is not an easy tool to use, requires both time and teamwork to effect well and should be regarded as a fundamental and ongoing part of the project work. Certainly, many organizations now regard the upkeep of the FMEA for any product line as a vital part of the control stage as well as the rest of the DMAIC or DFSS methodology. The various uses to which FMEA can be put are only distinguished in terms of the mental gymnastics required to use the tool; the basic framework remains commonly as shown in Figure 8.2, although it is not always a good idea to mix product, process and design FMEAs together. Since new design often covers products as well as processes, the application of the FMEA tool should be wide-ranging and used often and throughout the project. New design will frequently introduce what is effectively a new system, where the point of interest for failure has more to do with the component parts of the system failing to correctly interact and support each other. In the most extensive use, the FMEA tool can be used to analyse the risk of the business concept solution failing to meet customer needs, to analyse the failures associated with the new product,

Mode	Cause	Effect	Severity	Occurrence	Detection	Risk priority number
Unable to provide working room key	Out of blank keys	Failure to get customer to room	9	3	1	27
	Coding machine not operative	Need to use back-up process	4	5	3	60
	Coding machine fails to code correctly	Customer cannot get into room	7	2	9	126
	Door lock battery flat	Customer cannot get into room	7	3	7	147

Figure 8.2   Failure mode effect analysis chart

failures in connection with the new service and/or manufacturing process, and failures of the broader system and its interconnections. This is certainly a considerable amount of work!

The aim of FMEA is to identify all the possible failures that do or could occur and to rank them in an order appropriate to the business for corrective action. If there is a weakness in FMEA, then this is where it lies, as the target is to decide from a business, not customer, perspective what is most important and cost-effective to work on. Typically the steps required to complete an FMEA chart or diagram are as follows:

1 Decide on the objective for the FMEA – an existing product, a system, process or a new design feature.
2 Study the product, process map, system or new design function in detail.
3 Identify potential problems or failure modes and look for the root causes.
4 Rate the problem for severity, occurrence and detection using a scale of 1 to 10.
5 Compute the risk priority number, and prioritize the top-ranking part of the table.
6 Decide on and implement actions to reduce the risk, and then re-evaluate the table.
7 Update and maintain the table indefinitely as part of the (new) product or process control.

In using this tool difficulties may arise in the understanding of what the failure mode is, what is its effect, and how to score the different sections. Often a failure symptom or effect can also be a cause for yet more failure. Ingress of water in a car causes rust, and then rusting metalwork causes mechanical failure and so on. Many formal definitions of how to apply the tool exist, some of which extend to a great number of steps. Practical experience shows that often a more flexible approach to the immediate needs of the project and team is far more helpful. What is important is the ability to identify as many of the different ways the product, process, design or system could fail, rather than to follow a sequence of exact steps to complete yet another tool. Beginning with failure outcomes and then working backwards to effects is often much easier than starting with effects and looking for failures! A formal definition would cite failure as an inability to conform to either the process requirements or the intended design, typically based on the customer and business CTQs and CTPs for the product or process. Since it has already been shown that failure and error have an inherent risk of occurrence and damage, the most important problems are those with:

● a high risk of occurrence;
● high impact or damage outcome; and
● low likelihood of detection, and hence corrective action.

The risk priority number (RPN) is simply the multiplication of all three ranking numbers for each failure. The values used in the ranking should cover the full range from 1 to 10, which thus gives an RPN range from 1 to 1000. There are 'standard' tables for the number ranges; however, many teams will benefit greatly from discussion and adaptation of these tables to generate their own score sheets. Service projects in particular should consider developing standard tables for their individual industries; the severity rating of 10 is typically reserved in manufacturing for instances that kill or injure employees or customers, which is not common in hotel check-in, but clearly a possibility when using the lift. There will also be a need to discuss the outcome from a 'completed' FMEA, since the business or DFSS team will need to decide where to draw the line between acceptable failure and unacceptable failure that requires action. In existing products and processes the use of FMEA will identify special cause variation and failure and the team will then go on to devise an action plan to reduce the impact, occurrence or to improve the detection and correction. For any new design the work must be to identify potential failures that are a weakness of the proposed design as early as possible and then to change the design to reduce the RPN. This is a wonderful opportunity to 'get it right' from the very beginning, and the team should be encouraged to work through the FMEA approach at the earliest stages; they should fight shy of dealing with failure by simply adding inspection and 'exception protocols'.

If the study of the causes of catastrophic failure has shown anything, it will make quite clear the fact that failure is frequently about something not working *and* then something *else* going wrong, often almost as a consequence. In the recent nuclear industry accidents such as at Chernobyl and Three Mile Island, it can typically be seen that a standard component failed and was then backed up by a more manual operation, which then also failed. If the initial failure is common and the effect small, as is typical in service processes, then the manual bypass will frequently take over completely and increase overall cost and inefficiency. A very large number of calls to customer help-lines are about manually dealing with problems rather than preventing failure in the first place. Alternatively, if the initial failure is rare, such as in well-controlled systems, then the likelihood is that the manual back-up procedure has a very high risk of secondary failure since it is itself used infrequently. This goes well beyond a simple cause–effect approach to failure, and implies much more of a composite system at work, where the system and all its modes have to be understood and carefully considered. Such an application of the FMEA tool in the design of the new differs significantly from a more 'traditional' application of failure analysis; the real differentiator is again one of attitude. What is required from start to finish is a positive drive to identify and eliminate failure at the root rather than to work harder to detect and mitigate the effect. How much better to design a railway where the trains simply cannot physically meet in collision!

In this respect the use of the severity, occurrence and detection rankings may draw focus away from the real measures of failure – the impact of undeniable damage from a failed component of the new design, whether product or process, to perform as required. An interesting concept to consider is the division of the singular figure for occurrence into two separate constituents for probability of occurrence and likelihood of impact from the outcome. Projected failure for the new design is about both the probability of a failure event and the likelihood of subsequent damage, which may or may not be well related. In the check-in process, a failure mode is entered when a customer fails to check in to the correct room. This may be due to the basic causal event where someone walks into a hotel without a reservation, triggering a sequence of failures to deal with the immediate issue as well as the possible and subsequent errors. The probability of the primary event might be as high as one in ten arriving customers; however, each event may lead on to one of a number of failure outcomes. There is the failure to satisfy the potential customer if the hotel is full, the failure to allocate an appropriate room, and the real failure to preserve other bookings by allocating someone else's room in error. Since the ultimate damage caused is a compounding of the probability of the primary event with the possibility of the secondary event, as well as the severity of the damage in outcome, there is a strong argument within design for adding more weight to this area. Certainly, emphasis on the detection of failure is to be discouraged in favour of more appropriate action in the face of certain calamity. Clearly the fundamental damage is in the inability to allocate a customer to the most appropriate room in the shortest time frame, and FMEA should be used to identify and action weaknesses in the design. The failure of the epoch due to a large comet hitting the earth and wiping out civilization as we know it has a higher primary event probability than a single individual winning the jackpot in the national or state lottery. What must be considered is the fact that the first event can be neither detected nor prevented and is clearly not something that should rate high on the action list. Aeroplanes do crash into hotels, but the design action plan can only affect the practical issues and will not be able to move the hotel away from the local flight path. The second event, winning the lottery, has a low primary event probability, but since so many people play the lottery each week, someone somewhere wins on a regular basis. The likelihood of subsequent disruption for any hotel could be high, since many employees typically play in syndicates and a big win often results in multiple and immediate resignations. The impact and effect of not having half the staff turn up for work on Sunday after the big lottery win on a Saturday night should not be overlooked! Here, the primary event probability is low but significant. The possibility of a damaging outcome depends on the numbers in the syndicate as well as staff–employer relationships. The severity rating is high, even if the detection is good and therefore rates low. In reality, almost the only thing that can be done here is to reduce the impact through insurance, and to effect a lowering of the possibility of damage by improving staff relationships to the point where even big winners still want to come in to work the next day! The value gained from failure analysis is best seen in the practical and pragmatic use of the tools, and within design this may well imply adaptations to the tool use that coerce the focus of the team on the most achievable and appropriate.

ROBUST DESIGN AND LEAN MANUFACTURE

One of the great successes of the many incremental and continuous quality movements, such as *kaizen*, has been the gradual shift towards lean manufacturing and the just in time (JIT) principle. Anything consumed or expended that does not ultimately go towards the final product is waste and cost of poor quality. One of the best ways to ensuring lean manufacture is to remove any potential source of inefficiency. In many ways *kaizen* is similar to Six Sigma, in that it is both a philosophy and a set of tools. The philosophy emphasizes customer-focused quality and continuous improvement and that every employee must play an active part. The tools include a methodology based on something similar to the Deming cycle (plan, do, check, act) as well as the '5 Ss', the '5 Ms' and the '5 Whys', and the concept of waste or *muda*. The idea of the seven wastes or *muda* came originally from Toyota in Japan and the list includes:

- overproduction
- waiting
- transport
- inappropriate processing
- unnecessary inventory
- unnecessary motion
- defects.

This list can be extended and some people now advocate including waste of energy, pollution, space, complexity as well as waste of human talent in the workforce. The underlying fact to note is that waste elimination has more to do with actual production than it does with either quality or design; however, the designer of the new process must give every attention to the detail of how the process will operate. Badly designed processes will engender extra steps and create waste, whereas well-designed processes will facilitate, or even better will ensure, waste avoidance.

The first step is to identify the areas of waste, which for design will typically mean simulation and pilot studies before implementation. This is where good old-fashioned experience will pay dividends, as knowing what is likely to go wrong in the new design requires a little hindsight applied as foresight. Overproduction is often regarded as the worst kind of waste, particularly as it is quite natural and easy to do and contributes in one way or another to most of the other wastes later on. A real issue with overproduction is where some error or defect has been introduced without being noticed, and a large amount of stock has to be reworked, although this should never happen in a Six Sigma company! The waste of waiting is about much more than just time, and where there is a wait at a critical bottleneck the delay will often halt the entire process operation. Moving and transporting goods around is clearly not of value, except for transport and shipping companies. This will also extend to communications, and a good rule of thumb is a measure of 30 feet, as any paperwork or communication over more than this distance effectively splits any process with a move and therefore typically introduces inherent waste and delay. Inappropriate processing is important to design, as most processes will use tools and resources, which will either deliver satisfactory capability, or either too much or too little. Although Six Sigma almost indoctrinates the idea of zero defects (more practically fewer than four per million), there will be real waste in using too much capability in the new design. Naturally there is a balance between what is required today and what is a likely requirement for the future. Future-proofing is good, but is something that the business must decide on, not the designer. The typical waste of inappropriate processing today is the excessive use of new technology where something simpler, cheaper and more reliable would do just as well. Having any unnecessary inventory is clearly something that can be seen, felt and removed to good effect. In the ultra-lean JIT operation nothing is created unless it is required for the next stage, which itself has real risks of cascading failure when something goes wrong. However, excessive stocks can easily hide other quality issues by acting as a buffer zone for defective products and processes with excessive variation. Again there must be a good balance, and at the first launch of any new design the business may be happy to build in a little waste to ensure less risk of a more catastrophic failure. Once up and running, incremental improvements can often fine-tune the process. Unnecessary motion covers ergonomics and the well-being of operators and staff, and clearly if an operator has to bend and stretch to make sure no defect enters the product, then defects are going to happen more often at the end of each shift. In a Six Sigma environment, the waste of defects needs no further comment!

The '5 Ms' are really just a checklist, often used in fish-bone (cause and effect) diagrams, to ensure due consideration of all the principal components in any process. Many variations on the naming convention now exist, and a popular alternative is the '5 Ms and a P':

- materials
- machines
- methods
- measurement
- mother nature (environment)
- people.

Naturally, these will also be the principal areas for the introduction of error, defect and failure and good design will consider each sector in turn. The idea of promoting attention to detail implies a need to divide and conquer, since the whole design will often be far too big for just one person to contemplate. As process design is also a systemic activity, the division should be made at logical and discernible joints in the system and the above list is often a good point from which to start such a division.

The concept of the '5 Ss' again originated in Japan and is well practised by many companies from the shop floor to the managing director. The naming convention here becomes very complicated, as the Japanese does not translate well into English. There is an aligned list of English words beginning with 's', and a secondary list of more accurate words beginning with 'c'. The reader is encouraged to adopt the most comfortable arrangement!

- *seiri* – sort – clean-up
- *seiton* – straighten/simplify – configure
- *seiso* – scrub/sweep – clean
- *seiketsu* – standardize – conformity
- *shitsuke* – self-discipline – custom.

This is the preserve of the operating process in full swing and is one way of preventing many of the situations that cause the wastes mentioned above. However, the question needs to be asked as to why so many problems are there in the first place. Good design needs to provide the ability and encouragement to actively undertake the '5 Ss' in any process, manufacturing or service, and also to remove where possible the need for the '5 Ss' in the first place.

Clean-up is the task of removing anything unnecessary from the process or workplace, such as clutter that hinders smooth working. It can be undertaken using a 'red tag' system. Anything that has been tagged for a number of months and has not been used (when the tag is removed) should be archived or separated from the working area. Clean-up also includes rapidly fixing things that are broken and keeping everything neat and tidy. Nothing should be in any process except what is required. Configuring or orderliness is about having a place for everything and everything in its place, which extends the above to ensuring that all components of the process are ready to be used. Cleaning, and regular checking, is about a routine that encourages or enforces the first point. Often this will require checklists and the like, which will be a source for yet more error and failure, and so good design will build in such characteristics as openness to easy inspection. This is the reverse of 'out of sight, out of mind'. Conformity is about standards, used not only to keep the process running normally but also when things go wrong. Custom or discipline is about keeping to the defined process and the above practices, even when the rush of early enthusiasm has long since evaporated.

Excellent design will provide a product or service process where the item or workplace is self-cleaning, where spare parts are provided alongside the component that needs them, where things simply cannot be out of place and where standards are self-maintaining. It should also be impossible to cut corners and navigate around standards and procedures, which itself often leads to failure and error! The concept of adding fail-safe devices to products and processes is captured in the Japanese *poka yoke* or mistake-proofing. This typically centres on a device, ideally inexpensive but usually passive, which literally prevents defects from occurring. Since mistakes are almost inevitable, this approach aims either to act as a control or to provide a warning – most appropriately a control to prevent the cause triggering a defect and/or a warning to avoid the cause in the first place. Where two swing doors meet with an overlapping joint, then one door must close before the other. Using a large handle on one door and a smaller or no handle at all on the other will provide a warning as to which door to use first. This can be backed up with a small control device at the top of the doors that will only allow the second door to shut once the first is closed. Some hotel rooms provide a master light switch by the door, which is activated by inserting the plastic card used as the door key. This not only saves electricity upon departure (a control) but also reduces the incidence of walking out without the door key (a warning). Good fail-safe devices will be almost imperceptible and automatically effective for 100 per cent of all cases, but only operate when a failure is about to happen. Some types of 'fail-safe' in the service industry can be almost offensive, particularly when one is asked repeatedly during a meal, 'Is everything all right?' Here the fail-safe mechanism is an action rather than a device, and is being used as a last resort. More work should be carried out to identify the types of failure, such as not delivering what was ordered or the food being cold at service, and then looking to fail-safe the causes. There can be no doubt, however, that this is more challenging in the service process than in manufacturing!

One of the higher levels of attainment in *kaizen* and the quest for lean manufacture is the use of a *kanban* system. This Japanese word comes from the cards typically used to represent a communication signal, although it can also be represented by empty trays or spaces. Here the concept is to *pull* products and resources through a manufacturing process in which nothing moves without a signalled need from further along the line. Clearly this is a highly disciplined approach to eliminating waste and error, but it does require a tightly controlled and standardized system free of defects and with fairly stable demand. The modern development of lean supply chains works well where two businesses can closely interface supply and demand processes.

For completeness, the '5 Whys' tool is often used together with cause and effect analysis and consists of simply asking the question 'why?' up to five times, or more or less as necessary. The idea is to encourage the project team to work down to identify the root cause rather than simply concentrate on a symptom. In bringing Six Sigma to the service and transactional environment almost every one of the above ideas has been incorporated in the basic framework, particularly for the analyse and improve stages. Manufacturing and service processes are clearly inherently different and will often require almost diametrically opposing analysis and consideration. For the manufacturer making a widget, the manufacturing process should run with absolutely no overproduction, no excessive inventory, no waiting and certainly no defects. Taking the lean manufacturing principle into the service industry is not as difficult as it might at first seem, and many *kaizen*-like tools are easy to use and powerful in effect. However, further reflection will show that excessive leanness can cause more problems than it might be worth. In the large and busy hotel, waiting until such time as the next customer arrives before issuing a *kanban* to clean a room is not a good idea. The real distinction between manufacture and service is that service is experienced in real time and customers generally do not like waiting. It is essential to have a stock of clean rooms of every type ready and waiting for the next potential customer to walk through the door. The necessity of zero wait is so strong in some situations that lean no longer becomes sensible. In fact, for hotels the best concept is to drive the process to the reverse of the apparently lean just in time approach and to clean every room as soon as it becomes free. Rather than 'just in time', what is required is 'ahead of time', which works very well for such things as hotel check-out. Each customer wants to leave as quickly as they came in, if not faster, and check-out is usually the very bane of business travel. Accelerating the process ahead of time suggests check-out before breakfast, or even the night before. Some hotels have taken this idea to the logical conclusion, which is to check out when you check in. In the roadside Travelodge in the UK, check-in is open from mid-afternoon, when the arriving customer pays in full and takes a room key. Check-out upon departure during the following morning simply requires posting the key through a letterbox in the unmanned reception.

It is not the aggressive use of such tools that leads ultimately to perfection in both process design and operation, but rather the most appropriate use of the ideals behind the tools to achieve the higher objective of excellence in customer quality. Lean is good, but not always best in the wider perspective, and DFSS is about design with the widest possible viewpoint. There may well be a lean manufacturer of cars, with just in time and super-efficient production. However, this ultimately meets the end customer and consumer, where there will be either a stockpile of cars gathering dust and rust, or a customer waiting eight weeks for a factory order. Today the goal is for supply chains where no one moves unless the next in line sends a *kanban*, which, as the service provider knows all too well, is not how consumers either do or wish to operate!

CONSIDERING PEOPLE

There are two main areas for careful consideration when people are to be involved within any newly designed process. First, there is a need to consider the inevitable rate of error and mishap due to human frailty, and second, there is a more profound requirement to consider the role people will play in the well-designed process of the future.

Pursuing the reduction of all error and failure to the extreme highlights the inherent weaknesses of the human element. It is simply not possible for people to perform tasks without introducing errors, and the upper limit to performance seems to be close to a 1 per cent failure rate, perhaps one tenth of 1 per cent at best. This figure can be improved upon if using machines or automated tools as part of the process, but the fact remains that 'to err is human'. People make mistakes, and Table 8.1 shows the general classification of human failure, grouped by the two key aspects of willingness and knowledge.

When mistakes are made, the 'culprit' will either know or not know that an error has occurred, and will have consciously allowed or not wanted the mistake to happen. The willing and knowing type of error is rare and typically the result of a disgruntled employee or external agent. This is in the realm of fraud, security and how well companies treat employees. Not wanting to cause an error and yet knowing one has taken place is often due to misunderstandings and overwork. People pushed to the limit will allow errors to slip through simply because they can do little else, and again this is an issue for management rather than explicit design, although it should be considered at some point in the design project.

The real area of interest is where the error is committed unknowingly. If this is a willed error, then the cause is often lack of training or applied standards. It almost seems a contradiction that someone can will to cause an error, and yet not know that they have done so, but most employees are actually very eager to undertake tasks, even if they are likely to cause a problem as a result. This situation can be corrected providing it is made evident and the resources applied to deal with the root cause. In contrast the area of most interest in the design project must be that of the accidental or unintentional error, neither willed nor realized.

Table 8.1 Basic grouping of human error

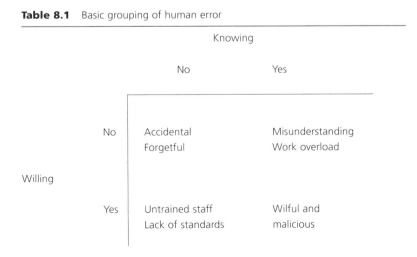

		Knowing	
		No	Yes
Willing	No	Accidental Forgetful	Misunderstanding Work overload
	Yes	Untrained staff Lack of standards	Wilful and malicious

Looking at the reasons why people make unintentional mistakes is almost pure psychology and well worth further consideration. Studies have shown that we all build conceptual models of the real world in our minds, based on past experiences, observation and feedback. We then launch into each day and try to make the best of what we find! The art of good design is to provide a good conceptual model with good visibility, positive mapping back to functionality with strong feedback, and appropriate constraints to prevent error. There are many aspects to this work, and it affects customers as well as the employed operators within a process. A book the design team should read is *The Design of Everyday Things* (by Donald A. Norman, 1988, MIT Press), which covers this area in detail and provides much food for thought. An example of the nature of human error, and how it can be prevented, can be seen in the difficulties often experienced with simple things like doors. I have noted an instance at Belfast International Airport at the end of the passenger exit corridor. This has glass doors of approximately double width, the right-hand side of which is a single swing door with a handle. The other half of the 'opening' is two pieces of plain glass, with notices on the glass and two posts slightly in front. The majority of passengers dutifully exit down the corridor and veer towards the right, which looks like a door. In fact it is an emergency exit, which is normally locked, and a small notice says just that. The left-hand side is actually a pair of sliding doors activated by a detector and the notices on them say 'No entry', but from the other side. The conceptual model is – look for something like a door. This is backed up by the handle and the fact that the left-hand side is barricaded by the two posts, which are really there to protect the sides of the sliding doors from luggage trolleys. I have not witnessed any accidents; however, the effort of pushing a baggage trolley violently to the left at the last moment must surely be wasted effort and a result of poor design!

Science fiction writers have for many years pondered the ultimate fate of mankind within the automated processes of tomorrow, with a typically gloomy scenario as to the outcome, and it would seem almost a foregone conclusion that people have no part to play. Perhaps we will gradually but inextricably move towards a society where every aspect of any process with a potential for failure is removed from our lives. Whatever the eventual outcome, it will be increasingly necessary for businesses and process designers to answer the blunt question – 'What will people *do* in our new process?'

Since people are so varied and ultimately of limited reliability, it might seem a good idea to do away with humans altogether. However, there are points during many processes, particularly transactional and service examples, where the human element is vital. We like to talk and communicate, and the human–human interface is still preferable to machines, providing the intercourse also meets our needs for speed, efficiency, functionality and the like. People loathe waiting to see the doctor, but really like to chat once they are at the head of the queue! This aspect of human nature can be developed to considerable use, providing that both customer and 'process agent' are given the time and the right environment in which to work. For any service process design where customer and process agent meet 'head on', the challenge is to ensure that both parties are totally comfortable. In many hotels the check-in desk is both tall and long and often has a back room to which the staff frequently retreat. The desire to place barriers, both physical and ethereal, between the provider and the served indicates a large degree of discomfort stemming from inability, insecurity, overload and poor process design. Face-to-face communication is both arduous and rewarding. However, to be capable of effective delivery over long periods staff need to be constantly able and willing, which implies ability of self together with a fully supportive process. Customers too need the appropriate signals to ensure that they can enter, participate, and disengage from the interaction with ease. A good point to check is whether or not the employee (and customer) is actually in control of the process. Lack of control is a sure recipe for not wanting to become involved, and this often implies ownership and practical empowerment over the outcome of the process. If the check-in clerk has to allocate rooms to guests, but has no control over the supply of rooms, then frustration is the assured outcome. Other points to look for from the employee perspective are:

- staff knowledge/information – or easy access to it;
- accessibility – promoted by a balanced workload;
- responsiveness – the process is a pleasure to work in;
- ease of use – nothing is difficult to do; and
- safety – when things go wrong no one comes to harm, physical or emotional.

In the more advanced technological countries around the world there is a continued shift of employment away from manufacturing and into the service industry and many organizations now run call centres. The more proactive organizations have realized the benefits in encouraging active and individual-centred communication with the customer, leading in many cases to increased satisfaction, higher loyalty and even increased sales. This can only be achieved by a holistic design that fully engages both business and customer and realizes the requirements and expectations of all parties. The process designer of tomorrow, as well as designing performance at five to six sigma, will need to utilize to best effect the key resources of the people in the organization. This requires an attitude towards the design of processes wherein people can reside comfortably, operate freely, and contribute reliably in a way that purely functional machines and computers simply cannot.

SUMMARY

- Customers have a well-expressed desire for the utmost reliability from both products and services, and it is failure in all of the many forms and areas that is typically the major issue in any new commercial offering. An important part of the DFSS project must be to reduce the element of risk of:

  - failure to deliver to basic customer needs – suitability of purpose;
  - deviation from customer-defined targets and limits – robustness from variation;
  - failure to satisfy the customer at the point of delivery – reliability in use; and
  - any occurrence of catastrophic failure – stability of design.

- The nature of failure is insidious and often enshrined in the popular articulation of Murphy's Law, which can be expressed as:

  - if something can go wrong, it will;
  - when something does go wrong it has the potential to cause the greatest amount of damage; and
  - failure comes ultimately from the simplest cause.

- The best approach to eliminating and reducing the impact of failure is to start with an attitude that recognizes the existence and importance of failure and then to deal with the root causes that lead to it. Specifically the design project must look to:

  - reduce the frequency of occurrence of failure;
  - reduce the costly impact of failure;
  - eliminate the root cause for failure and defect to occur; and
  - prevent the effect of failure from spreading.

- A powerful tool to help identify and quantify failure is failure mode effect analysis (FMEA). This can be used for products, processes, design features and systems, and aims to rate numerically each failure mode against the compounded impact from:

  - severity of damage;
  - occurrence; and
  - non-likelihood of detection.

- FMEA is typically used many times during the life of the DFSS project and should be treated as a living document to be handed over to the process owner at the project close. The outcome of the FMEA work is normally a series of prioritized actions and in the design project these will concentrate heavily on designing out the root cause of failure from the product, service or process.

- The practice of robust design, where products, services and processes are free from variation, failure and defect, can learn a great deal from the ideas and current best practices in lean manufacturing and the Japanese approach to continuous incremental quality such as *kaizen*. This area often includes the elimination of waste (*muda*), absolute tidiness in production processes ('5 Ss'), failure-proofing (*poka yoke*) and rigid signalling control (*kanban*).

- The sevens wastes or *muda* should be actively removed by designing out the causes and designing in controls and features to prevent:

  - overproduction
  - waiting and delay
  - transport and communication
  - inappropriate processing
  - unnecessary inventory
  - unnecessary motion
  - defects.

- The Japanese are noted for their high regard for cleanliness and the use of '5 Ss' stresses the regular, effective and sustained removal of any form of disorder or untidiness in the workplace. Although this is typically used to keep a production process working at peak efficiency, the concepts should be embodied within the new design to avoid untidiness and to facilitate and enforce the '5 Ss' ideals:

  - *seiri* – clean-up and fix, tidy and everything working;
  - *seiton* – orderliness, a place for everything and everything in its place;
  - *seiso* – regular cleaning and checking;
  - *seiketsu* – standardization of both normal practice and exceptions; and
  - *shitsuke* – discipline with strong management support.

- Failure-proofing or *poka yoke* is the introduction of an (ideally) inexpensive device to warn or control when a failure arises. Failure can be the result of a mistake reaching the customer and becoming a defect, and the design process should actively incorporate every approach possible that will reduce or eliminate the incidence and effect of such mistakes and failures.

- The visual approach to supply-chain management promotes the idea of signalling control or *kanban* to actively pull products and resources through processes. Although this can be very effective at eliminating waste and error, it does require a high level of control and standardization, low defect rates and reasonably stable demand.

- People generate process errors through the inevitable human mistakes, which probably amounts to about 1 per cent failure at best when unaided by controls, machines or external agents. Such errors can be classified into the willing and the known, and good design needs to consider all four possible combinations. The most critical area is the mistake made by the employee or customer that is entirely accidental. Good design will assist people to avoid such mistakes by providing a good conceptual model, good visibility, positive mapping to functionality, strong feedback and appropriate constraints to prevent error.
- Designers of processes will have increasing need to consider the position of both customers and employees within the process, in order to provide a stable situation where people can be comfortable, operate freely and reliably and contribute real benefit.

EXERCISES

Consider a typical major domestic process about which you have direct experience, such as cooking a formal meal like 'family Sunday lunch' or a meal for a party.

1 How robust is this process? Can you recount experiences of unreliable delivery of a meal and determine the cause of failure? What is the general attitude toward failure in this process?
2 Complete a simple process map for your chosen example, and then develop an FMEA table with about thirty entries. Compute the risk priority number, and devise a list of actions to correct the process.
3 Use the concepts of *muda* and the '5 Ss' on both the design and the execution of the process. How well does the concept of 'lean' help with eliminating failure and error?
4 How much of the problem is due to human error and what steps can be taken to prevent this? What fail-safe devices could be introduced to effectively block the physical cause of human error and process failure? Make a list of any fail-safe devices already in use.
5 If you were completely redesigning the process involved in producing and serving a major meal, what substantial yet cost-effective changes could be made to eliminate failure? Extend this to the commercial launch of a new restaurant or fast-food outlet.

PART THREE

Practical Issues

CHAPTER NINE

Practical implementation

As well as the theory and application of the DFSS methodology and tools, there are a number of practicalities that need to be carefully considered by any organization seeking to take the Six Sigma design approach on board. Success in DFSS stems not simply from its application but also from the measure of how well the adopting organization integrates the whole philosophy and concept with already existing tactics for developing new products and services. This chapter is intended to cover the practical issues involved with inanimate objects and the following chapter will deal with practical issues involved with people.

The ability of Six Sigma as a methodology and metric to attack and solve problems hitherto seen as difficult causes a great deal of inspection and consideration. The question most frequently asked is 'What is new in Six Sigma?' In truth there is not a lot that is new, as many of the tools used for the task of process improvement have been in use in main- or sidestream quality movements for a good number of years if not decades. It can be very challenging to distil out the very essence of Six Sigma; however, two factors seem to predominate where Six Sigma has been applied and used successfully. First, the methodology and framework used is important, and weaker methodologies may achieve less than is desired. The approach of choice is DMAIC – *define* the problem, *measure* the critical factors, *analyse* the root causes, *improve* the situation, and then *control* the process. As a methodology that is much more than just a framework in which tools are used, this approach can be very successful in dealing with an extraordinarily large range of challenging situations. For almost any problem where something is not quite right, the DMAIC approach will seek out the vital elements of both problem and solution required to implement successful change and improvement. The growing evidence of experience also seems to be pointing to the fact that the precise tools used are not quite as important as the methodology. This is equivalent to suggesting that if you want a job done well, find workers who can identify the problem using a structured approach and let them select the toolkit with which to work.

In direct contrast, the design and implementation of the 'new' may well turn out to be the exact antithesis of this approach. Early projects working on new design show that the methodology is not the key element for success. Indeed, within diverse industries and applications, the one thing that seems to change most often is the overarching DFSS methodology itself. What remains static is the list of tools commonly applied – a few heavyweight monsters that shatter the difficult nut that is the creation of the bold and the new and yet in a measured and effective way. Tools to deal with customer needs analysis, design and simulation, evaluation, implementation and failure prevention are almost universally applied to a wide range of industries and design projects.

This, then, might well seem to be the secret of universal success in Design For Six Sigma, in almost direct contrast to the success in 'Improve For Six Sigma'. Retain the universality in the use of the tools, adapting only the minor aspects of the tool for the project, but mould and adapt the framework methodology to suit the exact needs of business, industry, project and moment. Only time and use will prove the validity of this statement; however, if over time it were shown to hold true, then it would certainly explain why practitioners of DFSS from differing organizations find a continuing need to reframe the methodology but not the tools!

The real challenge of DFSS in its practical application is to arrive at an *adaptive* methodology that fits the industry and project emphasis, yet incorporates all the necessary elements to ensure that customer, business and technical design each contribute to the full. There is a danger that the fundamentals of Six Sigma and good design will be lost with any adaptation and that all that is taken on board is a thin veneer that simply covers over the existing cracks. It is important, therefore, if the methodology is to evolve, that the organization makes adaptations within an even broader and static framework strategy for the introduction of the 'new'.

DFSS AS PART OF COMPANY STRATEGY

Whatever DFSS methodology is used in practice, it is best operated as part of a much larger corporate strategy for new product or service introduction, implying therefore a sound NPI (new product introduction) process into which the DFSS project neatly fits. Many larger manufacturing organizations do indeed have NPI processes; however, best practice is unlikely to extend to the smaller or to the service-related organizations. Difficulties will arise from the lack of strategy plans, from wholly prescriptive strategies, from plans that are too short term in view and where there is a lack of communication downwards or inwards. A good strategy is one that is regularly reviewed and kept up to date, covers the full planning term to perhaps ten years or more, is fluid and inventive, and is part of an ongoing communication link between customer, business and operational management. The company that regularly listens to customers and employees, adapts strategy to suit and then communicates back to both employee and customer is in a far better position to benefit from new products and services. Certainly the hard reality is that no new product or service should ever be considered except as an answer to a well-understood and documented business need.

The typical NPI strategy will require much work ahead of any DFSS project, but will often support far more than just the one project or undertaking. The corporate strategy plan should be fully integrated into long-term planning and can be used to spawn a succession of DFSS and smaller Six Sigma projects either in sequence or in parallel for a wide range of products and services. It is the owner of the NPI plan who effectively commissions and oversees any one DFSS project, whereas in Six Sigma such work is often the shared responsibility of business and process owner. Again, the NPI owner will receive the completed project work from the team and will probably also need to act as a neutral chairperson in all formal proceedings. For the larger DFSS project, the end of the formal teamwork will often be the start of a number of subsequent Six Sigma improvement projects, conducted to fine-tune and stabilize the newly introduced process. The choreography of a multitude of such small projects will again have to be undertaken as a planned whole rather than as a number of independent activities, since they will often cover many process owners where conflict of interest may undo much good work previously completed by the DFSS team.

To get DFSS launched for the company's first DFSS project, a sensible approach would be to ensure that a background understanding of Six Sigma is in place, together with a corporate strategy for the introduction of at least one new bold product or service. This is in contrast with the smaller 'excursion into design' project, which is effectively an extension to 'Six Sigma improvement' – the smaller project can be typically treated as design within Six Sigma. An effective proposal would be to start with a small but nevertheless important design project, use a first-rate team of experts and Six Sigma enthusiasts, work in an area of great potential, use stable technology, drive customer focus hard and strive to bring all parts of the business together. Aim for speed of execution and an early acceptance in the marketplace, provide delivery of real value beyond the normal expectation, and fully exercise the trial and development of a new DFSS methodology for use within the corporate NPI. From this point of view, the introduction of DFSS is a project in its own right, and not something to be undertaken lightly.

PROJECT CONTROL

Even the smaller DFSS project will be relatively large, and when projects reach a critical size the management of the entire undertaking needs efficient procedures and control. It is not the aim of this book to provide a full project management methodology, but rather to point out that design projects generally require wide-ranging skills and input, and thus the marshalling and controlling of resources, including time, are often paramount. To control any project requires a time plan and scheduling of resources, as well as effective monitoring, communication and regular reporting. The major risk is that the project will slip and extend in time, which may imply heavy cost. The minor risk is that the project will fail to deliver to expectations, although customers may regard this as equally or more important than time or cost. Project slippage in terms of scope-creep can be controlled effectively by the use of tollgates, as well as by constraining the design stage and performing a design freeze; an example project tollgate structure is provided in the Appendix. Very large DFSS projects will benefit from the acceleration of the work by paralleling some of the earlier stages; however, this is more likely to compromise the effectiveness of the work rather than gain time in the long run. The whole basis of DFSS is that considerable time and effort is saved after the commercial launch rather than during the pre-design work, and up-front time-saving will come from a firmer approach that removes any unnecessary delay and conflict. Good project control, therefore, will ensure that each aspect of the work is completed once and once only, with all the necessary parties meeting regularly and effectively. Time slippage is more difficult to contain, particularly if the early allowances are unreasonable and the business is unwilling to promote the early stages of customer research and concept development to the full.

The importance of project governance and design freeze can be seen in the many cases of failure where the design has been forcibly changed or allowed to continue with alteration well past the 'point of no return'. The Swedish warship *Vasa* was the largest of its day when launched in 1628, under the direction of King Gustavus Adolphus. Taking three years to build and funded directly by the coffers of the crown, the ship was in effect commissioned by the king, who took an overly keen interest in the outcome. It was built by a prominent Dutch ship builder and based on the then best-known design for sailing ships of this kind, in which the fundamental practicalities of the design and shape allowed for a given tonnage of cannon on only one armoury deck. Less than a few nautical miles into the maiden voyage a slight gust of wind toppled the ship, which, with all gun ports open, quickly took on water and sank to the bottom of Stockholm harbour. The cause of this capsize is quite clear in that the ship was top heavy: the king had insisted on two armoury decks and had adjusted the number and weight of cannon, making the design top heavy. The ship had been tested before launch, with a crowd of men rushing from side to side and clearly demonstrating that there was a major problem; however, the king was at war and waiting for his new ship. A salutary lesson for all 'senior management' when using the power of rank rather than know-how and reason to influence the delicate balance and intricacies of the technical design and overall project!

Design is not typically a practice undertaken successfully by committee, and the common reality is that the more people involved, the more protracted and potentially disappointing the outcome. Indeed, the practice of using teams for proactive design is clearly an approach adopted in more recent years as technical design becomes increasingly complex. In the days of Brunel and Stephenson, just one person undertook much of the design work and where a team was involved the effort was hierarchical, well controlled and divided logically into sections. Brunel was well known for undertaking almost all of the design work himself, leaving only the finishing to associates and subordinates. The almost only early exception in this respect was the temporary design of steam locomotives by a committee at the North Eastern Railway in 1883. Led by Henry Tennant (no relation to the author), a committee designed a locomotive of which 20 were built and were well regarded by drivers and firemen. A contributory factor to the success of the design was that, rather than designing from scratch, existing components were brought together and rapidly modified to form a composite whole.

Successful design today requires a great deal of productive co-operation as well as the effective reuse of existing best practice. This implies 'design by committee' and therefore clearly requires some form of overall control and governance by effectively just one person. If a steering committee does oversee the project, then it is best formed by a three-way split between business, design and customer (typically by the 'quality' function, also acting as guardians of the DFSS methodology). Ultimately, however, someone has to take overall charge of taking decisions and funding the work, and neutrality and lack of partisanship in this role are characteristics to look for!

PILOT TESTING AND EVALUATION

The formal task of testing can be divided into two parts – design testing and post-design verification. Design testing should begin with the define stage and progress through to the design freeze. It should be concerned with ensuring that the design meets customer and business requirements. Post-design verification of the processes as well as the product must take place before commercialization. There can be no doubt that a major concern in any design project is the elapsed time between idea and commercial launch. What can be by far the most valuable stage, and the most easily skipped over, is that of testing and pilot trial. With what amounts to *almost* a product to hand, it is very tempting to go straight to commercial sales with either 'public' testing or no testing at all. Of course, testing to exhaustion before launch would mean serious delay. What is needed is a formal testing stage that is both effective and yet well contained.

Two points regarding pilot trials are worth noting. First, pilot testing is carried out to verify the new offering and to iron out slight wrinkles and practicalities. It is certainly not part of the ongoing design programme and any post-design-freeze test should have no (or very little) backward impact on the primary design. It is far better to allow any such impact to become part of the input for the next-generation project. Second, testing should be carried out to show that the product or service *fails*, rather than to show that it does not. Every product or service will fail, but only under certain conditions. Failure in the broadest sense includes capability failure, and taking any product, service or process to the limit of capability will demonstrate clearly what the ultimate commercial performance will actually be. This is again a matter of attitude and of balance: the attitude must be to evaluate fully the commercial offering but not to compromise the effectiveness of the project at such a late stage.

Since pre-commercial testing will engender a real cost and overhead to the project, the team must consider the full value of piloting for:

- hard testing of the product/service in a real environment;
- full loading beyond that expected for the worst-case scenario;
- the rapid investigation of alternatives with fine-tuning; and
- piloting run back to back with marketing and promotion as well as in-house training and a phased commercial launch.

The size of any competent pilot study will clearly depend on the product and service offering; however, the aim must be to ensure an environment that mimics real life to the full. If the product/service is a new hotel with 100 rooms, then the acid test must be to have 100 'guests' arrive late afternoon and actually stay the night. In reality this will be scaled down, but in doing so the risk is that parts of the systems that go to make up the hotel service will be underloaded. Critical parts of the system, such as check-in and room service, should be piloted at full capacity, even if only for a short time. It is often only when full capacity is reached or even exceeded that all the little problems come to the surface, and are naturally the times when the company is least able to cope or rectify faults! Piloting the hotel entrance lobby with a full-size model and real people provides an excellent opportunity to rapidly evaluate and test two or three carefully prepared alternatives. To make such testing a reality often requires a mock-up well ahead of the final construction of a new building, and so the proactive use of something like a large aircraft hangar will provide the space to build the model and to use and evaluate performance effectively.

Naturally, the use of people from outside is in preference to inviting company workers and members of the design and project team, who will have a tendency to tread far too softly to act out anything close to reality! Getting the most out of expensive pilot studies can include the use of the study for staff training, marketing and promotion, and possibly an integrated full public launch. Sending a product out to people to 'test' in their homes, or getting people to 'test' a new hotel or restaurant before opening night, should provide plenty of potentially 'free' publicity. Such publicity can apply equally well to internal staff as to external customers, since major change will need buy-in of new technology, processes and procedures. Involving employees is always a good idea for major new initiatives, and should be carried out throughout the entire project, but certainly the staff involved should be some of the first and not the very last to see and experience the new offering.

PROCESS CONTROL AND SPC

No DFSS project simply ends with the commercial launch, since this is really just the beginning of the full life cycle of the new product or service. Just as in Six Sigma, the objective is to hand over the project to a process owner, who will take the business responsibility for ongoing process control and maintenance of performance. The complexity here is that for the new design there is a multitude of entirely new processes and customer performance metrics to consider, not just one or two. The new design will typically encompass a range of products and services across many processes and will need a fair degree of continuing process improvement. 'Measure as you mean to go on' should be a motto throughout the entire project, since it will be the responsibility of the team to develop within the design the appropriate metrics and measurement systems to enable effective process ownership to take place. The critical to quality (CTQ) metrics developed during the early stages are a good place to start and need to be built into the final product, service and process to ensure ongoing measurement and monitoring of direct customer quality. This work must therefore include the design of data collection and analysis, together with reporting and feedback. Direct customer feedback can come from sales teams and marketing, point of sale, vendors, warrantee and registration cards, service agreements and repairs, although much of this is common in any company with or without Six Sigma. The fresh emphasis that Six Sigma brings is one of appropriate measurement of process performance, and early Six Sigma improvement projects will often suffer from an acute lack of good data with which to work. Most organizations measure too little or the wrong things; however, there is always a risk of unnecessary blanket measuring, and measurement data are indeed expensive to collect and process. What constitutes a good metric is only half the story, since poor data collection practice can remove almost any use even from good measures. Certainly it is at the point at which a new process is being designed that the future measurement system can be most effectively devised and integrated. Rather than struggling with the difficulty of determining what makes for a good measure, the design team is better served by gaining direct experience of the data collection issues faced in typical Six Sigma improvement projects. This alone is one very good reason for not beginning major DFSS projects until the organization has a good core understanding of Six Sigma in the first place. Another point to note is that the most effective measurement system is invisible and automated, right through to the production of control charts and corporate dashboards. Control charts are excellent tools for process control; however, such practices are foreign to the service industry and they are only likely to be used to any effect or at all if they are automatically generated. This imposes a considerable burden on the information system that will underpin the new commercial product or service, whereas the typical approach in writing new IT systems is to leave the 'reporting' to last. The process owner, and there may well be several new process owners for the larger DFSS project, will not want much more than a handful of simple computer screens on the corporate intranet, each showing a dashboard with process performance indicated in the most appropriate way. Such reporting needs should be negotiated at the early define stage and incorporated into the project, where they will certainly influence the selection and development of the technology and information systems used, if not the design itself. The hard fact that can often be difficult to convey to disinterested parties is that, if the customer sees quality as an issue of how long it takes to check in, then that measurement of check-in time must be collected, processed and reported for each and every customer. Further benefit will be gained from rolling up the whole range of measures to a single dashboard and in automatically maintaining an ongoing process sigma-metric value for each CTQ. Discussions with all the interested stakeholders may also shed light on potential future projects beyond the immediate needs of the DFSS project scope, and it may be possible to collect additional measurement data at little or no extra cost for future use.

As well as setting up the data collection and processing system for the new processes, the DFSS design process itself needs some form of process control and evaluation to ensure that it is working well to meet its own customer requirements. It is certainly in the interest of the sponsoring organization to see how effective the new design methodology is at providing a better result, and since every DFSS project is itself a process, it can be improved upon, but only if the right data are collected first. It might be typical of the organization just to measure project costs, time and resources; however, the Six Sigma approach implies due consideration of the key metrics that matter to customer quality and more emphasis should be given to input rather than output measurements. It will be a challenge to effect good process measurement on the design project for the very first attempt at DFSS; however, it will not be easy to demonstrate better performance if the existing approach has not been benchmarked first! As a minimum the DFSS team needs to take measurements similar to those in current use and then to look for better project process metrics as part of the ongoing improvement of the design process.

COMBINING DFSS WITH OTHER APPROACHES

For a variety of reasons DFSS must be deeply integrated into both the culture and the structure of an organization. This needs to work at least at two levels: that of corporate strategy for quality and excellence; and that of practical integration within the existing approaches to design. Although relatively few organizations operate a recognizable and effective NPI process, almost every company of any size will have some form of quality, IT, R&D, and sales and marketing departments. These departments, perhaps above all others, will have the greatest concentration of customer focus and creative activity or need, and this can lead to problems with the introduction of DFSS. Some organizations have accepted the formal rigour and structure of the methodology with enthusiasm; however, this is not always the case and the pure methodology is unlikely to fit every situation or need perfectly. The plain fact is that effective design relies on the input, support and co-operation of many departments, each of which has a slightly different agenda, focus, practice and culture. The most efficient design process is one that embodies almost concurrent activity, certainly in respect of the various inputs required from marketing, R&D, IT and so on. Any practical application of DFSS that is going to be substantially more than just surface veneer must unite both corporate vision and strategy with the practical expression of quality, customer focus and conceptual and technical design.

It might be possible to force an appearance of unity from all major stakeholders; however, only by carefully orchestrating the key players will the organization achieve true unity and efficiency. There is little point in having DFSS as the 'pet methodology' of just the IT department and sales, or perhaps the R&D department and quality, since discord elsewhere will nullify many of the major objectives. The business must commission and support, marketing must identify and promote, sales ultimately has to sell, R&D must create and inspire, quality (typically) must champion the customer, and IT or design often has to tie all the technical loose ends together and 'cut code'. What possible success could ever come from such a discordant group without a conductor to lead it? The danger is not that each segment is lacking any form of structured approach or model to work with, but rather that each continues to search out the most appropriate model for its sole use, thus maintaining a degree of discord across these disparate departments. DFSS is about concurrent co-operation, and it behoves the organization to actively unite the various models and approaches, if not completely on a practical plane then certainly at a strategic level.

ISO 9000 AND EXCELLENCE MODELS

Design For Six Sigma requires not just good design but also a strategy of excellence in customer-focused quality for the continual pursuit of new products and services, each with a successful commercial launch. At the strategic level this implies a need for some form of (quality) management to promote, facilitate and ensure that good practice is sought and maintained. A very popular approach to one practical expression of quality strategy is the ISO 9000 accreditation, which provides a degree of assurance that an organization has in place the structure for an effective quality management system (QMS). There are indeed many benefits to be gained from ISO 9000 accreditation; however, in itself it is absolutely no guarantee of either good performance or delivery of quality to the customer. Too many organizations accept either ISO 9000 or a similar tactic as sound practice and concrete evidence of the expression of excellence in quality, when it is more likely to be the end result of sufferance towards a demanding supplier. The basic quality management principles enshrined into almost every model of QMS today require that the organization clearly demonstrate:

- customer focus
- purposeful leadership
- involvement of (all) people
- a process (management) approach
- holistic systems thinking
- continual improvement
- fact-based decisions
- symbiotic supplier relationships.

The Six Sigma approach not only embodies every single one of these principles; it also extends a practical methodology that both facilitates and promotes these ideals, as well as encouraging active participation from every single employee. This is the powerful differentiator between a simplistic accreditation of a QMS and the practical expression of continuous improvement that is customer focused and uses data-driven analysis to underpin fact-based decisions. What use is a QMS that takes a 'snapshot' of processes in time through the periodic audit of staff? What is really required is a *culture* that says 'We are customer focused, we have a vision of excellence, we lead and involve everyone everyday in every way, we think processes and systems, we use data and facts to make reasoned decisions, and we promote mutually beneficial relationships with suppliers and customers.' From this point of view, the Six Sigma philosophy and practice is a profound supporter of all that is deemed good in world-class quality, and therefore it should be neither conceptually nor practically difficult to integrate Six Sigma and any other QMS.

The common ground between Six Sigma and the 'typical' QMS is clearly a form of continuous and customer-focused improvement, whereas the extension in application from 'continual improvement' to 'exponential new design' is a real challenge, and one that must be met head-on if any QMS is to extend to this area. Design does indeed work 'better' and certainly with greater ease when undertaken by a process of incremental and almost continuous small steps and refinements. This does not, however, provide either the customer or the business with what they really require and ultimately hinders the ability of the organization occasionally but rapidly and effectively to launch new products and services in the marketplace. The requirement of commercially effective design is that it is exponential, radically challenging the current limits to performance, but in a way that still delivers excellent quality to the customer. This demands a subtle shift in the QMS to incorporate such ideals as 'bold', 'risk-taking', 'exploratory', and the like and yet be measured and effectively risk-free. A good QMS for the design team will stress that:

> We aggressively seek out new products and services that radically alter the accepted limits to process capability and performance, and yet deliver reliable excellence and quality to our customers in a way that can be accurately measured and assessed.

Perhaps the element of Six Sigma that is for many people the most difficult to attune to is the lack of formal accreditation or standard approach that can be neatly boxed, audited and then certified. This now extends not only to the methodology, but also to the tools and practitioner training, as if audit and control (although important and useful in their place) ever produced excellence and creativity on their own! Maybe, in some curious way, this is the one element that actually works to the favour of the customer. The word 'continuous' appears in many QMS manuals; however, the process of documentation, audit and accreditation is rarely continuous, and often freezes the moment the ink is dry on the certificate. The needs of the customer, and the challenges of the competitive marketplace, are certainly continuous in their change. Six Sigma (if done correctly) lays down a defined goal of perfection as set by the customer. This will certainly need continuously updating; therefore a culture founded on the Six Sigma concept is more likely to promote and facilitate the practical expression of sound quality management. It must surely be almost impossible to 'audit' culture, and the integration of Six Sigma, or any formal QMS, together with 'design of the new' should retain a high degree of bravado and flexibility as well as formal rigour and audit.

There is a growing number of business excellence models, aimed at establishing some form of appropriate management framework that provides a strong directional lead towards an end goal of notable distinction. The European Foundation for Quality Management (EFQM) has developed a business excellence model that promotes:

- leadership and constancy of purpose
- management by processes and facts
- people development and involvement
- continuous learning, innovation and improvement
- results orientation
- customer focus
- partnership development
- public responsibility.

Again the foundation principles can be seen to match closely with the common ground of best practice in this area, perhaps with a stronger focus on a practical demonstration through certain key areas. The aim here is to provide more of a practical tool than a conceptual ideal, which will assist with the measurement of current position and gaps in performance, and perhaps kindle potential solutions. Indeed, the application of Six Sigma methods and tools might be one such practical solution, yet with a certain element and contribution of strategy and quality management of its own. Some companies take Six Sigma as the embodiment of their entire quality system, yet others position Six Sigma within and subservient to a more fashionable QMS. There is an argument for using Six Sigma as the overall strategy and driver for a culture that leads to an expression and practice of all that is good in quality and excellence, which can then be governed and audited by means of some form of 'standard' QMS. In this respect Six Sigma is probably the dog that wags the tail, whereas ISO and the like are tails that may attempt to wag the dog. If Six Sigma is simply seen as a methodology, then it may become too neatly packaged and contained within some other inappropriate QMS, whereas Six Sigma has often demonstrated sufficient structure and substance to act as both methodology and framework QMS in its own right.

If there is indeed a secret to be found within DFSS that will unleash a torrent of untapped wonder and potential, then it must reside in the unification of the disparate groups required for the design and development of a new product or service. The 'Dilbert' cartoon is an excellent parody of engineering (technical designers) versus management, secretaries, sales and marketing and the rest of the company. The sad fact is that all too often managers design, designers fill in office secretarial paperwork, secretaries sell, salespeople conduct market analysis and marketing manage the company. Simply shifting this back into synchronized step will not solve the problem: what is required is a unity of purpose and strategy across each of the contributing departments, yet retaining enough individuality to ensure sound application to the specific tasks and needs of each group.

THE IT ENVIRONMENT

A number of information systems designers and developers firmly believe that they execute the ultimate expression of pure design since they 'create something out of nothing'. This is indeed a very misguided realization of this singular design activity and must be a fundamental cause of many of the problems within IT development today. The person who creates something out of nothing is just a randomly inspired artist who applies paint to a blank canvas with neither purpose nor direction. What anyone in this position in IT should say, and this also applies to anyone in design generally, is that they 'create something of (commercial) worth out of a customer specification'. Even better still if the artist were to begin with a well-defined pallet of paints rather than nothing at all! The requirement for the practical design of software is clearly to use form and function from past and present work (the reuse of code) and to ensure design for both business and customer in a well-structured and efficient way.

The failure to apply structure, rigour and strategy as well as practical common sense to the development of software is not one-sided, but includes customer and business alike. Over many years I have created a great deal of systems design and code, most of which was 'out of nothing' and most of which ultimately amounted to and contributed nothing. A complete customer database and reporting structure, created because of a perceived need, was unused and eventually scrapped after collecting data of incredible value for five years from behind the scenes. A major addition to an existing system, to deal with expected new business from colour photocopiers, was again created out of a 'sales hunch' rather than a true and measured need, and was used for just five deals in five years, never returning any commercial benefit. The lessons for the IT design team are profound. Yes, design is creative, but no, it must never be out of nothing, from nothing or indeed for nothing. Often far removed from the end user, and with little control historically of either specification or development, IT systems have gained a justifiable reputation for the development of something the customer never really wanted in the first place. Here is an excellent place to introduce DFSS; however, much work will be required to change both culture and practice. The necessity, just as in the DFSS methodology itself, is for structure, rigour and a strategy focused on delivering to the business requirements via the customer needs. One of the several and more structured attempts to formalize the process of design within IT is the Software Engineering Institute (SEI) capability maturity model (CMM). This outlines a framework for the development of software that considers not only the product, the software itself, but also the process by which the software product is developed and delivered. Rather than stemming from a purist ideal or philosophy, the model contains recognizable levels of practical and outward expressions of excellence in software development and design. These levels relate to the process as much as to the organization, and are graded as follows:

1 Initial – an *ad hoc* process
2 Repeatable – basic project management
3 Defined – documented, standardized and integrated
4 Managed – process and products are measured and quantitatively understood
5 Optimizing – continuous process improvement.

This is the beginning of enlightenment toward the view that software development (which is certainly a key part of design today, and will become increasingly so) is not only a design process but also one that needs continuous improvement. Naturally the use of technology, particularly information processing and computers of one type or another, is set to become a mainstay of the commercial offering in both new products and services. The advent of the electronic revolution, with mobile and electronic commerce now a mass reality, clearly modifies the capability of many processes in ways that almost defy belief. There is no reason why any supportive design process such as IT should not itself undergo due scrutiny and change.

There is a very strong similarity between CMM and DFSS in both expression and purpose, and the use of process metrics to understand and thus enable continuous process improvement is common to both. Any debate as to which is the greater of the two is of little real benefit, but it is worth pointing out that commercial design today requires technology, particularly software, and no large DFSS project will flourish without IT. It is also true that both ideals begin from slightly different positions and a merger between software project and DFSS project will often require much compromise and co-operation. DFSS is, perhaps for the moment, stronger in customer focus and business commitment, whereas CMM and the like focus on practical expression more than strategic empathy. DFSS is about the embodiment of commercial design, from business and customer through to production and control, whereas CMM perhaps focuses more on the immediate and challenging task of overhauling the software design process. In practical terms some organizations may find that a direct adoption of a DFSS-based design process will achieve as much as the CMM would, perhaps with stronger Six Sigma cultural links to the rest of the business. Alternatively, in going directly for something like the CMM, both IT and the organization as a whole will typically encounter a great deal of support from any existing in-house Six Sigma experience and culture. The experience of witness shows that much effort is required to blend IT and Six Sigma, and the DFSS approach often contributes strongly in the first three stages, whereas the IT function holds court for the technical design. Neither can complete without the other, but this can be just a marriage of convenience rather than a matchmaker's dream. It is often necessary to undertake one or even two weeks of workshops, detailing the practical expression of the methodology in use by both teams, followed by a joint evaluation and formal merger. In many cases it could be argued that DFSS applied to IT projects has compromised and shifted from a stance on the moral high ground; however, the moral must be that practical compromise is much better than a stand-off between two giants. The design project simply cannot live isolated from IT, and IT needs to join the ranks of those who recognize the power of the formal process and of continuous improvement, supported by metrics, structure and rigour. However, in the battleground of compromise and merger neither side should forget either the business or the customer!

MARKETING AND SALES

These, perhaps completely separate, departments are a crucial area for productive customer contact as well as supporting new product instigation and commercial launch. They will frequently play an important part in any NPI and thus can contribute a great deal to the DFSS project, as well as benefiting themselves from a more structured and focused approach to the instigation of new products and services. Integration and adaptation of DFSS in this area has potential for major payback since it will cover the full project life cycle from initial concept development to final launch. Since there is a great deal of customer contact in this field, the Six Sigma philosophy of customer and business focus will not be new, although the concept of a structured and rigorous process for the development of new ideas through to final entities may be received with caution.

Salespeople are among the most creative and ebulliently communicative within any organization, and can often provide valuable input and contribution to any Six Sigma project, particularly for DFSS. Such people are frequently privy to and understanding of details about customers that cannot be easily captured in formal analytical surveys, and will often have a very good idea of what the market both needs and is willing to accept. Naturally, sales and marketing people rarely have a sparkling talent or the patience for technical detail and design. However, combine a salesperson with a technical designer, get them working together fruitfully, and there is an increased likelihood that the combination will come up with an idea for something new that can be both built and sold. The motto for practical and successful commercial enterprise is this: 'Do not market something that you cannot design, and do not design something that you cannot market.' In short, real achievement is underpinned by getting each and every practitioner in their individual field to undertake their job, in unison, as part of a working team. Salespeople make very good team members, as do marketing people, and with care a DFSS approach within a Six-Sigma-enabled organization can work well across these areas. The challenge is to introduce elements of measurement, analysis and verification to screen out wild and inappropriate ideas where there is a tendency to sell unsuitable products. A further challenge is to reduce the often considerable amount of handoffs and delay in the whole process of marketing and selling. Typically these areas may have hands-on productive time of less than 15 per cent, with new ideas bouncing back and forth between people and departments for months if not years. Since DFSS is about a team working together rapidly and effectively, it may be necessary to first process-map and improve the new product development, marketing and sales processes!

RESEARCH AND DEVELOPMENT

The full spectrum of R&D activities is indeed wide-ranging, passing from highly stereotyped boffins in white coats to a more pragmatic group that can make almost anything work using sealing wax and string, often incorporating elements of the 'Heath Robinson' genre. Pure R&D should be positioned at the very start of DFSS projects, even perhaps well outside of the mainstream activity and typically as part of the NPI process for development of new concepts for business solutions. In enjoying membership of a more formal structure and with strong monitoring and feedback, the R&D function might be better introduced and employed within the DFSS methodology itself as part of the controlled stages for conceptual development and design implementation. The difference between the two positions is more a matter for the practical realization of what is after all a very creative activity, with a shift of position from 'front' to 'in the middle' actually affording the R&D department a chance to acquire feedback from engineers, designers and customers as well as the business. Research can be very dry and a more focused viewpoint as part of the larger group will require and deliver a sharper business focus, although this position and information may not always be popular!

My father worked for a time with the early Rank xerography photocopiers in the early 1960s, often providing technical support on site trying to make the machines do what the salesperson had promised the customer they would. The first machines to be produced clearly had an unsure marketplace and considerable incentive was provided to the sales team to sell proactively. Such was the bonus that a young but enterprising salesman, who managed to sell three machines in three months, netted a salary equal to that of the senior design manager who had overseen the entire commercial development of the xerography project. Naturally this caused a great deal of resentment, but still today leaves unanswered the perplexing question of who should in fact be paid more and who less. Without R&D there are no new principles or new technologies to underpin the new products of tomorrow. Without design and development there are no new working prototypes, without manufacturing and engineering there are no new products to sell, and yet without any actual sales there is no new money in the bank. The question of just who, or more rightly, which department, is more worthy in the pursuit of excellence for the commercial 'new' (as opposed to the academic search of the 'new') must be the hardest question to answer. In an almost glib reply the truth must be 'the customer', since if the new photocopier was that good at meeting a customer need, and thus sold outstandingly well, then everyone else in the business clearly benefited. It is when the customer says 'no thanks' to the new offering that the worry should really begin. The ultimate challenge for DFSS is to bring together the necessary skills and contributions of a very wide team, and this is a challenge relating to the management of people.

SUMMARY

● Success of DFSS requires the use of a well-defined set of tools, within an adaptive methodology. Business success in adopting DFSS therefore requires a wide framework strategy for the introduction and development of new products and services.

- DFSS must be treated as part of a successful corporate strategy for new product introduction (NPI). Sound strategies are those that are regularly reviewed, cover the longer term, and are fluid and inventive and well communicated both from and to customers and employees.

- Control is a key aspect for successful DFSS projects, which are typically 'design by committee' and where 'one person' must ensure sound governance as well as effective scheduling, communication and reporting. The use of tollgates aids the prevention of scope-creep, time slippage and poor focus and reporting.

- Pilot testing and evaluation before commercial launch is an important part of final testing, although it should not be seen as having a major influence on the design itself. Although it can be time-consuming and expensive to conduct, real-life testing provides the opportunity to:

  - undertake testing in a real environment;
  - test under load to verify process capability at failure;
  - rapidly investigate and fine-tune alternative solutions; and
  - include more effective training, marketing and a phased launch.

- The DFSS project does not end with project close, as each new process must be handed over to one or more (potentially new) process owners. To enable effective ongoing monitoring of performance, the basic CTQs need to be continually maintained as measurements collected, appropriately analysed and displayed using statistical process control. Additional measurements for future Six Sigma project work may also be needed. The onus will be on the project team to devise and integrate an appropriate metric system into the design of the new processes. This approach should also be extended to measuring and reporting on the performance of the design process itself.

- The DFSS project team should include all the departments that will contribute towards the final product and service, and it is important that the DFSS approach is integrated into the company structure and culture, particularly for the IT, R&D, marketing and sales departments. DFSS can be integrated with or alongside many existing approaches, but needs to work at both the strategic and the practical level. A number of practical or strategic frameworks exist to guide towards excellence in quality management, which in summary typically promote:

  - purposeful leadership with a constancy of purpose;
  - management by process with a results orientation;
  - customer focus and a systems approach;
  - management and decisions based on facts and data;
  - continual improvement, learning and innovation;
  - involvement and development of all staff; and
  - mutually beneficial partnerships and public responsibility.

- The particular challenges involved in integrating DFSS with other departments and approaches include promoting a more structured process of formal design and development, together with a strong customer focus and the use of measurements to improve both product and design process. Efficiency in commercial design will come when the many often disparate skills are brought together to form a highly concurrent and co-operative team with a common methodology.

CHAPTER TEN

Management and people

No amount of planning, structure, rigour and customer focus will deliver the perfect design project unless the organization fully utilizes a project team with just the right mix of personalities, skills and knowledge base. A critical element in the success of DFSS in each of the stages is a willingness for pragmatic change, and either lacklustre or overbearing attitudes will quickly stifle creativity and progress. An important part of DFSS therefore is the ability to manage project teams and creative designers, and yet remain within the boundaries laid down for the project by the business ownership. Team composition and management is important in Six Sigma, but takes on a far greater importance in DFSS simply because of the creative nature and larger size of the project and tools used. In many companies the Six Sigma Black Belts are also known as 'change agents'; indeed one or two companies dispense with 'Black Belt' and refer to the Six Sigma practitioners as just 'agents', secret or otherwise! Typically the significance of every aspect of Six Sigma becomes magnified within DFSS and the requirement for change agents now becomes a need for 'change activists' – people who make big things happen fast, yet in a controlled, considered and measured way.

This is not simply a matter of telling the team members to be good change agents or change activists; it requires a culture and attitude towards change, progress and the customer that pervades the entire organization. It is one thing to say 'this project is important'; it is another matter altogether to actually mean it and demonstrate so through daily actions. This chapter is titled 'Management *and* people' and not 'Management *of* people'. The difference is vast.

TEAM SKILLS AND TRAINING

It is important to identify and fully satisfy the need for a sound skill set and training within the project team. Typical project structure will vary from being either slightly to being very different from that of a 'standard' Six Sigma project and the larger DFSS projects may require two or more teams (conceptual and technical design) to run semi-concurrently. Expect as a minimum a team of five or six, extending to a composite group of perhaps twenty or more. In the very large projects the work can be neatly divided into sub-groups, making individual team composition limited to a better five or six but requiring well-defined interaction between the separate teams. Whilst smaller projects will close within six months to one year, the larger projects will run on for several years and it is to be expected that members will continually join and leave the group over that time. There will be a degree of fluidity in team composition that will necessitate ongoing training and team management, as well as a corporate culture to accept change even down to the daily experience of the project group. A key issue during the life of the project is the retention of knowledge and experience within the group memory; the development of a team handbook containing all the facts and figures that everyone needs to know can be very useful. Beyond this an appropriate balance for the annotation of meetings and record keeping is required since too little will allow vital detail to slip, whereas too much will blunt creativity and pace.

The tools used in DFSS are small in number but very large in application and may be used quite infrequently. Repeated 'just in time' training is often required, supplied and supported by a small number of key experts such as Master Black Belts (MBB). The DFSS MBB is a Six Sigma expert and trainer/coach, but with additional training and expertise in the DFSS tools, as well as a passion for creativity and change. Such people should also have a good grounding in some form of technical design as well as the core business of the organization. Teams need to contain a good mix of people, including:

- Six Sigma experts, often one or more Master Black Belts and Black Belts
- business experts, including directors or senior operational managers
- customer experts, perhaps sales, marketing or customer service agents
- technical experts in the particular field of development
- creative experts and designers, and perhaps also 'team facilitators'.

It is also a good idea to include people from the widest possible range of the base organization, particularly people from the actual area or product under development. Bringing in people from a senior business level achieves a high degree of status for the project as well as a great deal of business acumen, and helps build bridges to the new process owners. It is not a good idea to include everyone with a stakeholder interest, since such people will clearly have at least some agenda to make future life easy for themselves! Such people should, however, be included in a larger circle of all the parties invited to discussions and reporting meetings. Communication needs to be two-way – outwards from the project to the business and inwards from the business to the project. The project tollgate reviews can be informal or formal, depending on the size and importance of the project; however, it is clear that the communication of important detail should not be left until these meetings. As a more formal list, the distinct groups who will play an active role in the project management will include:

- the business leadership
- project leader
- process owner(s)
- Master Black Belt
- Black Belt(s)
- team members, and others.

Training requirements will certainly be much greater than for Six Sigma for a number of reasons, not least because of the more complex and technical subject matter involved. With such a broader spectrum of team membership it is highly likely that the individual past experience of Six Sigma will vary, and a good starting point is to draw the group together with an introductory training session. It is to be assumed that the core DFSS team will be full time for the entire duration of the project; only smaller projects are the exception to this rule. Bringing the team together for training therefore also helps with forging a working team from the disparate membership, and this does take both time and effort. Typical DFSS training revolves around a team attending one week of theory interspersed with project workshops; however, this may need to be fronted by basic Six Sigma training first. Specialist training for the particular subject areas is also useful and can cover individual tools as well as more esoteric subjects such as innovation and creativity. The full list of required training might therefore include all of the following:

- Six Sigma training – theory and practice
- team-building skills and training
- project management, including fiscal and resource management
- DFSS methodology structure
- specific tool training:

- benchmarking
- customer survey and analysis
- quality function deployment
- failure mode effect analysis
- simulation and modelling

- innovation and creativity skills
- reporting and presentation skills.

All of this should be regarded as a real and positive investment by the organization and certainly not as an expense with dubious return. For the initial and large projects, training will involve two or even three one-week stints, with extra training over the project lifespan. Once the organization as well as the individual has adopted the basic skills, future projects will clearly require less formal training with perhaps infrequent refresher courses. It should be noted, however, that sending teams to DFSS-specific training, where the majority of members have no prior experience of Six Sigma, will result in confusion and a dilution of impact. DFSS is an extension to Six Sigma, both tools and ideals, and the basic groundwork of Six Sigma theory and practice must be completed first. Ideally no member of the DFSS team will attend without having first-hand experience of at least one successful Six Sigma project.

As well as considering the requirements of the whole team and the corporate body, the individual within DFSS needs to display the characteristics of a proactive change activist. Aggressive change and innovation require many strengths, all of which extend well beyond the confines of the individual to a wider group and so the characteristics of change must be seen in the total environment around each person. What must be sought is a lucid demonstration of:

- clear focus and objectives
- motivation and leadership
- confidence and trust
- membership of an inclusive team
- empowering communication, both speaking and listening
- self-worth and self-esteem
- strength and stamina.

These are all 'soft skills' and may well contrast very sharply with technical and formal design! However, it is only with a clear objective, with strong motivation and motivational leadership as well as supporting trust and confidence that people can step forward boldly to promote change. Productive teamwork can be extraordinarily powerful in what can be achieved, but the secret lies within comfortable membership and full inclusion, where self-worth and self-esteem as well as effective communication flourish. Communication is as much about listening as it is about speaking, and it can be quite worrying to see how little of either actually takes place at committee meetings! Personal strength and stamina is important too, since a great deal of personal and group energy will be required to expedite productive innovation and change.

The greatest component in the corporate toolkit used to advance new products and services is quite simply a team of change activists. Such people lead themselves and can often be both individually and collectively the bane of more stoic management styles. If an organization is at all interested in developing, acquiring and then retaining such people, it must place change and activism at the core of the culture and practice, and this means starting with the corporate leaders.

THE BUSINESS–CUSTOMER CONFLICT

Three hundred years ago the majority of the UK population lived in small rural communities. Transport was by horse and cart or carriage and often took days. Other forms of communication mostly did not exist, medical knowledge was primitive, science was at an early stage and commerce was restricted mainly to cottage industry. From then to now the elapsed time spans only four complete lifetimes and yet the change experienced by anyone during just one life is simply astonishing. However, the personal change that accompanies anyone from their early twenties to the grave can be very limited and typically in later years the desire is to avoid assiduously any form of personally experienced change. As well as the natural and inherent personal need to evade change, there is also a strong corporate need to do so, and the management structures of many companies simply build walls and barriers around their own discrete business functions. One of the easiest barriers to erect is the one that seems to form quite habitually between business and customer. Indeed, many companies would be quite happy to continue without any customers at all and might even perform better as a result!

There is an astonishing potential for conflict between the needs of the business and those of the customer, and this conflict is rightly the preserve of the corporate management. In DFSS the aim is to incorporate into the project plan every single customer – including employees, stakeholders and shareholders, regulatory bodies, end users and consumers. With such a large input of often competing, compelling and primitive needs, it seems almost impossible to please everyone completely, and typically it is the business that has the final say, perhaps with a tendency to overly manage customer expectations as a result. One of the greatest challenges within DFSS is the need for a change in attitude towards the customer from company management and those in positions of control and authority. The direction of any one organization is not just happenstance or the whim of the customer, but rather it is selected and executed through a chain of senior directors and managers who act out the embodiment of the corporate mission statement in their daily lives. The way in which any one company generates, selects and then promotes new concepts and ideas for products and services is fashioned through the corporate culture and leadership, just as much if not more so than it is through the corporate design methodology. Attitude and culture can both promote and hinder change, sometimes depending on the outcome of a few chosen words or the simplest of actions. Change inevitably incorporates an element of risk and if either the corporate or personal body fails both to accept and manage a degree of risk associated with the customer and product or service, then change will simply not take place.

The word 'entrepreneur' is often taken to mean a business person or adventure capitalist, and typically implies personal and business exposure to a considerable degree of financial risk. Good design is about excellence in satisfying customer needs and requirements, which may mean exposure to an assortment of risks when the design becomes a commercial undertaking for profit. Business management of necessity requires risk management and fiscal governance, but can become far too much a matter of risk management by simple mitigation or elimination. Over-management of commercial risk often totally stifles good proactive design and a true entrepreneurial spirit, since the easiest thing to manage is often customer expectation. Lower expectations mean lower demands and complications, whereas higher expectations mean a greater challenge for both business and design, and yet also a greater potential to satisfy customer need. When customers want more space in aeroplane seating arrangement, the organization that not only delivers but also contains costs and thus prices will certainly win. In seemingly tightly constrained situations this can often only be achieved by bold adjustments to the inherent capability of the existing design – the same number of seats but each with more space. If the business manages the commercial risks by insisting that customers can have more space, but at an extra cost, then creativity and bold design will be constrained. If the business manages the customer needs by giving more room at the same cost, then it could certainly suffer from damaging competitive disadvantage. If, however, the business promotes both customer and creative design, a better way forward may be found that delivers both. Looking back over history, the lessons of the past show that technology and design often do indeed deliver increased capability, but that commercial enterprise does not always proactively use a measure of both new design and technology to deliver to the customer. The secret of Six Sigma and good design is to deliver what the customer wants and at a price that beats the competitors, through boldly pushing back the limits to process capability. Corporate management can achieve this only when all the factors are given due balance and consideration, which may require more emphasis and empathy towards customer satisfaction than solely the fiscal probity and governance of the corporate entity.

SCORECARDS, REWARD AND RECOGNITION

The returns from a successful DFSS project must be much more than just good design together with an implementation plan, and it is important that a sense of achievement is demonstrated for all concerned. It is not only the business that has an interest in the outcome of the project, since both employee and customer will have reason to benefit from a new and beneficial product, service or process. Clarity of the gains achieved from both the new design methodology and the newly designed product or service can only be seen if effectively measured and monitored. The project team should regard the collection and analysis of process metrics around the project performance as standard practice; however, the need to obtain objective feedback from the full raft of interested customers is certainly a greater challenge.

Scorecards can be used to measure and monitor customer and supplier reaction to new products and services, both directly and indirectly. Early successes in Six Sigma initiatives are important to gain acceptance of the methodology and concept, and DFSS is no exception. However, the first few projects are more likely to take longer and require more effort in the early stages than in existing approaches, and so any early and short-term monitoring will often return a very biased opinion. The aim must be to avoid short-term measurements for either the basis for reward and recognition or for a basis on which to judge and evaluate the DFSS methodology itself. Short-term focus will only engender a view that encourages inappropriate constraints and short-cuts to appease the business. Long-term focus will be on reduced costs and fewer errors from the performance of the new products and services in the field over a period of many months and years, as well as a more rapid development cycle that can launch swiftly and successfully. A good scorecard will therefore include many of the following elements on which to measure and report:

- customer reaction to the innovative new ideas in the product/service
- employee reaction to newly designed and improved work processes
- reductions in field maintenance, recalls and production changes
- speed and depth of penetration and take-up in the marketplace
- increased overall sales and customer loyalty, including feedback from sales and marketing
- reduced time to prepare for the next generation of products and services
- lower design and development costs and increased overall speed from launch to 'hands-off' close
- competitive and market dominance signalled by independent review and appraisal
- stronger teamwork across the technical and non-technical departments involved.

This list can clearly be extended in use and the careful monitoring of a new product or service in the future will indicate where disappointment or failure can be attributed to the original design or design process. This will ensure that DFSS undergoes inspection and improvement, since it is likely that the real benefits from DFSS will arise only over the very long term.

Internal project team reward will be a factor in reinforcing both personal and corporate acceptance of the more rigorous and structured approach towards design. Since the teams involved will often include a broader than usual spectrum of skills and experiences as well as cultures, simplistic rewards such as bonuses or handouts are unlikely to appeal to everyone. Traditionally any apportioned bonuses have been the preserve of salespeople and certainly not everyone is motivated by money alone. Designers and engineers often gain reward from the public recognition of their work, which can extend for many years of successful use in the marketplace. Reward for design creativity, customer focus, reduction in future costs and adherence to the methodology are important, since all are potential cost-savers for the business, and benefits gained should be shared equally among those responsible. However, if the fiscal returns from the correct application of good design only come over many years, it seems almost folly to provide short-term incentive and reward. There are no easy answers to this difficult question, but the challenge must be to retain a long-term incentive that in some way penalizes the failure to deliver excellence in commercial design over the whole life of the product or service. This implies a need to impart a share in the success of the new design, and certainly 'share options' tied strongly to the performance of one particular brand or service, rather than simply the entire company, would be one targeted way to reward long-term success from excellence in design.

INNOVATION AND CHAOS

Research has shown that there is a clear correlation between the level of innovation within an organization and its freedom and depth of communication. However, it may well be that effective communication is not the principal driver for innovative change, but rather is an important factor in creating an environment where innovation can thrive and come to the fore. What drives innovation is pure creativity and inventiveness within a sympathetic environment, and clearly the aim for the proactive organization is to foster the best possible climate for the creative design team to work in. Surprisingly enough, it is the relatively poorly understood area of chaos theory that allows a better consideration of how to set up and maintain effective and creative teamwork, and the answer is not simply in having one single concentrated team of people communicating closely. Rather what is required is a culture of proactive change, where the team lives on the edge of chaos, in neither a state of equilibrium nor one of total disorder.

Chaos is the state observed when a number of elemental objects or entities interact in disequilibrium, apparently operating at random and without purpose or pattern. The study of physics implies that a fundamental principle in this universe is that order always passes to disorder and chaos, never the reverse. However, it is thought by some that in certain unique circumstances chaos naturally gives rise to what seems to be a spontaneous order, almost in reverse of the natural law of entropy. This is the secret of creativity and change, where on the edge between chaos and order is a sphere of real growth and potential. It is quite clear that change cannot occur in a highly ordered state, where rigidity and conformity exclude variation. Likewise, utter chaos is totally random and incoherent, excluding any chance of the emergence of any form of pattern or structure. What is required is a large degree of chaotic variation with a pull towards structure that forms patterns out of the disorder, some of which then lead to growth and new levels of understanding. The only place where change can naturally be a way of life is in the gap between the two extremes – on the edge of both order and chaos. This, then, is the conundrum for constructive change: how to achieve the unique conditions required to run a team, or even a whole organization, on the edge of chaos. The answer is to liberate the team members and allow them to become a system of autonomous agents, networked together to form non-linear dynamics. Every 'system' can oscillate to some degree and will always have a natural frequency of oscillation. By driving the system at its natural frequency, violent oscillation (major disequilibrium) will occur, and it is from such major upheaval and chaos that order has the potential to be brought forth.

To achieve 'chaos to order', a system needs to oscillate – which implies some form of mass or a degree of inertia, some form of linkage or interconnection, and a force or stress directed to restore the *status quo* when the mass is displaced from stability. Translating this to a 'system for innovation' within an organization implies that people provide the inertia (teams with resistance to change), the linkage comes from inter-team communication, and the force is derived from a degree of conformity and imposed rigour and structure. All that is needed to set the system in motion is some form of displacement from the normal position, which can easily occur when the business throws a new design challenge to the team. In practical terms, innovation comes from retaining several (not one) autonomous teams, networked together where communication underpins such networking. To obtain the very best from such teams, the extent, frequency and methods of communication are vital, underlying once again the importance of communication in any proactive and innovative organization. The three key factors required to support innovative chaos are to be found in dispersion, connection and oscillation, that is:

- create autonomy – diversity with few constraints and a free-flow of information;
- create connection – common language and meaning, networked in various ways; and
- create disturbance – experiment, drive feedback, iterate and stress.

Autonomous agents are to be found in disparate teams where both freedom and structure reside. There needs to be a degree of belonging as part of a group, with dependency and responsibility, but there also needs to be a degree of wholeness as an individual acting alone. It is very important to break up the DFSS group into smaller teams. It is also important to connect these teams together, but only lightly. Formal inter-group meetings should occur only two or three times per month, but outside of formal meetings the members must be allowed and encouraged to network at will. It is also very important to allow and encourage disturbance and experimentation, which can be achieved artificially by challenging and stressing the team. Notably it has been the Russians who have arrived at the more innovative technology in such areas as space rocket engine design, rather than the Americans, who had far more money and resources at their disposal. Stress can come from restriction on resources, which then leads to greater experimentation, communication and order from chaos. Note, however, that this all involves time, and constraining the team with an unreasonable timescale will simply dampen rather than enhance the potential for creativity.

Autonomy, communication and displacement applied correctly and over a period of time will naturally provide the very best environment for innovation and change. All that is required to maintain such a productive state is to recognize and reward innovative ideas and to propagate the best ideas through to commercial products and services using a DFSS approach. With care the 'edge of chaos' state can be maintained and even encouraged beyond the boundaries of the DFSS project. The Six Sigma culture is an excellent breeding ground for the ideal conditions for living on the edge of chaos. The common language, networked layers of practitioners both in and outside of the immediate organization, and the dynamic nature of process improvement all help to create autonomy, connection and disturbance. The real issue for DFSS teams is to ensure that several teams or layers are used, to ensure continual experimentation, and to keep the formal rigour of Six Sigma and quality standardization out of the group dynamics. The danger is that, driven to the extreme, Six Sigma will constrain and eliminate all sources of variation from an organization, removing all forms of experimentation and thus ultimately any chaos and change. Some variation in every organization is indeed useful and highly beneficial and Six Sigma (like any formal quality management system) has a danger of being exploited by 'quality police' to such an extent that utter conformity will kill for ever the true nature of change.

CONCLUSION

Design for Six Sigma is a collection of concepts and tools that are naturally complex and perhaps seemingly rather disjointed, which makes a journey such as this through the theory and practice potentially confusing and may leave the reader with a sense of having 'lost the plot' several chapters ago. Six Sigma generally is more of a journey than a destination; DFSS is more about a journey of discovery where the discovery is perhaps even more important than the journey itself. In Six Sigma as an approach to process improvement, the journey is all-important, with the destination always somewhere higher up the mountain path towards a peak of perfection. In contrast, DFSS is about finding a true understanding, which can just as easily occur at sea level as half-way up a mountain. Design starts with what often turns out to be a ceaseless journey of exploration, and what matters far more than the journey is the knowledge and understanding acquired before, during and after travelling. The outcome of our journey will often be to arrive back where the journey began, yet having gained knowledge and understanding for the first time – which neatly sums up the conundrum of DFSS. If those who successfully apply the practices and principles that have been explored within this book feel, after completing just one DFSS project, that they are back where they started from, then it is likely that all is well. What is more important by far is, do you know the place – customer, *gemba*, product, service, process and design – for the first time? Do you really know what the customer wants, and what it is your design needs to deliver to achieve world-class quality? Do you really know what failure is and how to eliminate the chance and impact of error? Success in DFSS comes from a ceaseless and aggressive exploration of all the things that matter to excellent design, and to come right back to where the exploration started, the original business concept solution and yet to really *know* this place for the first time. Then, and only then, can the team turn the conceptual solution into a world-class design that will deliver world-class quality. To achieve great things in DFSS requires many skills and tools, but above all it requires an attitude and practice that encourages each of the following:

● listening to the business
● visiting the customer *gemba* – frequently and staying long
● hearing the voice of the customer
● designing creatively, boldly and well
● measuring and evaluating with Six Sigma as a rule
● banishing the root of failure and error
● implementing with impunity and confidence.

Designing well, and with a target of Six Sigma performance in mind, is hard indeed. The rewards for the organization that succeeds are simply staggering – the small part of the commercial world in which you design will indeed be your oyster.

SUMMARY

- DFSS projects will need at least one and possibly several teams each of about six members. Team membership needs to cover many skills and should include:

    - Six Sigma experts such as Master and Black Belts
    - business experts such as senior managers
    - customer experts – sales, marketing or customer service agents
    - technical experts from the product or service field
    - creative experts and designers
    - perhaps also 'team facilitators'.

- Project teams will require a background experience and knowledge of Six Sigma and will often need to begin with one week of training covering the DFSS methodology and team-building skills, followed by further training as required. The full range of team training should include:

    - Six Sigma theory and practice
    - team-building skills
    - project management
    - DFSS methodology
    - particular tools such as benchmarking, customer survey, quality function deployment, failure mode effect analysis and simulation and modelling
    - innovation and creativity skills
    - reporting and presentation skills.

- Individuals in a good DFSS team will each champion change as well as personal growth and will need to act as 'change activists'. The environment and project team that supports and promotes such change activists will demonstrate:

    - clear focus and objectives
    - motivation and leadership
    - confidence and trust
    - membership of an inclusive team
    - empowering communication, both speaking and listening
    - self-worth and self-esteem
    - strength and stamina.

- The real and challenging conflict between business and customer typically arises over expectations of product or service performance, and corporate management may resort to promoting the control of customer expectation to help constrain the financial risk. While businesses do need sound fiscal governance, it is important that customer expectations are aggressively met through proactive and bold design. Limiting customer expectation will ultimately lead to both stifled design and poor performance.

- Scorecards are a good way to monitor and report on design and product/service performance. They should look at the long-term benefits of using DFSS and should report on:

    - customer reaction to the new product/service
    - employee reaction to new work processes
    - field maintenance, recalls and production changes

- marketplace penetration and take-up
- long-term sales and customer loyalty
- elapsed time to the next generation of products/services
- design and development costs as well as time from project launch to close
- independent appraisal of competitive and market dominance
- effectiveness of teamwork across all of the departments involved.

● The format for employee reward and recognition should be balanced to account for the diverse expectations of the various groups within the DFSS project and should firmly concentrate on the long-term appraisal of success. Fiscal as well as recognition rewards can be tied to long-term 'stock options' associated with the particular design brand or service.
● Change and innovation take place on the 'edge of chaos', which requires:

- autonomy – diversity with few constraints and a free-flow of information
- connection – common language and meaning, networked in various ways
- disturbance – experimentation with driven feedback, iteration and stress.

It is important to keep a degree of chaos and variation in the organization and the design process; otherwise all creativity and proactive innovation will be stifled.

Appendix

DPMO-TO-PROCESS SIGMA CONVERSION TABLE

The process-sigma metric is formally calculated from the number of standard deviations (sigma) which fit between the mean and the (nearest) acceptable customer limit for a process, providing the process performance follows a pattern similar to that of the normal distribution. The part (or tail) of the normal distribution which falls outside of the customer limit equates to the 'defects' experienced by the customer, the whole distribution equating to all possible opportunities for such a defect. This can also be described as a fractional part of a million, often referred to as the 'defects per million opportunities' or DPMO. This fraction of the normal distribution falling outside of a given process sigma can be found from calculated tables, and can be applied to situations where the process shows a non-normal distribution or is more complex. Once a 'defect' and an 'opportunity for a defect' have been defined and counted, it is often much easier to both use and understand the DPMO-to-process sigma conversion table than it is to calculate the process sigma from the actual distribution. Without having to understand normal curves, means and standard deviations, Table A.1 allows anyone with a simple calculator and a count of 'defects' and 'opportunities for defect' to arrive at a process sigma value, for any process.

Note that Table A.1 includes the standard 1.5 sigma shift for short-term sigma. To convert between short-term sigma (the best possible process capability) and long-term sigma (or process performance, which is equivalent to the number of standard deviations between customer limit and mean) subtract 1.5 from the sigma value given in the table. Values in the table have been rounded to four or less significant figures, and will have some degree of inaccuracy, although it is unlikely that greater significance will ever be either appropriate or needed.

To calculate any given value, the following formulae can be used in Excel or a similar spreadsheet. NORMSDIST is the standard normal cumulative distribution (the area under the standard normal curve for a given value of z), and NORMSINV is the inverse of the standard normal cumulative distribution. For Excel (as for most software), the multiplication symbol is * and the division symbol is /. Rounding can usually be applied by specifying a number format for the cell.

The equation for converting DPMO to process sigma is:

$$process\ sigma = \text{NORMSINV}(1 - (dpmo/1\ 000\ 000)) + 1.5$$

The equation for converting process sigma to DPMO is:

$$dpmo = 1\ 000\ 000 * (1 - \text{NORMSDIST}(process\ sigma - 1.5))$$

DCCDI METHODOLOGY TOLLGATES

What follows is an outline of the typical tollgate requirements and deliverables for each stage. Full project reviews can be completed with the project team, business, customer representatives and the 'quality function', where each party should accept or reject the work completed to date. Dependent

Table A.1 DPMO-to-process sigma conversion table

Process sigma	Defects Per Million Opportunities									
	0.00	0.01	0.02	0.03	0.04	0.05	0.06	0.07	0.08	0.09
0.0	933 200	931 900	930 600	929 200	927 900	926 500	925 100	923 600	922 200	920 700
0.1	919 200	917 700	916 200	914 700	913 100	911 500	909 900	908 200	906 600	904 900
0.2	903 200	901 500	899 700	898 000	896 200	894 400	892 500	890 700	888 800	886 900
0.3	884 900	883 000	881 000	879 000	877 000	874 900	872 900	870 800	868 600	866 500
0.4	864 300	862 100	859 900	857 700	855 400	853 100	850 800	848 500	846 100	843 800
0.5	841 300	838 900	836 500	834 000	831 500	828 900	826 400	823 800	821 200	818 600
0.6	815 900	813 300	810 600	807 800	805 100	802 300	799 500	796 700	793 900	791 000
0.7	788 100	785 200	782 300	779 400	776 400	773 400	770 400	767 300	764 200	761 100
0.8	758 000	754 900	751 700	748 600	745 400	742 200	738 900	735 700	732 400	729 100
0.9	725 700	722 400	719 000	715 700	712 300	708 800	705 400	701 900	698 500	695 000
1.0	691 500	687 900	684 400	680 800	677 200	673 600	670 000	666 400	662 800	659 100
1.1	655 400	651 700	648 000	644 300	640 600	636 800	633 100	629 300	625 500	621 700
1.2	617 900	614 100	610 300	606 400	602 600	598 700	594 800	591 000	587 100	583 200
1.3	579 300	575 300	571 400	567 500	563 600	559 600	555 700	551 700	547 800	543 800
1.4	539 800	535 900	531 900	527 900	523 900	519 900	516 000	512 000	508 000	504 000
1.5	500 000	496 000	492 000	488 000	484 000	480 100	476 100	472 100	468 100	464 100
1.6	460 200	456 200	452 200	448 300	444 300	440 400	436 400	432 500	428 600	424 700
1.7	420 700	416 800	412 900	409 000	405 200	401 300	397 400	393 600	389 700	385 900
1.8	382 100	378 300	374 500	370 700	366 900	363 200	359 400	355 700	352 000	348 300
1.9	344 600	340 900	337 200	333 600	330 000	326 400	322 800	319 200	315 600	312 100
2.0	308 500	305 000	301 500	298 100	294 600	291 200	287 700	284 300	281 000	277 600
2.1	274 300	270 900	267 600	264 300	261 100	257 800	254 600	251 400	248 300	245 100
2.2	242 000	238 900	235 800	232 700	229 600	226 600	223 600	220 600	217 700	214 800
2.3	211 900	209 000	206 100	203 300	200 500	197 700	194 900	192 200	189 400	186 700
2.4	184 100	181 400	178 800	176 200	173 600	171 100	168 500	166 000	163 500	161 100
2.5	158 700	156 200	153 900	151 500	149 200	146 900	144 600	142 300	140 100	137 900
2.6	135 700	133 500	131 400	129 200	127 100	125 100	123 000	121 000	119 000	117 000
2.7	115 100	113 100	111 200	109 300	107 500	105 600	103 800	102 000	100 300	98 530
2.8	96 800	95 100	93 420	91 760	90 120	88 510	86 920	85 340	83 790	82 260
2.9	80 760	79 270	77 800	76 360	74 930	73 530	72 150	70 780	69 440	68 110
3.0	66 810	65 520	64 260	63 010	61 780	60 570	59 380	58 210	57 050	55 920
3.1	54 800	53 700	52 620	51 550	50 500	49 470	48 460	47 460	46 480	45 510
3.2	44 570	43 630	42 720	41 820	40 930	40 060	39 200	38 360	37 540	36 730
3.3	35 930	35 150	34 380	33 620	32 880	32 160	31 440	30 740	30 050	29 380
3.4	28 720	28 070	27 430	26 800	26 190	25 590	25 000	24 420	23 850	23 300
3.5	22 750	22 220	21 690	21 180	20 680	20 180	19 700	19 230	18 760	18 310
3.6	17 860	17 430	17 000	16 590	16 180	15 780	15 390	15 000	14 630	14 260
3.7	13 900	13 550	13 210	12 870	12 550	12 220	11 910	11 600	11 300	11 010
3.8	10 720	10 440	10 170	9 903	9 642	9 387	9 137	8 894	8 656	8 424
3.9	8 198	7 976	7 760	7 549	7 344	7 143	6 947	6 756	6 569	6 387
4.0	6 210	6 037	5 868	5 703	5 543	5 386	5 234	5 085	4 940	4 799
4.1	4 661	4 527	4 397	4 269	4 145	4 025	3 907	3 793	3 681	3 573
4.2	3 467	3 364	3 264	3 167	3 072	2 980	2 890	2 803	2 718	2 635
4.3	2 555	2 477	2 401	2 327	2 256	2 186	2 118	2 052	1 988	1 926
4.4	1 866	1 807	1 750	1 695	1 641	1 589	1 538	1 489	1 441	1 395
4.5	1 350	1 306	1 264	1 223	1 183	1 144	1 107	1 070	1 035	1 001
4.6	968	936	904	874	845	816	789	762	736	711
4.7	687	664	641	619	598	577	557	538	519	501
4.8	483	467	450	434	419	404	390	376	362	350
4.9	337	325	313	302	291	280	270	260	251	242
5.0	233	224	216	208	200	193	185	179	172	165
5.1	159	153	147	142	136	131	126	121	117	112
5.2	108	104	100	96	92	88	85	82	78	75
5.3	72	70	67	64	62	59	57	54	52	50
5.4	48	46	44	42	41	39	37	36	34	33
5.5	32	30	29	28	27	26	25	24	23	22
5.6	21	20	19	18	17	17	16	15	15	14
5.7	13	13	12	12	11	11	10	10	9	9
5.8	9	8	8	7	7	7	7	6	6	6
5.9	5	5	5	5	5	4	4	4	4	4
6.0	3.4	3.2	3.1	3.0	2.8	2.7	2.6	2.4	2	2

on the size and importance of the project, passage to the next stage can be halted unless a unanimous or majority vote is obtained in favour of continuing.

NPI – TOLLGATE ZERO

To confirm and expedite the effective launch of the project.

Concept:

- primary idea in outline detail
- corporate strategy for development in the project area
- simple business risk analysis – do versus don't do.

Market:

- target market with demographics and outline customer expectations
- preliminary CTQs and gap analysis, sales forecasts
- current competitor and self benchmarking.

Multi-generation plan:

- three-stage outline plan with stage one as proposed project
- details from previous projects and any historical work to date.

Funding:

- outline project budget, both time and money
- resource requirements for both people and technical needs
- outline project charter and corporate sponsorship.

DEFINE – TOLLGATE ONE

To confirm the foundation and scope of the project.

Business strategy approval:

- basic product and/or service description
- target market and customer description and segmentation
- updated MGP and business plan
- cost and benefit analysis
- concept FMEA and risk analysis
- project financial budget plan.

Scope:

- project definition document
- description of goals and deliverables
- analysis of impact on existing processes
- customer survey and CTQ documentation.

Project management:

- team details, champion, process owner(s), (M)BB, team members
- team charter document finalized
- team-training requirements and resource needs

– project workbook and reporting structure
– full project plan with timescale, milestones and resource requirements.

CUSTOMER – TOLLGATE TWO

To confirm the full understanding of customer requirements.

Customer requirements:

– voice of the customer survey results and final analysis
– product and service description from a customer focus
– benchmarking analysis in detail.

Critical to quality metrics:

– full house of quality (first) and detailed customer needs tree
– detail of each CTQ with specified targets and limits
– risk analysis for CTQ conflicts and omissions
– results of internal business customer analysis.

Risk analysis:

– FMEA conducted on outline design concept
– preliminary cost of poor-quality calculations and projections
– first review of project exit strategies.

CONCEPTUALIZE – TOLLGATE THREE

To confirm the development of a sound design brief which meets customer and business requirements.

Functional requirements:

– full house of quality (second) with option selection details
– functional description of the product/service down to a detailed level.

Concept design refinement:

– product and/or service concept on paper and to sufficient detail
– full design specification to sufficient detail to pass to next stage.

Performance evaluation:

– process capability (sigma) evaluation and summary
– performance difficulties highlighted for technical design improvement
– critical to process metrics identified and targets set (where appropriate)
– final cost of poor-quality calculations and projections
– second-pass project exit strategies and completed business FMEA.

DESIGN – TOLLGATE FOUR

To confirm the development of a fully executed design ready for implementation.

Technical design:

– additional houses of quality as required

– full critical to process metrics and targets completed
– full and detailed process maps
– full technical design specifications.

Simulation and evaluation:

– computer simulation models devised and approved
– simulation results analysed and design refined accordingly
– process load testing and design reviews.

Preliminary control plan:

– control metrics identified
– FMEA analysis on product/service, process and system.

IMPLEMENT – TOLLGATE FIVE

To confirm and expedite the commercial readiness of the design.

Pilot study:

– planning, roll-out execution and evaluation of pilot
– pilot results analysed and design refinements approval
– real-life capability analysis completed
– customer and stakeholder feedback analysis
– failures and omissions identified and correction plan instigated.

Implementation and commercialization plan:

– procedures fully documented
– staff/customer training plan
– marketing and support preparation
– phased commercial roll-out begun.

Final control plan and full documentation completed.

COMMERCIAL PRODUCTION – TOLLGATE SIX

To close the project formally and stand down the team.

Formal project close:

– reward and recognition for team and associates
– documentation and control finalized and installed
– evaluation and lessons learnt with feedback to business.

Process improvement plan:

– list of spawned Six Sigma improvement projects
– long-term monitoring and customer feedback plan.

MGP feed forward:

– information and control plans to process owners
– information to business and development teams.

GAZETTEER

Good design is frequently and easily to be found in the real world; however, it is perhaps only the utmost excellence in good design that stands the ultimate test of time, so history is often a good place to seek out some of the finest examples. For the native to the UK and also for the visitor from abroad, what follows is a short list of places to visit and contemplate the abilities of some of the greatest design engineers.

Whilst every attempt has been made to list only places of broad design interest and with reliable availability and access, visitors travelling from a distance should check details beforehand.

PONTCYSYLLTE AQUEDUCT

Three miles east of Llangollen. Designed and built by Thomas Telford for the Ellesmere Canal Company, this was astonishingly bold and the wonder of the age when completed in 1805, and remains almost exactly as built. There are 19 spans of 53 feet making a total length of 1007 feet and a maximum height of 127 feet over the river Dee. The canal water is contained in a cast-iron tank just under 12 feet wide, supported on masonry piers, and is remarkable for the simplicity of design as well as the profoundly successful use of the then relatively new material of cast iron.

IRONBRIDGE

The Pontcysyllte aqueduct can be compared with the Iron Bridge (Ironbridge, Telford) which was the world's first cast-iron bridge, dating from 1779. It has a 100-foot span and uses no bolts! The Ironbridge Gorge Museum at Coalbrookdale was the location for the beginning of iron foundry and retains several other interesting exhibits.

ISAMBARD KINGDOM BRUNEL

An extraordinary engineer and designer, he is worth study in his own right, having completed in a short lifetime some 25 railway lines, 5 suspension bridges, 125 other bridges, 8 pier and dock developments and 3 major ships. He was capable of astonishing originality, and his ideas were generally bolder and grander than anything that had gone before (and in some cases, since). Typical of Brunel, any existing solution was rethought and existing technology reconfigured in new ways, yet with due consideration of both the smallest detail as well as the overall design. Often thought highly extravagant, his greatest strength was in the confidence and seeming limitless ability to tackle any challenge. He was certainly not one to count the cost of every element of design, yet his personal legacy to Victorian engineering remains clearly unsurpassed!

LONDON

Although really the work of Marc Brunel, the world's first sub-aquatic tunnel, under the Thames, was supervised by Isambard Brunel, and is now in use as part of the London Underground. Travel to Wapping on the East London Line; the southern end of the platforms provides a (disappointing) view of the twin-tunnel entrance, with the lights of the next station seen reflected on the rails. The stairs and lift for the station are situated in the original access shaft.

The Science Museum at Kensington holds an exceptionally fine display of a wide range of early steam engines and other artefacts from the industrial age. Similarly excellent museums of science and technology exist at Manchester and also Birmingham. Railway museums at York, Swindon and Didcot (and many others) demonstrate the rapid progress of design and technology in this field. Didcot houses an interesting replication layout of mixed broad- and standard-gauge track.

Brunel designed Paddington Station as the London terminus for the Great Western Railway. The building was improved two decades later, again by Brunel, and the roof is a classic example of his work. The original layout of platforms, goods yard, station buildings and hotel was regarded as the best-designed mainline terminus of its day.

BRISTOL

Almost the mutually adopted home of Brunel, Bristol retains probably the largest collection of Brunel's engineering and design impact to be seen within one location. Journey down from London Paddington on the original GWR route via Chippenham and Bath to Bristol Temple Meads (note Brunel's original old station at Bristol) – not much evidence of the broad gauge remains apart from the wider-than-average cuttings along the route. The Clifton Suspension Bridge across the Avon Gorge was actually built after Brunel's death and to his design, but remains in busy and practical use. His steamship the *Great Britain* resides in the dry dock from which she was launched and is notable for many revolutionary design features; take a walk to the Cumberland Basin and locks to see the dock-entrance widening undertaken by Brunel, required to allow the *Great Britain* to leave! A statue of Brunel stands by the road to Queen Square from the centre (walk away from the Hippodrome towards the railway station). Sadly, the statue of Brunel at Paddington, with the engineer looking along the platforms towards the west, has been moved to the side entrance in the recent station refurbishment of the Underground access. It was Brunel's noted ambition for his Great Western Railway that it would form the first part of a route to America via Bristol and steamship.

Index